True Storytelling

True Storytelling is a new method of studying, planning, facilitating, ensuring, implementing and evaluating ethical and sustainable changes in companies, organizations and societies. *True Storytelling* is both a method with seven principles and a mindset to help managers and researchers to work with change. *True Storytelling* stresses that we need to balance the resources of the Earth, our wellbeing and the economy when we are dealing with change.

It is not only a book about how to prevent climate change, it is also a book about how we can navigate through crisis, create less stress and achieve better life in organizations and in society as a whole. You will learn how to create innovative start-ups with a purpose and fund money for sustainable projects and good ideas.

The book combines practical cases, interviews with managers and CEOs, theory and philosophy to define the method and to teach the Seven True Storytelling Principles:

1 You yourself must be true and prepare the energy and effort for a sustainable future
2 True storytelling makes spaces that respect the stories already there
3 You must create stories with a clear plot, creating direction and helping people prioritize
4 You must have timing
5 You must be able to help stories on their way and be open to experiment
6 You must consider staging, including scenography and artefacts
7 You must reflect on the stories and how they create value

This book is a guide to implementing these core principles to boost leadership practices, create a storytelling culture and staff buy-in. The method is also useful as an analytical tool for organizations, managers and consultants in order to prepare, plan and execute the implementation of strategies. It is valuable reading for researchers and students at master level as well as leaders and consultants in charge of ethical and sustainable changes.

Jens Larsen is a storytelling researcher and the founding partner of the Danish consulting company Old Friends Industries. Jens has written books about ethics and leadership and worked with managers from brands like IKEA, Novo, Microsoft, Mærsk and public organizations and NGOs like Red Cross.

David M. Boje Ph.D. is a Professor at Aalborg's Business College and Regents Professor and Professor Emeritus at New Mexico State University. He teaches qualitative storytelling science methods at Cabrini University in Philadelphia. He is editor-in-chief of the Business Storytelling Encyclopedia. Boje gives invited keynote presentations on storytelling science, water crises, and the global climate crisis, in Zoom sessions, all around the world.

Lena Bruun has 24 years of professional experience as a manager, advisor and consultant within the public and private sector; including Roskilde Municipality, The Museum of Rock, Pop and Youth culture Ragnarock and a communication consultancy. Lena is partner in Old Friends Industries.

True Storytelling

Seven Principles for an Ethical and Sustainable Change-Management Strategy

Jens Larsen, David M. Boje and Lena Bruun

Routledge
Taylor & Francis Group
LONDON AND NEW YORK

First published 2021
by Routledge
2 Park Square, Milton Park, Abingdon, Oxon OX14 4RN

and by Routledge
52 Vanderbilt Avenue, New York, NY 10017

Routledge is an imprint of the Taylor & Francis Group, an informa business

British Library Cataloguing-in-Publication Data
A catalogue record for this book is available from the British Library

Library of Congress Cataloging-in-Publication Data
Names: Larsen, Jens, 1965- author. | Boje, David M., author. |
Bruun, Lena, 1967- author.
Title: True storytelling : seven principles for an ethical and sustainable change-management strategy / Jens Larsen, David M. Boje, and Lena Bruun.
Description: 1 Edition. | New York : Routledge, 2020. |
Includes bibliographical references and index.
Identifiers: LCCN 2020016935 (print) | LCCN 2020016936 (ebook) |
ISBN 9780367425722 (hardback) | ISBN 9780367549275 (paperback) |
ISBN 9780367425739 (ebook)
Subjects: LCSH: Organizational change. | Leadership. | Storytelling.
Classification: LCC HD58.8 .L3756 2020 (print) | LCC HD58.8 (ebook) |
DDC 658.4/06--dc23
LC record available at https://lccn.loc.gov/2020016935
LC ebook record available at https://lccn.loc.gov/2020016936

ISBN: 978-0-367-42572-2 (hbk)
ISBN: 978-0-367-54927-5 (pbk)
ISBN: 978-0-367-42573-9 (ebk)

Typeset in Sabon
by Taylor & Francis Books

We dedicate this book to all who are working for a True Storytelling, sustainable future.

Boje dedicates this book to his grandchildren (Juliete, Oliver, Hudson, and Natalie in New Jersey and Shiva Sun in Canada) so they may have the planetary life-giving Gaia to survive in the Anthropocene.

Jens dedicates it to his two kids, Viggo and Augusta, for their curiosity and friendship.

Lena dedicates it to her children, Albert and Emil, for being hopeful despite everything.

Contents

Preface

True Storytelling is a new ethical path for sustainable change. It is a foundation for life, and a method for research and change that can guide us on our path towards a truer and more sustainable future.

Let's start with some True Storytelling!

We are researchers of storytelling, living in self-quarantine. It's the time of the Coronavirus pandemic. David is living on a small ranch in New Mexico. David and his wife have just cancelled all their travel plans, and like everyone else, they are in Zoom meetings, making calls to friends and family, taking care of their animals, and each other, at home. Lena and her husband are on a small island an hour by boat from the coast of Denmark, working out of home and teleconferencing with their sons. And Jens is with his family in their apartment in downtown Copenhagen. He is working from home, looking down on the lonely streets, which used to be noisy and full of people. And every evening at seven o'clock he opens the windows, waving to neighbours, clapping and singing to pay tribute to the social workers and people working at the hospitals.

The Coronavirus struck right after we sent the True Storytelling book to Routledge. Now the book and the ethics of a True Storytelling life existence have a whole new meaning. The principles we crafted still apply, but you, the reader, will have to make the new connections. There are too many traumatic stories of death and misery. People are scared. Some have panicked. Store shelves are emptied of what everyone needs to survive. It is a time when there are many negative, quite tragic stories.

What are we doing about all this? We are collecting local stories, meeting digitally with colleagues, and trying to figure out how True Storytelling can help people get a sense of how to navigate in their many narratives that are being spun around the Coronavirus. We are perhaps reflecting on our life style and the social and economic choices we have been making that are part of the bigger picture. To get in touch with the planet, its quantumness, the way everything is interconnected in global supply chains, in air and train travel, in waiting rooms and classrooms where bodies mingle with zoonotic risks of more outbreaks. A new normal is happening. We are all together on this planet coming up with new ways of Being, new ways of being family, being part of Nature, recognizing that we are already Nature, and cannot separate from it.

So David is building a greenhouse, learning how to farm and grow things, to be in harmony with Nature. His ancestors go as far back as there were Bøjes on the planet, and that's maybe more than 10,000 years he estimates – they had been small farmers, caring for plants and animals. But wait, about 50 years' ago, the Bøjes left family farming and joined service businesses, became part of a capitalism too addicted to oil, became part of the problem leading up to pandemic after pandemic, with more forecasted to come. There are thousands of viruses, most undiscovered, so if we don't get a True Storytelling we will keep fooling ourselves into believing that business-as-usual, a return to that normal, is the way to proceed.

Jens is having a break for the first time in many years. He is rediscovering being around his family, eating together, sharing stories from the day – reading books, poems, writing stories and coming up with new ideas about how to connect and share ideas about True Storytelling with people from New Zealand, South Africa, India, Argentina and the US.

Lena is facing a personal challenge waking up each morning, trying to deal with the fact that she cannot perform and chase goals as she used to. She is transforming from a human doer into a human being. Is it possible to just be present without daily check lists and KPIs; who is she when she is not doing but just being?

The Coronavirus is just one out of the many crises that we have to deal with in our lives, overwhelming as it may seem. The financial crisis of 2008 was another, and the climate crisis is the most important and scary crisis, although many people have a hard time relating to it because it is moving slowly compared to the Corona and financial crises.

The book is a way to help you navigate in crises in search of a true and sustainable story but it is also a book about how to create less stress and a better life in organizations and in society as a whole. It is also a book about creating innovative start-ups with a purpose, and fundraising money for sustainable projects and good ideas.

Before we invite you into the Seven Principles of True Storytelling, we want to acknowledge some people.

We wish to acknowledge the inspiration and help from our spouses and of course, our dogs and cats. We appreciate the wonderful support from the people at Routledge. The Danish philosopher Ole Fogh Kirkeby has been an inspiration. We give special thanks to the people – managers, artists and companies – who contributed with interviews from their own life and to Marita Svane and Kenneth Mølbjerg Jørgensen for their work in antenarrative and terrestrial ethics, to Grace Ann Rosile for her work on ensemble storytelling and ensemble leadership, to Mikkel Bruun for helping with translation and to Maiken Bork Clausen for her sense of the political perspective on True Storytelling.

Introduction: What is True Storytelling?

Introduction

This is a book about how each one of us can help create commitment to more sustainable change and help ourselves and others in the search for the truth. It is not only a book about climate change and how to create a more sustainable production and more awareness about how we use the resources of the Earth, although that is the most important task. It is also a book about how we can create less stress and better life in organizations, among students and in society in general, about how we can create innovative start-ups with a purpose, help artists find their voices, fund money for sustainable projects and good ideas. It is about how we can help ourselves, people we care for and the world around us in the search for a better future and true story.

Research tells us it is hard to implement changes – 70% of organizational change implementations do not persist.[1] It is said that implementation processes are strategies too costly for the 1%. But research finds that the small group of senior executives has become an elite who are scared of employee participation, and they worship the British philosopher Herbert Spencer, best known for his idea of 'the survival of the fittest,' who believed God wants the rich to get richer and the poor will always be a given. Fortunately for the 99% there is a way to engage ensemble leadership (we are all leaders in the fight against climate denial and the elitism of Spencerism).

We believe in ensemble leadership and together-telling as an important part of our approach to initiate change. To use storytelling when working with change is nothing new. It is rather old news. Jesus, Buddha and Muhammed used storytelling to get their moral and teaching through. Indigenous people have their own way of storytelling as opposed to Western storytelling with a beginning, middle, end. Great leaders, and bad leaders alike, have used storytelling. Companies have used it for branding purposes, politicians as spin and fake storytelling. Over the last two decades narratives and storytelling have been used to create empowerment in organizations and in communities, but has also created a lot of confusion about what is up and down, meaningful and meaningless.

But the facts of climate change have created a totally new agenda as the French philosopher Bruno Latour put it in his book *Down to Earth* (2018). Latour stresses that the political field has changed – it is not only about left and right but about who wants to take action on the climate and who don't.

We believe this has a radical influence on how we approach everything – for example, leadership and also the art of storytelling – and we believe it is time to stand up for a more radical approach. We call it True Storytelling. Our purpose is to call for an ethical approach in the search for truth.

What do we mean by True Storytelling? True Storytelling is an ethical standpoint – True Storytelling adopts the ethics of answerability, knowing that we are accountable for our doing and being in the world.

The short answer is that True Storytelling is a relational process ontology (Boje, 2019b) and a way to stand as an ensemble against 'Fake Storytelling' and climate change deniers. It is not just relational to humans, but relational to all species. We stand with Donna Haraway's (2016) multispecies storytelling, not with the humancentric. We are not speciests. True Storytelling is not "the godhead of seeing everything from nowhere" (Haraway, 1991: 188). We stand with the Danish poet Theis Ørntoft and the Indian author Amitav Ghosh when they stress that future storytelling needs to relate to the climate crisis.[2] We stand with the indigenous peoples' approach to storytelling (Cajete, 2000), believing storytelling is more than the Western concept with a beginning, middle and end but is a complex flow of energy and stories and small fragments of stories. And that storytelling, as said before, includes the land and all living species. We stand with Hannah Arendt and her concept of natality[3] – everything needs to have the time to be in rebirth and that it is important to have a sensibility towards nature when we reflect.

Our approach in this book is essayistic. Essay in French means 'to try.' We move between case studies, personal experiences, storytelling and philosophy and science in our search. We stand with essayist Joan Didion's (1990, 2007) novels – how she conveys her moral sensibility, intertwines personal asides with descriptions of her characters. She bridges the personal with the experience of material conditions.

In the book we use stories about the singer and songwriter Johnny Cash, the surfing universe, great literature and arts to illustrate and unfold our ideas. The book consists of an introduction to the concept of True Storytelling where we explain the background and the philosophy behind it. Then we present seven chapters with seven True Storytelling principles. Each chapter explains a principle through stories and examples and it will give you some idea on how to work with it. We finish with a chapter with workpapers and what we call 'anti tools' you can use in your work with change. However, the main purpose is to inspire and open your mind for a different approach to view how you can work with sustainable change in search of your true story.

Seven Principles, one model

We (David Boje, Jens Larsen and Lena Bruun) have developed Seven Principles to enable success with transformational change. You can think of them as tuning forks for when you work with sustainable change.

1 True: You yourself must be true and prepare the energy and effort for a sustainable future
2 Making room: True Storytelling makes spaces that respect the stories already there
3 Plotting: You must create stories with a clear plot, creating direction and helping people prioritize
4 Timing: You must have timing
5 Helping stories along: You must be able to help stories on their way and be open to experiment
6 Staging: You must consider staging, including scenography and artefacts
7 Reflecting: You must reflect on the stories and how they create value.

True Storytelling principles are an ethical approach to self-correcting the Fake to get closer to the True. We have developed True Storytelling as a philosophical and storytelling science scaffolding.[4] It is an ethical and sustainable approach to work with change and development, for example, related to climate change, mental health, start-ups, communities and fundraising.

There is a chapter for each principle so you can learn them one by one. It is important to understand for the outset that all seven principles can be used in combination. Throughout the book we apply the True Storytelling model inspired by the seven principles that David Boje created with our Danish colleagues, Kenneth Mølbjerg Jørgensen and Marita Svane.

Abstracting is about pulling oneself up from the complex world to get a more philosophical overview of the matter, but putting oneself into an overall narrative is what companies do when 'branding' themselves, and it's useful to keep people moving in one direction. The downside of *abstracting* is that it is often about one heroic person, one plot, one theme, leaving out the diversity of people who are making things happen. It also leaves out the changing, dynamic situation – once something is branded, it is very hard to change and develop a new *futuring*. What we mean by that is that a company, country etc. with a strong story can be hard to change. The story can almost paralyze the company and if things change with, for example, the Coronavirus, the company cannot move into the future because it's stuck in this one-plot, heroic story which fits perfectly with the old world.

We think it is important to have a Danish storytelling model. To be concerned, as we are, to ground the abstract, doing more together-telling than just the 'strong man' telling us all what is what. In Danish the word for Truth is '*sand*' (*sandhed*), but it is also the word for 'grains of sand.' In Danish, 'truth storytelling' is '*sandhedsfortælling*' and it does not have a

Figure 0.1 The five entangled processes of True Storytelling – a 'sand' tale

direct English translation. We like the double meaning: 'sand-as-truth' and 'sand-as-grains-of-sand.' 'Truth' and 'sand' are both about a multiplicity, so there are many truths and many grains of sand. *Abstracting* into one 'grand narrative' leaves out all the grains of truth, in the myriad of little stories left on the 'branding room' floor, as all those edited-out stories narrows into just the one narrative-fits-all.

The seven True Storytelling principles are part of a methodology of *sandhedsfortælling* that we call 'self-correcting' – to get closer and closer to the grains of truth – and, at the same time, we are well aware of the fact that there is not just 'one' narratable truth. Don't you just hate it when your boss hears one side of a story and, without asking for your side of the story, without listening, without researching, checking, makes a decision about you, leaving you on the defensive? To learn to listen to many sides of the storytelling, before plunging into a decision is an important practice of True Storytelling. We therefore stand with Charles Sanders Peirce's (1931/1960) attention to fallibilism and his way of 'self-correcting' our storytelling so we might take some steps away from 'Fake Storytelling' to True Storytelling. We stand with Karl Popper in refuting the fake, and not just confirming *post hoc*. We stand with Nietzsche (1910: 109): "Everything in the domain of morality has evolved, is changeable, unstable, everything is dissolved, it is true; but *everything is also streaming towards one goal*." 'Fake Storytelling' will become weaker and it is True Storytelling that is "gradually implanting itself in us on the same ground" (110). For Nietzsche, this process of 'grounding' will take thousands of years, with our guilty conscious for all the fake being but the first step to reclaiming "ancient wisdom" (114).

Since we are all Danish (David is an American with Danish roots), the philosopher Søren Kierkegaard and '*historiefortæller*' (storyteller) Hans Christian Andersen and the founder of the Danish Folk School movement Niels Frederik

Severin Grundtvig constitute our ancestral moorings. We have been working with our Danish colleagues, Kenneth Mølbjerg Jørgensen and Marita Svane, on the model in the above figure.[5] 'Antenarrating' refers to pre-constituting processes before (*ante* to) a coherent story or narrative forming, and to various *bets on the future*. Instead of just *abstracting* into some universal narrative plot or story line, we want to be *grounding* in nature, in the sociomaterialities. Instead of one past, *rehistoricizing* is many pasts, including pasts that never were, and pasts that are being uncovered with each presenting emergence. We look at *futuring*, the many futures, including futures that could have been, and futures that never will be.

True vs fake

Philosophers are quick to reply, 'there can be no true storytelling' because truth is an illusion, just a social construction, or worse the delusion of 'Cartesian Theater' or more problematic 'Cartesian Materialism,' and that our sensemaking (sensory perception) is reducible to billions of brain neurons projecting on some inner theatre we reify into a storytelling self that does not exist, confusing neuron synapses with real experiencing of the world we can never know (Dennett, 1993). Such reductionism of storytelling denies the 37.2 trillion living cells of our embodiment, and how we are walking climate, exchanging cells with ecologies of living cells in the world (Boje 2019a).

Our standpoint is that True Storytelling is the sands of our existence in the world. It is not the reductionism of neuro-psychologists trotting out the reductionism metaphor, 'Cartesian Theatre.' Nor is True Storytelling a Kantian retreat to universal categories, or Aristotle's 'house of reason' or Wittgenstein's interminable language games,' nor is it the prison of the text with nothing beyond. We are ontologists, not social constructivists. As Walter Benjamin ([1936]/1955/1986/2007) predicted, "storytelling is coming to an end." We believe it is because 'Fake Storytelling' is becoming increasingly powerful in 'Fake News' and has no moral compass. Facts don't seem to matter to Fake leaders. The fake is becoming the new 'real.'

Fake Storytelling is dangerous to the survival of all species. Fake News puts the anecdote ahead of scientific, makes climate science into a debate. Is it impossible for all storytelling to escape the problem of True and Fake. The risk of the Fake is taken for granted in science in that a single anecdote, or the case study "cannot provide reliable information about the broader class" (Flyvbjerg, 2001: 66). Still sometimes an anecdote is a way into people's hearts:

> This baby sea mammal captured people's hearts. She just died from eating plastic. A young dugong, a relative of the manatee. Sometimes a case study touches our hearts. "Everyone is sad about her passing, but this is an issue that must be urgently resolved," officials from the Department of Marine and Coastal Resources in Thailand said on Facebook. "If we want to conserve rare marine animals so they remain in existence with us, every sector, every person must help with marine trash."[6]

We think it's important not to toss out the case studies. *Where I Was From* by essayist Joan Didion (2003: 3) begins with her great-great-great-great-great-grandmother Elizabeth, born in 1766 who killed ten men: "This may or may not be true or it may be, in a local oral tradition inclined towards stories that turn on decisive gestures, embroidery." Didion's essays turn to how:

> A good deal about California does not, on its own preferred terms, add up. The Sacramento River, the main source of surface water in a state where distrust of centralized governmental authority has historically passed for an ethic, has its headwaters in the far norther ranges of Siskiyou County. It picks up the waters of the McCloud and the Pit Rivers above Redding, of the Featherand the Yuba and the Bear below Knight's Landing, of the America at Sacramento, of the San Joaquin below Steamboat Slough, and empties through San Francisco Bay into the Pacific, draining the deep snowpacks of the southern Cascades and the northern Sierra Nevada.

Didion exemplifies True Storytelling by entangling her personal anecdotes with materialist accounts of geohistory. She keeps *rehistoricizing* any official past by weaving in many forgotten pasts, punctuating the present with many accounts of Sacramento Valley's entirely artificial environment, while bearing witness to horrid futures arriving instead of what might have been. We are not saying she has found absolute truth, only that by challenging past hegemonic accounts, identifying emergences presenting themselves, and witnessing the *futuring*, Didion is not lost in *abstracting* more and more grand narratives, but instead keeps on *grounding, rehistoricizing*, and *futuring*, deconstructing layers of storytelling in order to create spaces for change.

Our essayist book on True Storytelling will give examples from our efforts to make United Nations Sustainable Development Goals (SDGs) come 'true'. For instance, the police that speak 'true' in crisis situations, education (particularly our passion for the Danish Folk School movement) that experiences 'true' in its problem-based learning, the 'true' stress students are under in neoliberal regimes of truth, the mountain-walking we do with leaders, and coaching each of us to find our own True Storytelling path. As well as our practical work experience and consultancy work, we have been helping organisations, both private and public, to act 'true' and thereby succeed in heading for their goals – goals that will last. With trial-and-error we are constantly reviewing and adjusting our own efforts to be true either as consultants or employers as well as employees in the process. We are not saying we find 'absolute truth.' Rather, we follow Charles Sanders Peirce 'self-correcting' method, modifying expectations of future experience in regards to tests of our inference by self-reflection, conversing with others, conducting experiments or quasi-experiments, persisting in our essayist inquiry so, "we shall gradually be brought around to the truth. This gradual process of rectification is in great contrast to what takes place with rudimentary induction where the correction comes with a bang" (Peirce, 1931/1960: 7.115).

True Storytelling results in morally ethical and sustainable practices, as opposed to fake storytelling as spin, greenwashing, or fake news driven by the myth of the strong man or strong woman solo leader, or a group of executives attempting to be smarter than all of us together-leading. We call it 'True Storytelling' because it is inspired by a different kind of storytelling and because it is about ethics and the trueness of the whole 'togetherness' storytelling.

We share with you how to implement and create ownership of true and sustainable changes in the inseparability between 'Human-world' and 'Nature-world' because humans are one of many species within the world of Humans-in-Nature.

True Storytelling is about how we can take care of the Earth and become more sustainable. And, therefore, it is also about human sustainability and an economic and social sustainability that respects all life on the planet. It bridges the gap between ongoing changes and longing for meaning and trueness – by following Seven Principles of True Storytelling.

It fulfils the goals of:

- creating a more sustainable way for human, resources and economy
- initiating innovation and creativity
- creating strong and healthy communities and teams
- success with sustainable strategy implementation
- secure, profound impact in the organization
- obtaining efficiency and results
- creating start-ups of all kinds of enterprises (arts, business, NGOs, etc.)
- supporting employee satisfaction and reduce stress
- building up a stronger brand inside and outside the organization
- success with fundraising.

Analytical tool

True Storytelling is also a method, an analytical and diagnostic tool for organizations, NGOs, managers, workers, staff, consultants and human beings to prepare, plan and execute the implementation of 'morally-answerable' sustainable relationships between the human-world and our own inseparability from the nature-world. True Storytelling provides a link between the individual and the collective level in the organization, the community or society that strengthens developments and the natural environment through 'moral answerability' to stop being the bystander who says and does nothing as situations get worse.

We have a different role for case studies which fits our essayistic approach. The general view from the scientific method is that the case study is anecdotal, good only for a pilot study, and one should quickly move on to surveys or some other rigorous research methodology. Donald T. Campbell (1966) says a case study is not only unscientific, it is unethical to observe a group one time only. So why does Bent Flyvbjerg (2001: 66) declare that the denigration of the "detailed examination of a single example" leads to several misunderstandings, to an over simplification of the nature of the case study?

1 Since Plato and Socrates, the abstract universal has been considered more valuable than contextual grounding in the particular. Yet, some amazing breakthroughs began as case studies.
2 If case studies are not generalizable then they cannot contribute to scientific development. Yet physicists perform case studies all the time.
3 Case studies are only good for generating hypotheses in the first stage of research, and then more rigorous methods take front stage. Yet, qualitative inquiry continues to deconstruct quantitative methods for their reach.
4 As Karl Popper puts it, case study has an inductive bias toward confirmation and verification of the researcher's hypothesis, when what is needed is disconfirmation, falsifying a theory, and refuting assumptions. Yet, it is possible to do refuting as part of the storytelling research.
5 Generalizing from a single case study can miss the 'black swan' unless they keep sampling the entire population. Yet, we can keep sampling until we account for all swans.

We will apply a 'storytelling science' methodology Boje and Rosile (2019, in press) called *self-correcting*. Self-correcting combines induction with abduction and deduction, and is rooted in a proposal by Charles Sanders Peirce (1933–1937, 5.580, which hereafter means Volume 5, section #580): "In an induction we enlarge our sample for the sake of the self-correcting effect of the induction." True Storytelling applies Peirce's tests in a self-correcting triadic of Abduction-Induction-Deduction. Peirce's Abduction is the initial intuitive inference, that gets explored by Induction inference inquiries, and put to four sorts of tests to self-correct one's Deductive inference:

1 Refutation test of self-reflexivity is the first step, and if that does not deconstruct a theory, question abductions, then the next tests can be undertaken:
2 Critical storytelling conversations with others that becomes co-inquiry, co-sharing (not a semi-structured interview, which is just interrogation, so one-sided),
3 Studying the science involved include Native Science (Cajete, 2000), and
4 Doing experiments and/or interventions to get closer to the contextual situation.

Self-correcting storytelling science is a method for arriving closer to the truth by what Popper (1963: 318) calls a trial-and-error approach to scientific method. Of course, we do not get to an absolute truth, or a universal principle. Rather it is a kind of self-correcting to get "closer approximation to the truth" by trial-and-error, and all the while "critically discussing" to show what is "not true," to refute and falsify our own theory our own hypotheses, our own assumptions (Popper 1956/1983: 20, 23, 25). Peirce (1933–1937: 6.473) develops the self-correcting approach to make a proposition of the truth:

> Gradual Induction, which makes a new estimate of the proposition of truth in the hypothesis with every new instance; and given any degree of error there will *some time* be an estimate (or would be, if the probation were persisted in) which will be absolutely the last to be infected with so much falsity.

Core message: what is True Storytelling?

True Storytelling is possible, if and only if, every 'Fake Storytelling' premise and false conclusion is challenged as an incomplete story. This means refuting false storytelling rivals and countering examples of counter-narratives, so there is a high probability of finding 'True Storytelling.' Our search is for the whole story, instead of buying into just one side of the story. True Storytelling is defined here as a self-correcting 'storytelling science' methodology, a way to get to a closer approximation to truth, but with the humility of knowing we will never arrive at the 'absolute truth.'[7]

How to work with True Storytelling

What is a principle?

A principle is defined here as a way to do self-correcting 'storytelling science' by refuting our beliefs, practices, and assumptions so get closer, without ever arriving at absolute truth. Below we have put the principles into a model to illustrate how they interconnect.

We will use this image to light up the Seven Principles of True Storytelling in the following seven chapters, one by one. Think of them as surfboards, each suited to different wave conditions to understand the entire storytelling, *grounding* and *futuring* what waves to ride, given the surf conditions. *Abstracting* does not make

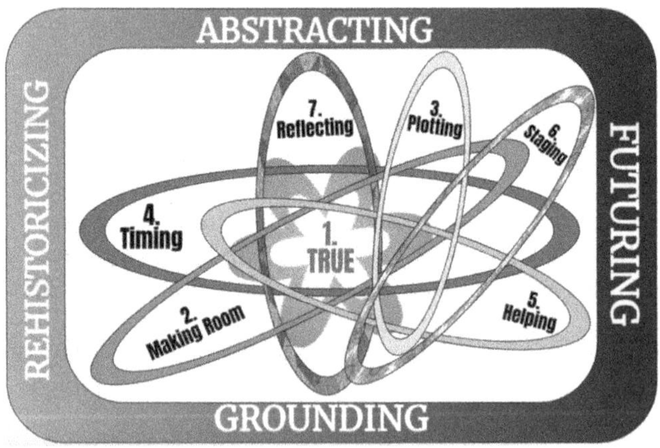

Figure 0.2 True Storytelling Principles

good surfers! Surfing means *grounding* in the waves, an intuitive sense of the wave patterns, timing when to ride a particular wave.

We have been working with 'Seven True Storytelling Principles' in Denmark's Sorø Municipality and six businesses, to create a better *ethical relationship* between the 'Human-world' and 'Nature-world.' Sorø is moving from *abstracting* to *grounding* as it is discovering we are all part of the one 'Living world.' Together, Sorø and we have listened to 'Mother Earth.'

As William James (1907: 96) put it over a century ago, "Things tell a story." The 'Nature-world' of all *'living 'things'* is telling one living story and the 'Human-world' of *'human-created things'* is building 'artificial-worlds,' denying its own inseparability from 'Nature-world' and sometimes telling an 'untrue' story. True Storytelling means moving from one story, told by one leader that pretends to fit all, into *we the people and we, all the species, all have* 'living stories' to tell! It is *grounding* and being able to do *futuring* of many possible worlds-in-the-making that are *rehistoricizing* that gets memorialized in so many different pasts.

How do we begin our search? Ask the question, 'what is your story?'

This is not your resume. It is a question about your existence in *place* and *time* in your life, in the *mattering* of what matters. Antenarratively, pre-story may be unstoried, even narrative, non-narrativized. Most people have never done the moral self-reflection on their own story. Judith Butler (2005) call it 'giving an account of oneself' and by that she declares it is actually one's responsibility to give a 'moral account.' "No one can live in a radically non-narratable world or survive a radically non-narratable life" (Butler 2000: 34). For Bakhtin (1993: 3), being morally answerable is not the same thing as being the bystander who watches a tragedy and does nothing to intervene. It is easy to give a Fake Storytelling of one's life by being the bystander in the once-occurrent eventness of Being. True Storytelling is more important than ever before because reports like Better World Better Business and surveys shows that young people want to work for companies and organizations which have a good and meaningful purpose and a sustainable future in a world in existential crisis.[8] It's not only about the money. People want to make a difference and they want to live a meaningful life in a multi-species storytelling world (Haraway, 2016). After years of stress and talking about economic growth and more economic growth, before well-being, there are more and more young people longing for meaningfulness through what Haraway calls 'Staying with the Trouble.' We suggest that people of all ages are longing for True Storytelling, disbelieve what leaders tell them is true, and care enough to intervene.

Together-telling

True Storytelling is about how, in together-telling, we can create and co-create the answer to that longingness for meaning (Boje, Larsen & Brunn, 2017).

Together-telling is about being dialectical without becoming anti-dialectical, being dialogical without turning anti-dialogical. That, too, is 'Staying with the Trouble.' As Aristotle puts it:

> Things that sound contradictory should be examined by the same rules as in dialectical refutation whether the same thing is meant, in the same relation, and in the same sense. We should therefore solve the question by reference to what the poet says [herself/] himself, or to what is tacitly assumed by a person of intelligence.[9]

Compared to top-down leader approaches to change management methods, True Storytelling takes it further into existential questions of our time – how do we (the multi-species storytellers) begin co-creating together? True Storytelling is not about spin and greenwash or whitewash. True Storytelling is not advice on how to manage corporate narratives as bystanders.

When the stories we tell are not yet true and alive, we can use a method of self-correction to find our surfing waves again. 'Self-correcting' is a method of challenging what we take to be True Storytelling and refuting every fake and false claim to the situation. So we get closer to, yet never uncover, absolute truth. This True Storytelling method is done by *together-telling*, getting people in-the-know together to get as many sides of the living story, and start *grounding* and *futuring*.[10] *Together-telling* is not a 60-minute collection of phrases on a flipchart. It is not one boss telling us what will be done. It is not the people at the top deciding they know better than all the people working in the organization, nor is it just the human species lording it over all other species in the natural world. Rather, *together-telling* is defined here as getting everyone in touch 'together' with our inseparability from Nature-world, and how humankind is only one of millions of species, and does not get to use up all the planetary resources in the name of an absentee shareholder. *Together-telling* can take days, weeks, and months so all the stories, including the counterstories, get heard, so the abstracting grand or master narratives get to understand the counternarratives.

There are multiple futures and multiple pasts. There is the future that will never be and the past that never was. There is the business-as-usual future and alternative futures that can become actualized by changing our ways of being in the present. By becoming aware of multiple pasts and multiple futures, we can begin to create a space for preparing in advance for a future that is not yet. True Storytelling "implementation requires involvement and co-operation to succeed" (Boje, Larsen & Bruun, 2017). This book is about passion and finding meaningfulness for each of us and moral answerability for the problems we have created. As Donna Haraway (2016) puts it, 'Staying with the Trouble.' Instead of Anthropocene, she calls it the '*Chthulucene,*' how humans and non-humans are inextricably linked in sym-poiesis instead of auto-poiesis. Auto-poiesis means to bring something into being that did not exist before. Sympoiesis is more about multi-species storytelling, bringing things into existence that help the living planet of all species. It is about how together we can build more liveable futures for all species. *Chthulucene* is not just a word, it replaces *Human Relations* with *Kin-Ship* of all kinds of species in a multi-species storytelling. It is a pathway out of the troubled waters of neoliberal Spencerism economic growth damage to our ecosystems. It is an answer to the gloom and doom world telling of Anthropocene scholarship by 'Staying with the Trouble' of our damage to the planet systems. It is the power of storytelling of our entanglement with all species. It is not the self-making narratives of neoliberal individualism. It is not clearing away the present and the past to make way for some future pathways for coming generations. It is a sceptical reception of the 'Fake Storytelling' of the Capitalocene. Instead of the bitter cynicism of game over, it is a pathway to multi-species flourishing by opening spaces for different futures to business-as-usual. We draw upon research, existential philosophy, native science, storytelling science, and cases from the real world.

The principles are a kind of a tuning fork, as mentioned earlier, to tune the strategy by self-correcting a series of cases, experiments, interventions, and lots of critical self-reflection. We are excited about three kinds of reflectivity (Bell & Willmott, 2019):

1. Epistemic reflexivity – where our ways of knowing follow a discipline, but we must admit to being ontologists, checking it out in ways of Being
2. Constitutive reflexivity – which, in our terms, is about antenarrative processes constitutive in the pre-narrative and pre-story before coherence into narrative or story.
3. Disruptive reflexivity – which we apply by disconfirming the stories and narratives with counterstories and counternarratives, attempting to refute and falsify our own theories and abductions, to come up with better ones.

And we believe in grounding ourselves in a terrestrial ethics approach to how we, for example, can work with actually implementing the UN goals instead of them being a 'brand,' a way to talk about, but not do, what is needed.[11] Our argument is that if the UN is just branding economic growth instead of degrowth we will not live to see average global temperature increases stay below 1.5° C.[12] True Storytelling is a way for people, organizations and countries to be in a multi-species world, living a balanced life for humankind and for nature. Kallis, Kostakis, Lange, Muraca, Paulson and Schmelzer (2018: 291) contend that "degrowth signals a radical political and economic reorganization leading to reduced resource and energy use." Put simply, the degrowth hypothesis is that it is possible to organize a transition and live well under a different political-economic system that has a radically smaller resource throughput. Put simply, the UN SDGs have been colonized and continue to be co-opted by a continued-growth-business-as-usual agenda, without considering living well in a 'degrowth' political-economic system (Boje, 2019d). We ask 'how did the growth paradigm (Schmelzer, 2015) become hegemonic in the UN SDGs, and how can its hegemony be dismantled?' Lowe (2015: 109) asserts: "The scientific evidence for anthropogenic climate change, peak oil, global environmental problems and limits to growth more generally is clear, but denial is still widespread." Prádanos (2015) call for a pedagogy of degrowth to deal with the complex socio-environmental challenges of the Anthropocene.

We submit that True Storytelling is needed to counter the denial of climate science evidence financed by Exxon ($30 million) and the Koch brothers ($127 million), and resonating in social media echo chambers (Watts Up With That (WUWT) and Global Warming Policy Forum (GWPF) Bloomfield & Tillery, 2019).[13] Milojević and Inayatullah (2015: 151) call for a narrative foresight that can "move future thinking from a focus on new technologies and generally to the question of what's next, to an exploration of the worldviews and myths that underlie possible, probable and preferred futures." 'Probable' means those bets on the future that are not yet certain to become 'true' but we can foresee a probable loss that is likely or unlikely to be true. Climate change is a highly likely probable event. Since Exxon has known since 1982 that its industry practices are responsible for climate change, it is time to hold them accountable for the consequences of their actions and inactions, just as was done to the tobacco industry once their denier strategy was shown to be a probable way to delay long enough to eke out a few more billion in profit.

As a way to create change, we follow the self-correcting method and action research using the seven principles in True Storytelling helping people finding the true; being open and respecting stories already there; trying from all the small stories to create and emerge a clear but open plot which give some direction in a complex world; working with timing in the short and long run; helping stories along and supporting experiment, bets on the future; working with how to stage a true story but also remember to reflect on if the story 'now' is sustainable not only for the people, the community but for the earth and all species.

Before we end the Introduction, we want to go back to the story about the Danish municipality where we carried out the action research with True Storytelling and the self-correcting method. We will describe it in different phases mentioned below.

It progressed in several phases (I to V, in the above illustration). Each is a cycle repeated to form a spiral of True Storytelling principles, by integrating several cycles of Abduction-Induction-Deduction (A-I-D) using the methodology of 'storytelling science.' Jens Larsen's research question for his dissertation, at Aalborg University, was 'How can we use UN SDGs and True Storytelling principles to create a more sustainable and ethical future for the Municipality of Sorø and the companies and business?' This is both about sustainable production and the wellbeing of citizens.

Phase I Beginning conversations with a Danish Municipality

Jens: "It all began with me inviting the head, Søren Kjær, of Sorø Municipality to a meeting with David and I. David and I asked for some challenges to

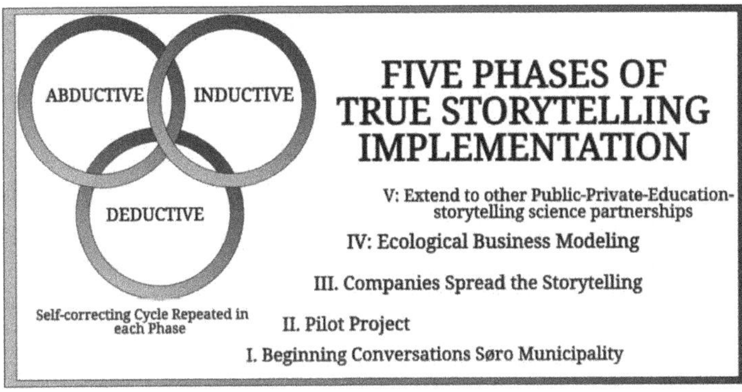

Figure 0.3 Dynamic mapping of True Storytelling Principles: implementation in Sorø Municipality

Figure 0.4 Sorø Project with business storytellers' relations to UN SDGs

explore with storytelling science applications. Søren suggested we help them with a project to implement the United Nations 'Sustainable Development Goals' (SDGs) which was a part of their strategy. At that time (2018) they were pioneers in working with SDGs. We asked him about the Principle 1 (True) questions: Do you believe in this approach? Do you have the energy and commitment to sustain for the long term? And we ask ourselves if we did believe in the project? Was it right for us to do at this time?"

David and I had a conversation interview, at that time, with Grace Ann Rosile (we don't do semi-structured interviewing because it's too one-

> sided). She suggested that we rearrange the SDGs into means and ends. This made the whole project more doable. In January 2019, I made an introduction to the whole Sorø Municipality staff of management. Intuitively I sensed that to begin with Principle 2 respecting the stories of sustainability, was how I needed to begin with Sorø. I also noticed that what stands out about Sorø are old forests and lots of lakes, and the Heron is quite at home there. David was asking me, "What spirit animals are in Sorø Municipality?" The Heron represents wisdom, good judgement, and grounding in achievements. The Heron symbolizes stillness, tranquillity, and what is needed to recognize future opportunities.[14] Later on I researched the history of Sorø and found out that it has a long history going back to the Middle Age, the Enlightenment and connections to storytelling and spirituality. Great storytellers and thinkers like H.C. Andersen, Ingemann, Ludvig Holberg and Grundtvig has a connection with Sorø.

We look more into the history of Sorø in Chapter 1.

Phase II Pilot project

Jens:

> As a pilot project, Sorø leaders asked me to write a magazine article about six businesses that are located in their municipality. I developed my analysis of Phase I conversations, and initiated conversation interviews with the six businesses. It was a way of Sorø 'making room' for what was already present now – Principle 2: Make room: respecting the stories already there. At the same time, I was working with Sorø to enact all seven True Storytelling principles. I had to begin with trust building from the get go. I had noticed in Phase I, that I had begun the first few conversations without sharing who I was and what I believed in. This is an example of an abductive hypothesis, something I was aware of intuitively, but also a phenomenon I know I have to get more scientific about, by employing inductive conversations and other tests of the 'self-correcting' storytelling method. After the first few conversations, I learned to relax and have back-and-forth conversations. I even disclosed more upfront that I stutter, and I noticed it's a kind of invitation for them to share, if they like, their own life challenges. For example, in the storytelling conversation with one of the company owners, he shared his living stories about a personal challenge, it completely changed his outlook on how to be a leader, what was important in having business be part of the community, and so on. Building trust is important for each of us. They ask, but they don't say it aloud: "who is this guy?" and "what is he going to do with us?" I learned in Phase I and more in Phase II, to be in the conversations more authentically, and how to sort out which principle was important when, in order to move forward.

Phase III Companies spread the storytelling

Jens:

> I do not have III and IV figured out, but I have an intuitive awareness that these will be happening. My abductive hypothesis at this point, is that each of the six businesses I have performed conversational interviews with, and two more that seem the right next ones to do, these eight all have some kind of living story transition, a way in which they have begun 'grounding' themselves in spiritual ecology. I ask "what is the [living] story of your company?" For example, a company which create gardens from nature stones, we had a conversation about storytelling leadership. She said it was to give 'stones' their due as having old energy. Stones, from a quantum storytelling standpoint, are part of the spiritual ecology, with living energy. A third business, that entrepreneur told me his dad was the first person in Denmark to think about the importance to the future, of harvesting rainwater. I have another abductive hypothesis: I always seem to be working between stepping into the future, while at the same time needing to remember the lessons of history. It is something I learned from Kierkegaard. While there is no one common theme to the six, soon to be eight business storytellings, there is something unique, how we need as a business community to take care of the Earth for our grandchildren's sake."

Phase IV Work with ecological business modelling

Jens:

> What seems to be unfolding (my abductive hypothesis) is that there are municipalities and businesses out there who want an ecological business model (something we get to in Principle 7), and it is reflecting all the way through the project from my reason to agreeing to it, to the potential we see working together as an ensemble.

Phase V: Extend True Storytelling Principles to other public-private-education-storytelling science partnerships

Jens:

> I have to see where this idea is going before I act. But as an abductive prediction, I would think that we can extend ensemble storytelling and the seven True Storytelling principles into public-private-education-storytelling science partnerships that have some sort of Terrestrial Ethics grounding as their focus. This means that there is some kind of spiritual awakening

along with the 'storytelling science' as organizations and communities rethink a lot of things, and get in touch with their own loving stories.

The project has grown since the beginning and will involve not only the municipality but 30 companies, NGOs and different stakeholders in the whole region of Zealand west of Copenhagen. We will return to this case throughout the book and our research project in Sorø will go on for years to come.

Besides Sorø, we have conducted workshops and projects with companies, organizations and municipalities in Denmark and the States in which we facilitate True Storytelling Principle application to problem situations. Abductions are the seminar member's intuitive predictions of what is going on. Induction is the inquiry into those productions that are tested in up to four ways: a) reflecting by individual writing and sharing in groups; b) doing conversations with additional people about the situation; c) applying various science disciplines to the problem situation; d) do intervention projects (experiments) that test the abductive predictions. Deductions come from research and from the testing of the evolving theory and assumptions. The self-correcting occurs as the A-I-D cycles are enacted and tested, to attempt to refute the theory of the situation and assumptions.

What are our own 'living stories' as co-authors?

If you want to work with True Storytelling it's important to know your own story. The land and the place you come from, your grandparents and your parents' stories, people you have met, books you have read, music you have heard etc. You need to become alive and organic and become friends with your stories or else they can become your enemies when you are working with others stories in search for the truth.

Jens

Storytelling has always been a part of my life. I grew up in a little village, Svinninge, one and a half hours west of Copenhagen, Denmark. There was one long street running through the village with shops, taverns, the city council, a cinema and the headquarter for the electric company. People were walking up and down the street, kids playing, cars driving by. My mom and dad had a store. In the early years they sold tobacco, wine, newspapers, lotto, sport betting etc. Later, because of my dad's passion for hunting, we sold guns, rifles and equipment for hunting and fishing. All kind of people came to that store. The local salesman, the big farmers, working-class people, bums, kids and elderly people. In the back of the store the hunters and salesmen were telling stories and, in the kitchen, people were telling stories while my dad counted the lotto coupons long time before the web and online services. These years in my childhood I think I learned the art of hanging out and listening to stories to quote one of my heroes, the American non-fiction writer, Gay Talese.

My mother died when I was 17 and my dad when I was 24. My sister and I inherited the store and sold it after a while.

I come from a family which combines two different classes in society. My mom is the only child of a big farmer and a religious family and my dad is from a working-class family. I have a photo with him and his two sisters and brother standing outside a shack near by a field where they dug for peat to use for fire in the wintertime. My dad's dad is in wooden shoes and an old jacket. Everybody is looking down as they were afraid of the camera except my dad looking up with a straight back.

Since I was a kid I have always written. I still have some of the old notebooks. I write to understand life and what I think (to quote Joan Didion). My best class in school was literature. I loved to write essays and discuss the stories and poems we read. And I still do today. I love to use stories and art to think with and enlarge my life.

I remember my first journey, a year of hitchhiking across the US back 1985, when I was 19 years old, with my good friend Peter, standing one morning at the beach in Big Sur at Highway One in California. It was still cold and you could feel the fog on your skin and hear the waves from the Pacific Ocean hitting the rocks. I made a promise to myself – I wanted to write stories, be among friends and travel around the world. I'm not the first young man who has made such a promise, and later I have made myself many more promises that are long forgotten, but that one I kept.

Over the years I have been working with storytelling, written biographies, interview books with CEOs and the best writers, poets and songwriters. I have been working for the theatre creates plays where I have collected stories from real people's lives and the Danish film director Lars von Trier's scriptwriter Peter Asmussen rewrote the stories into a script. One of the plays got the Danish award for best directing and was later played in Stockholm and Berlin.

I have taught people to write, both doctoral students and experienced researchers, and for the last 24 years I have taught people the art of essay-writing at the 150 years' old Testrup Folk School. I have written books about ethics and leadership and founded the company Old Friend Industries based on the wish that friendship could be the driver which could bring people together to make a difference. I have always been inspired by the Danish Folk School movement and it is an important part of Danish history, an education for life, not only for certain skills. I have worked and developed what we called New Nordic Leadership as a more trustful approach to leadership and lately co-founded the Nordic School of Arts and Health.

It has always been more than just work. It is something deeper, a journey looking for a True Storytelling, to mention what this book is about; it has always been about how to be in the world and how to deal with the complexity of life.

When I was young, I spent the summers in my parent's summer house, which I have inherited now with my sister. I loved to surf. Here in Denmark it was windsurfing, the feeling of the wind, the waves, being in the now and try to be a part of nature, forgetting myself – which never has been my strong side, but something I always have been attracted by – a feeling I can compare to writing and good and meaningful conversations and Zen meditations. In my definition, this book is not only a book about how to implement sustainable change, it's also a book about how to be in the world and live a true and sustainable life in close connection with nature and other human beings. And I think my quest is to help people and organizations to find their own true story, and working with Lena and David on this project, is surely a part of my own true story.

Lena

My living story is I worked to implement a new kind of storytelling experience, the Ragnarock Museum for Pop, Rock and Youth Culture in Roskilde Denmark. It is not the usual celebration of a band, but a story about how the youth – through music, dance and living – changed the world after the Second World War. The story is told using True Storytelling principles in the development of the exhibitions; staging, plotting, reflecting, making room for peoples' stories. The 12-year-long journey making the museum also mirrors the storytelling approach, as I believe the museum never would have succeed if we had not (however unaware) been following the five entangled processes moving from *abstracting* (the philanthropic idea) to *grounding* (who are we really), to *futuring* (what it is going to be; too many opinion on that issue) and *rehistorizing* (new counter stories and time challenges make constantly impact on how to proceed). I then met Jens, and then David, and we initiated the True Storytelling Principles by mixing our living stories together.

I grew up in the 70s in a left-wing family; my mom was a red stocking of the Women's Liberation Movement, my dad a psychologist dragging me to endless demonstrations against capitalism, imperialism, nuclear plants, weapons and fighting for equal rights between women and men. I heard awful stories and good stories listening to political discussions and songs, music and performances as well as my mom's friends bashing men and 'the system' (actually, mostly the latter, as they blamed 'the system' and not only the men for being suppressed; a reflection for the #MeToo movement).

When I was 11 years old, I told my dad that in order to change the world, as I had already experienced how fatal the climate is today, I would not be a politician, but change the big companies and injustices from within – through being a part of them, doing it with them. It became my mission to work with both management and employees and stakeholders to find common grounds. I have worked with culture, urban planning, public relations, fundraising and organisational change in municipalities, museum, institutions, corporations, boards etc., all with the same target of accomplishing something sustainable together with people. Always with the same trial-and-error approach being super scared that I was on the wrong path – or jumping on a wave – leading people the wrong way. Always in doubt as to what I was doing and then again with an intuitive sense that it was somehow the right thing to do. A dear friend of mine once said "You are like Gandalf; we are not really sure of what you are doing, but we trust you, as you seem to believe it yourself." I was not aware of the storyline of my work or person, as my private life undergoes the same weirdness, until I met Jens and David.

To please my father, I once considered writing a book. However, I felt much more comfortable, as Jens visualises it, standing on the surfboard riding the waves on and on in real-life-time. I often felt I was drowning, when things went wrong, as they always do. However, a new wave would soon appear, and I would get the chance to make it right again.

I am an external examiner in leadership, organisation, strategy and communication at Copenhagen Business School and Roskilde University, and besides making me more clever and able to benefit from it in my practical work life, the biggest joy I get is to help the young (stressed up) students to feel confident by themselves and their work. Learn them and make them experience the huge satisfaction reflecting on their hard work and academic achievements.

For many years I wondered how come I never had a hobby or passion besides working and family. Very often I have been lying, inventing hobbies, to satisfy people at dinner parties etc. But the truth is, that I enjoy ongoing self-development and self-insight and that is why the work on True Storytelling with David and Jens is a natural personal wave on which to surf.

David

My living story is the centuries-old quest for the relationship between the humanity of past generations to all living things of this generation. For a long time, I was uneducated, but was the first in my family to attend college, and somehow graduated, kept going to get a PhD, an assistant professor at UCLA, and then my life came undone – my marriage, my tenure, relationships to everything, all undone. Here-and-now, I do apprentice-blacksmithing to keep me connected to my indigenous-roots, to a great grandfather who had a blacksmith's shop in Goldendale, Washington, and to all the blacksmiths on family farms for a thousand years before. I am a shamanic practitioner aiming to *rehistoricize* my Celtic indigeneity because that is the living story life that unfolds in me today. I was born into Catholicism and adopted into Jainism after I met Grace Ann Rosile and became vegetarian, someone with compassion for all life – in that conference food line, and in that first nanosecond of our relationship, all that mattered in my life changed forevermore. I had claimed, in that nanosecond, a new future and keep caring for it, manifesting it. I am not just a 'storytelling researcher,' not just a 'writer' about stories, or someone traveling the world to do True Storytelling keynotes, and teaching doctoral students how to do 'storytelling science.' These are identity-narratives to situate me in social networks, these *markers* are far from my 'living story.' My 'living story' is deeper in places, in times, and in my aliveness. I come from a place called 'Spokane,' the city where I was born, but also the 'Little Spokane River' that flows into the Columbia River and into the Pacific Ocean. I come from ancestors, all farmers, from as far back as I can trace my family tree, to Holstein in the 1700s, when it was still part of Denmark (on my dad's side) and from Scotland and Wales (on my mother's side) and before that Boje's (on both sides). I am Celtic, and that means 'once upon a time' and to this day, 'I am Celtic' 'tribal' and 'indigenous.' Being farmers and living in relation to growing plants, trees, and animals ended in my dad and mom's generation, and our indigeneity was thoroughly colonized three centuries before that. Discovering the web of living stories – I am committed to living here and now – has taken a lifetime to reveal. I am a spiritual being in a world of spiritual beings, and a nomad between many kinds of worlds. This is my living story, and it all became about True Storytelling when I met Jens, and Lena, and we embarked on this project together. The first time the three of us came up with the concept True Storytelling[15] was in 2016 and the year after we had the principle ready (Boje, Larsen & Bruun, 2017).

Then, over the last couple of years, we have explored, discussed and tried to define the principle through case studies – not the usual one-shot cases, rather we do self-correcting storytelling science. Using the principle in projects, workshops, coaching with start-ups etc. we develop our own deductive theories, question our abductive propositions, and finetune our inductive inference methods. We know we cannot get to absolute truth, but we can refute the fake telling, especially in our own work.

We have failed and we have met a lot of critics shaking their heads, but also found great support from people who believe in True Storytelling and use it as a path for the future. Or as the quote from Theodore Roosevelt says:

> It is not the critic who counts; not the man who points out how the strong man stumbles, or where the doer of deeds could have done them better. The credit belongs to the man who is actually in the arena, whose face is marred by dust and sweat and blood; who strives valiantly; who errs, who comes short again and again, because there is no effort without error and shortcoming; but who does actually strive to do the deeds; who knows great enthusiasms, the great devotions; who spends himself in a worthy cause; who at the best knows in the end the triumph of high achievement, and who at the worst, if he fails, at least fails while daring greatly, so that his place shall never be with those cold and timid souls who neither know victory nor defeat.[16]

This book is for all the people who dare to stand inside the arena to try to strive to do the deeds, as Roosevelt put it, although they sometimes fail and get dirty and lose.

Notes

1 See 'Mckinsey Quarterly (2008): Creating Organizational Transformation' and 'McKinsey Global Survey Results (2010): What Successful Transformations Share,' accessed January 2020 at www.mckinsey.com/business-functions/organization/our-insights/what-successful-transformations-share-mckinsey-global-survey-results

2 Interview January 4, 2020, in the Danish newspaper *Politiken*.
3 Arendt, 2001: 23–42.
4 Together (Boje, Larsen & Bruun, 2017) developed the principles of True Storytelling, and began collecting case materials. Boje (2012, 2014, 2017b, 2019b) continued to develop the relation between quantum physics and storytelling using Heidegger's (1962) notions such as before of forehaving, beneath of foreconcepting, between of forestructuring, becoming of forecaring, and bets of foresight (bets on the future). Boje, Gergerich & Svane (2016) develop these same Heideggerian notions in relation to antenarrative processes. Work in review by Kenneth Mølbjerg Jørgensen, Marita Svane, and David Boje has added foregrasping, a Heideggerian term about one's embodiment awareness that is a 'beyond' the limits of narrative and story. Our body knows what is 'true' before the storytelling commences. Thus antenarrative has matured from its initial Boje (2001) 'before' and 'bets' of antenarrative, to the six B-notions, adding, beneath, between, becoming, and beyond.
5 For more on this storytelling model, see Boje, Svane & Gergerich, 2016; Svane, Boje & Gergerich, 2015; Svane, 2014; Boje, 2001, 2011; Jørgensen & Boje, 2009; Jørgensen, 2011
6 *Washington Post*, accessed August 19, 2019 at www.washingtonpost.com/science/2019/08/17/this-baby-sea-mammal-captured-peoples-hearts-she-just-died-eating-plastic/?wpisrc=nl_most&wpmm=1
7 Boje and Rosile (2019, in press) provide the application of self-correcting method for people doing masters theses, and doctoral dissertations. Work on the self-correcting storytelling paradigm was also derived from Boje (2019a in press, 2019b, and 2019c).
8 busiesscommission.org 2015 Survey, accessed August 19 2019 at http://report.businesscommission.org/report
9 Aristotle (1954, section #25).
10 *Together-telling* is a notion from work by Rosile, Boje, Herder, and Sanchez in an article recently accepted in the journal *Business and Society*. It builds upon work by Rosile, Boje, and Claw (2018) on ensemble leadership, in which we all together are leaders, in heterarchy instead of hierarchy, or some notion of an over-compensated cadre of top leaders with everyone else marginalized and silenced to the bottom layers of the pyramid.
11 For more on terrestrial ethics, see https://davidboje.com/Gaia an initiative to create a Gaia PhD.
12 Without action, according to UN, the world's average surface temperature is likely to increase by 3° C this century: www.un.org/sustainabledevelopment/climate-change/
13 'Exxon knew about climate change since 1982 and spent $30 million on climate debate [denial] advertising,' accessed August 20 2019 at www.scientificamerican.com/article/exxon-knew-about-climate-change-almost-40-years-ago/ 'Koch Family Foundations spent $127,006,756 directly financing 92 groups that have attacked climate change science and policy solutions, from 1997–2017,' accessed August 20 2019 at www.greenpeace.org/usa/global-warming/climate-deniers/koch-industries/
14 For more on the Heron see Imelda's website, accessed June 3 2019 at https://trustedpsychicmediums.com/spirit-animals/heron-spirit-animal/ Also see David Boje's website https://davidboje.com/Shamanic for how to do meditations in Lower World to find your own power animal helping spirit.
15 We had several ideas for the name for the concept (sustainable storytelling, ethical storytelling, etc.), but Maiken Bork Clausen suggested the name True Storytelling.
16 Theodore Roosevelt quotes, accessed August 19 2019 at www.goodreads.com/quotes/7-it-is-not-the-critic-who-counts-not-the-man

1 Principle 1

You yourself must be true and prepare the energy and effort for a sustainable future

This chapter is about working with UN goals and climate change and about how the singer and songwriter Johnny Cash found his true story, together with the hip hop producer Rick Rubin, and how they recorded the best album in his career. It's about how organizations and society can find out what is true and sustainable and powerful.

In a world with so much information, so many answers, ideas and so much going on, how is it possible to find out what is true for you and the people and strategies you are working with? And how can you find the right way to prepare the energy for a sustainable future?

The first principle is the foundation of True Storytelling. The principle says: "You yourself must be true and prepare the energy and effort for a sustainable future." The principle stresses the importance of finding a strategy for your life or for your organization, company or country which is true, which means it is sustainable in a human, and a multi-species planetary-context, and not just in an economic sense – you and the people you are working with believe in it and are energized for the long haul.

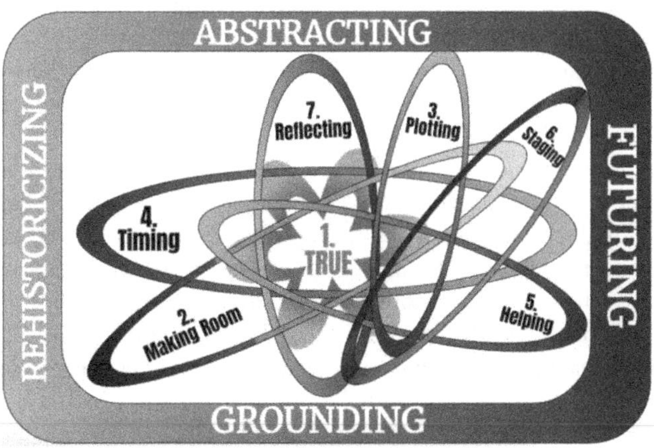

Figure 1.1

In this chapter we will try to define the principle, but also the concept, of 'true' as an ethical and sustainable way of life. Furthermore, will we define the concepts of antenarrative-*forecaring*, as important concepts which help you in your life and work, with implementing sustainable changes.[1] True has many grains; there are many sides to true. And, finally, we will give some advice and tools for working with Principle 1 in praxis, for example, in a private or public organization, municipality, in fundraising or in coaching. The self-correcting method of storytelling science means making mistakes and finding better ways, through trial-and-error.

To warm you up, we start with some questions. For Principle 1, please begin your *together-telling* with these five questions:

1 What is a true and sustainable strategy when it comes to nature (biosphere), human (and non-human) and economy?
2 Did you check it out?
3 Do you believe in it?
4 Do you have the knowledge to do it?
5 Can you sustain it (get energized and not burn out) in the long term?

Ok we are ready …

We must be true together and prepare the energy and effort for a sustainable future. How do we do this? For us, it is about being in dialogue and doing *together-telling*. In the next paragraph we want to show how the different concepts of the model come into play and how it can help you to get new perspectives on Principle 1 and the challenges you are struggling with.

In *together-telling*, I listen to what is true for you, preparing our co-energies, and our joint-efforts for a sustainable future, together. This is multi-species storytelling (Haraway, 2016). We begin the process of checking it out, together, self-correcting and together-correcting to find our way forward. This *futuring* means working together, caring in advance, for a particular future, out of the many potential futures, that we believe in doing. We each have our own webwork of unfolding living stories, and, by listening to one another, we gain the knowledge to do the changes together. *Together-telling* means we are sustaining one another so we don't get burned out, and can do something that has value for many generations beyond our own. As we do the *futuring* we are *rehistoricizing*, claiming some past out of the many entangling pasts. Some are here-and-now apparent, highlighted because of the future we are manifesting and what we are here-and-now attending to. Doing our 'living story webwork' here-and-now is how one living story begs for another to be told, and you interrupt my telling to tell one of your own, and then another one. This is what it means to be *together-telling*. This is managing our change management together, and *grounding* it in community relations, in organizational relations, in customer and supplier relations. But we are far from done with *grounding*. The entire supply chain, the customer ways of using what we are producing and distributing, has its own 'will' which is greater than us together, a wholeness unfolding with its own agency, its own consequence, its own hidden costs. Every supply chain, and the distribution chain to the customers, is using planetary natural resources, is appropriating them for better or for worse. By *grounding* we are zooming-in, then zooming-out again to understand our complicity. We zoom-in to the quantum field level, the waveform of energy at subatomic context. We zoom-out to multi-species storytelling, and to the cosmos. In moving our conscious awareness from *abstracting* and reflection in a meeting room, to getting embodied (our 37.2 trillion living cells), to being in our sensemaking *of the world-making*, how our change management strategies as Human-world are already inseparable and undeniable apart of 'Nature-world' in the way our ways of living story life and work, are complicit and morally answerable to what ways 'Living World' is unfolding has to be First Principle, '*True*' in the sense of being about the 'Whole Story' of our existence. We are not just logical, we are spiritual beings, and artistically living a life that has ethical coordinates.

The story of Johnny Cash and how he found his true story and made a comeback

To illustrate the *together-telling* and self-correcting method and model, we will start with a story about the singer and songwriter Johnny Cash and his work with the producer Rick Rubin. In the late 80s and early 90s Johnny Cash lost faith in himself. Somehow, he lost the true story which he had created up through the 50s, 60s and 70s with a certain signature, style and attitude. In 1992, Johnny Cash was out of business. The radios didn't play his songs, he was too old and he could not find a company for his new records. At that time, he was playing at places like cheap low-rent Las Vegas residencies around the country.[2] On February 27, 1993 he was playing a concert at The Rhythm Cafe, Santa Ana, Los Angeles. A few days earlier the hip hop producer Rick Rubin had phoned his manager and asked for a meeting. "He shouldn't be playing at that place. He was a legend. I went to see him after the concert."

Rubin is famous for producing The Beastie Boys, Metallica, Slayer and other heavy metal bands. Rick Rubin continues: "I don't like a certain kind of music, I simply like great music. My job is to help people to find their own voice and set them free."

Johnny Cash recalled the meeting:

> I said: "What're you gonna do with me, that nobody else has done, to sell records for me?" Rick said: "Well, I don't know that we will sell records. I would like you to sit in my living room with a guitar and two microphones and just sing to your heart's content, everything you ever wanted to record." I said: "That sounds good to me."

Johnny Cash visited Rubin in his home at Sunset Strip in LA. He had some recording gear in his living room. It was an ADAT tape recorder and two microphones. "Just play something," Rubin said. Cash took his guitar and played. Rubin explains:

> Much of the job is about creating an environment in which the artist feels safe, so that they can allow themselves to be more vulnerable. There's something very beautiful in seeing someone allowing themselves to be vulnerable. I think that, more than anything, is my job.

Rubin is a big man with a big beard who walks around barefoot. While Cash were playing, Rubin lay on a couch and listened with his whole body, not only with his ears. He is inspired by Zen, an aspect of Buddhism which stresses the important of awareness and being in the now.

Rubin explains: "Even if you had heard a particular song your whole life, when he sang it, all of a sudden you understood it, or thought about the words in a different way, or took the song more seriously."

You can say Rubin used his body as a tuning fork and every time he had a feeling in his body due the music he reacted. We can also say he used his body as a truth-awareness, to find something which is important or true – the body never lies. Principle 1 is this kind of embodiment, grasping form beyond the future arriving in the here and now. It is a manifestation of a conscious capitalism in the theatre of capitalism.[3] If we analyze it and use our model and the four approaches on each principle, Rubin's listening with his body and Cash's playing is the grounding of the true but Rubin and Cash also draw upon their history: Rubin of working with different bands and Cash's whole career. Rubin put in a vision or concept on an abstract level working with Cash and both of them worked out how to bring his music, or the music they created together, into the future. As they get along and do their *together-telling*, they are doing the process of self-correcting. And when Walter Benjamin (1936) in his famous essay stresses there is no storytelling anymore, this is a way to come back to a truer storytelling.

The same approach has been taken by the Danish music producer Lars Skaerbaek:

> "It about creating an atmosphere with no pressure or ambitions. Very often the best takes are the first takes. The artist come into the studio and I ask them to do a sound check or rehearsal. I introduced it like a kind of warm up exercise but very often we decide to use the first takes on the final track."

Skaerbaek's approach is almost the same as Rubin's – it's a way to find something which is true for the artist. To create a room of no-performance. It is more to catch the right moment while it drives or moves by. Another Danish musician, Lars Top Galia,[4] from the Danish legendary punk band Sort Sol, stresses the importance of finding the true in the sound. "If you push the artist in a certain way to please a market or an audience it always ends up as a failure." The political philosopher Hannah Arendt (1958) writes about how to push the past and the future to leave room for the present where something new can emerge. Perhaps it could be a metaphor for what these producers are doing?

We must add that it is not always the producers and artists who have success, which means the concept of truth in the sense of art is hard to grasp. To quote a great artist, the American writer Jonathan Franzen: "The novel is often complex cause it is trying to grasp the truth and the true is complex".[5] The great German painter Anselm Giefer put it this way: "The truth is always grey or has different nuances of grey. It's never clear" (Hustvedt, 2012).

Antenarrative theory

We can unpack the shades of grey and the truth by using antenarrative questions as a way of getting closer to the truth:

1 What was *Forehaveing* BEFORE? This is the antenarrative process of *rehistoricizing*, by preparing in advance for what one is about to be having. An example is how parents prepare in advance before having (*forehaving*) a baby. The mother watches her diet, and quits smoking. The father takes classes in parenting.
2 What is *Foreconcepting* BENEATH? Beneath the narrating and storying is all that is preconstitutive, the language, symbols, and gestures understood in the context of a society or company in order to make sense enough to create a story or narrative of a newborn (the baby language, names of baby furniture, language, and so on).
3 What is *Forestructuring* BETWEEN? Parents have to cope with a whole different context of infrastructure that supports or interferes with having a newborn: the insurance agents (not in Denmark, the healthcare is free), the medical establishment, the grandparents, the religious institutions everyone belongs to or avoids.

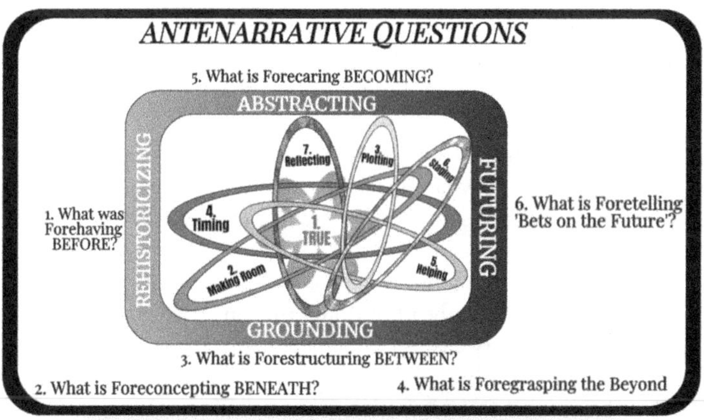

Figure 1.2 Six antenarrative questions for True Storytelling strategies

4 What is *Foregrasping* BEYOND? Beyond is the body, the new to arrive body of the newborn, the changing body of the mother, the body of the father, and so on. Each body can grasp the beyond, in advance, ahead of being able to articulate a story or a narrative with any coherence. The body never lies, and it speaks truth but sometimes the mind does not listen or denies what the body is telling, antecedent to the mouth being able to speak, to tell.
5 What is *Forecaring*, the BECOMING? The foetus has not taken its first breath, has not arrived to breathe the same air as the parents and doctors, and so many more people, animals, and plants. The Becoming of the child in birth, maturing, and eventual death is all about the primordial aspect of coming into the world, becoming human, learning to Be-in-the-world, and to Be-of-the-world, inseparable from Nature.
6 What is *Foresight*, the 'Bets on the Future'? The parents, in advance of the birth begin to whisper to the foetus, "be a doctor' or "be an engineer." Everyone is trying to influence the future, to bake their own bets on the future. Each bet on the future is an antenarrative process, a preparing both the teller and the one who listens (spouse, grandparents, the foetus) for a pathway in life. The infant is born into their living story world before they can crawl or form words, or even say 'Mama' or 'Dada.'

What antenarrative processes are all about is reconstituting the True Storytelling world of the parents and the child in advance of the birth, then in advance of the child attending school, and so on. There are preparations for the future, acts of *forehaving, foreconcepting, forestructuring, foregrasping, foresight*, and *forecaring* (Boje, & Rosile, in press 2019):

6 Bs
1 How is the BEFORE (*forehaving*) narrative or story possible?
2 What is in advance BENEATH (*foreconcepting*) in symbols, languages, understandings that make the narrative or story possible to accomplish?
3 What is BETWEEN the actors and material-actants, in their *forestructuring*, that pre-constitutes narrative or story?
4 What is the BEYOND (*foregrasping*) that is the embodied, pre-narrative, pre-story way of intuiting?
5 What are the *bets on the future* made with *foresight* (or *foretelling*) by various parties in what Weick (2012) calls antenarrative assemblage?
6 What is the entire BECOMING, *forecaring* of the enterprise?

This is one example. Every organization, every nation, and humanity as a whole, has its antenarrative processes ahead of doing the narrative–counternarrative, and the living-story–counterstory aspects of being in a storytelling world. The antenarrative questions can help a family, an organization, or a nation zoom in on the minute details of life and work, or zoom out on the macro pattern, the multifractality of life (Boje, 2018a; Deleuze, & Guattari, 1987).

The research approach of antenarrative and True Storytelling is aligned with the French ISEOR Institute of Socioeconomics in Lyon, with our colleagues Henri Savall, Veronique Zardet, Marc Bonnet and Amandine Savall.[6] Mikhail Bakhtin, Judith Butler, Donna Haraway and Hannah Arendt have respectively provided the 'moral answerability,' 'moral accountability,' and 'ethical political,' for us to help you to do the kinds of True Storytelling, reflective of oneself in the eventness of once-occurrent Being, to attempt to live one's life by True Storytelling principles.[7] For its spiritual ecology we draw upon the 'Native Science' work of Professor Gregory Cajete.[8] Walter Benjamin and Gertrude Stein believed that 'storytelling was coming to an end,' its practices subverted since the industrial revolution, with prohibitions on workers singing and otherwise telling what is true, for fear of reprisal from the hegemonic ways of narrative in an information society.[9] Benjamin was first to do antenarrative, before it became so named.[10] Donna Haraway's (2016) multi-species storytelling is hopeful.

The overall idea of a 'True Storytelling' is to create coherence and meaning between – on a macro level – an organization's or society's strategic efforts, and – on a micro level – the commitment by people, employees and managers to implement the strategies in the organization or community, and do work within the planetary limits of Earth's carrying capacity for all species. This is why we believe in '*grounding*' in multi-species storytelling, and getting down to the Terrestrial reality, the planetary limits of corporations, governments, and consumers' accumulations of stuff.

It is a significant point that the macro level does not work without the micro level and vice versa. There must be a strategy on the one hand and someone to execute it on the other hand. One might say that it is an expression of power levels in the society or organization and that one can suppress the other if the strategy is not communicated and accepted. The trick of implementation is to tie the two levels (micro and macro) together. True Storytelling as a bridge builder also becomes an organic and dynamic method that needs continuous care. It is by virtue of the interaction, between the individual and the organization as a unit, that innovation is delivered and results are created for them. This is not a quick fix, but an ongoing process between the macro and micro level.

The story of Cash and Rubin, and the quotes of the Danish musicians, are great examples of the concept of the six antenarrative questions, which are a very important part of Principle 1.[11] What was Before a narrative or story cohered? Narrative and story come from the situation people are embedded in, in this example of musicians having their recording gear, its prehistory, which is still happening, despite our not being able to put a master narrative or a living story onto it.[12] It is part of making a 'bet on the future' and 'preparing' or 'planning' in advance for the future one wishes to arrive in the here-and-now. To make music one needs *foreconception* (music language, music notes, music signs on music sheets). To have a music industry, there needs to be *forestructuring* of what is between the music being made and it being heard in a concert or a recording technology. To be a musician requires an embodiment, a feeling for the music, that is the 'beyond' a *foregrasping* of a melody or lyric so it can come into being. The becoming, its *forecaring*, is all about nurturing the music; a heart of care means letting the music enliven one's spirit. Many bets on the future are being made, and each is an opportunity cost. Manifesting one kind of music by a group of musicians means their talent is not manifesting some other style of music. These six antenarrative processes are the musical stuff out of which musical grand narratives and musicians' living stories are happening, interrupting other living stories. You cannot tell one living story without telling another, and one more, oh and the one just forgotten.

Actually, organizations and managers and people in general are very good at planning but very often they do not create ownership of the right strategy or process because the whole process lacks antenarrative *forecaring*. To understand the difference between planning and *forecaring* we can explore what 'care' means. 'To take care' is to be aware of or take responsibility for another person. The Danish word for it is '*omsorg*' and it means to make a circle around somebody sorrows and it is often compared to 'motherhood'. It is an embodied concept. You have to be out there among the people listening, to understand what the true story is now and what people are worrying about. To care 'before' means to care for the future, to create an atmosphere where the right ideas can emerge. If we are doing *forecaring* and spend time with people, like Rubin did when he worked with Johnny Cash, we have a big chance to change the things to come. *We have to build a bridge where people can cross.*

Rubin create a space of trust when he does *forecaring* (becoming of care) and in this space new ideas or antenarrative *foreconception* (the beneath) and *foresight* (*bets on the future*) can emerge. The antenarrative process of *foresight* is like bets in a poker game. We can never be sure but we have to have the courage to experiment with bringing a new future into being. Some bets are too risky, a gambler's dilemma. Some are not different enough from the status quo to be called new.

Somehow, if we want to explain it in a more abstract way, Cash was in-between a dominant narrative of himself as a burned-out country singer and the counter narrative about how he and his audience used to see him. What Rubin did was to make room for some new living stories and antenarrative to emerge. Rubin was doing something that was antenarrative, and at other times using anti-narrative.[13]

True Storytelling is about prospective sensemaking, the fashioning out of antenarrative processes, the many pasts, and many futures, arriving in the present here-and-now. This is often a pre-conscious, prestory, pre-narrative, unstoryable, unnarrativizable coming into awareness of embodied grasping the beyond. There are dialogical and dialectical processes, as well as anti-dialogical and anti-dialectical processes, in the situated dynamics of storytelling.

An example of these new ideas or bets on the future could be how Rubin suggested that Cash should play a song by Cris Cornell, frontman in the American grunge band Soundgarden, *Rusty Cage*. "My fans will hate me,"

Cash answered. In other words, they are antithetical to the song, and anti-dialectical as well as anti-dialogical. Cash is caught up in struggles between musical styles and genres in the polity of music discourses. And perhaps some of them did hate him, but Rubin reinvented Johnny Cash and made him bigger, more respected, more powerful and truer than ever. After the first record, *American Recordings* from 1994, they worked together until Cash died in 2003.

Why did we tell this long story about Johnny Cash and Rick Rubin? Because it illustrates the core of Principle 1 and how you can work with it doing *together-telling*, doing *forecaring* and working with the antenarratives.

Using the *together-telling*, self-correcting method at a Danish Municipality and its companies working with UN Sustainability Goals as a new strategy

In the examples above, the music producer Rick Rubin showed how to do *forecaring* and how to work with the self-correcting method. How you do it always depends on the situation, but as the example with the music producers shows, it is about creating a space where stories and *together-telling* can emerge. We want to illustrate this with an example from the project where we work with the municipality helping them implement SDGs. As an important part of Principle 1, we are interested in the entire story and not just a small part of it. The example is a People's Gathering about the UN goals they held in August 2019; before this we had had conversations with local companies and citizens from the municipality.

This conversation is from a recording of three people being interviewed by David. The reason for looking at these parts of the interview is to show a broader example of how we work and how we try do *forecaring*. You can find a complete version of the interview in Appendix II. Before we go into the conversations, here is just a bit about the UN goals.

The United Nations Sustainable Development Goals (UN-SDGs) are the largest change process consultation ever attempted in the history of humankind. The Intergovernmental Panel on Climate Change (IPCC) 'frames' climate change with "largely narrow, science-oriented" terms in a kind of science-storytelling that goes to newspapers and digital social media, who in turn re-story and reframe the IPCC storytelling in broader impacts and adaptations, to the policymakers and various stakeholders worldwide, who make decisions (Wardekker, & Lorenz, 2019).

In Sorø, a blue (right-wing) party supports a neoclassical economic approach to the UN-SDGs. The focus is on economic growth and progress as the ultimate SDGs within the constraints of the budget. The good news is that in a conservative rural community, implementing most of the SDGs is a priority for city council and local businesses.

The Municipality of Sorø was one of the first municipalities in Denmark which made the UN goals their strategy. The population is 30,000 people and it's an area with lakes and forest and farming land. The main city, also called Sorø, has a population of 11,000 citizens and is surrounded by four smaller towns and villages.

We went, as said before, to Sorø on August 17, 2019, to their festival celebrating the UN-SDGs. I (David) gave a talk and then stayed around, and did storytelling conversation interviews with a dozen exhibitors, and the mayor. I sometimes challenged a story, offered a counterstory, or just tried to do self-correction of my own assumptions and theories. I was exploring Principle 1: You yourself must be true and prepare the energy and effort for a sustainable future.

Interview with the Mayor

DAVID: "What is your story about?" [We think that's a powerful question because it is very open.]

MAYOR OF SORØ: "It is amazing to me that we have taken this initiative to have this vision in 2022. We have chosen nine out of the 17 goals. We are actually on an island. The lakes surround the island. And of course, a lot about the sea is not appropriate to us. But something could be similar with our sewage or wastewater. If that is going to float over and into the lake"

DAVID: "Yeah, that would be a big problem. You might get some complaints."

MAYOR: "Yes, in Denmark we've got a green flag. We've got a blue flag. It's ok to go there and swim. There's no problem about that. So the problem is similar. We have to transfer the 17 goals to Sorø."

DAVID: "Right."

MAYOR: "OK, so that has been a very interesting process, involving all the population of Sorø, and so forth. So it was a good experience for us to invite people, to invite Connie Hedegaard, the earlier European Commissioner for [Climate Action 2011–2014] and so forth. So I am glad we have so many people even though we have bad weather."

DAVID: "Rain is a good thing. So how do you explain this municipality Sorø has done more. It is not just talk, talk, talk. You actually have programs and implementation."

MAYOR: "All the heating in Sorø, you have a central distribution center, where we make all the elating and electricity. Before we had these sustainable goals, it was used by natural gas."

DAVID: "Natural gas, Yeah."

MAYOR: "Afterwards we said we have to make some new things. We'll have it with biofuel. We have to make a partnership, goal number 17, with all the collectors of garbage cans, and they also collect, we have a lot of trees, a lot of forest. And then the people are going to cut trees in the gardens, we collect it in one place. And we use it for the biomass to make the heat. It's CO_2 zero. Before we did natural gas with a lot of CO_2 emissions. So that is an example of where we said 'we have to be CO_2 neutral in 2030.' We have changed this kind of fueling. That's one thing. And, of course, in our elderly help."

DAVID: "Yeah."

MAYOR: "We have the normal gasoline and diesel cars, when we have money enough we will go to hybrid cars."

DAVID: "Yeah, I just bought one. I'm so happy."

MAYOR: "So that's another way where we have changed our attitude to showing people which kinds of initiatives we are taking. Goal number 13, climate: Bring down the CO^2 emissions."

DAVID: "Yeah that's so wonderful."

MAYOR: "So we have a very specific plan. So it is necessary for us it also be economically sustainable because we don't have, we can't pull up money for everything. So, it has to be step-by-step, we are promising a small community with 30,000 inhabitants, will not save all the world. We will make and we will be clear in which kinds of initiatives we are going to do."

The conversation began with an open question: "What's your story about this?". The Mayor told the story about the land and the water, moving into how the citizens got involved and the different actions they have been taking. Somehow the Mayor's story unfolded by itself with a few comments from me, but almost no questions. I knew the Mayor has an apple farm, so I took the Mayor's answer and used it as a personal question, just going with the energy of the conversation:

DAVID: "You have an apple farm, and do you practice these things with your farm?"

MAYOR: "Actually, two years ago we don't make it as a commercial thing. No NPK [Nitrogen (N), Phosphorus (P), and Potassium (K) fertilizer] and so forth.... And in Denmark if you don't change the trees, to be effective, every ten years."

DAVID: "Ahh, I didn't know you have to change the apple trees every ten years."

MAYOR: "If you do it commercially, because in Denmark if you are growing the trees, the leaves is growing such a way [motioning with his hands] and you do it, actually like grapes. And you have a line, and you put up..."

DAVID: "How do you know the apples are going to taste good. Because there are so many, like 4,000 different kinds of apples."

MAYOR: "Yeah, but no, you have normally one sort." [Both of us laugh]

MAYOR: "For a thousand trees."

DAVID: "Wow, you have a thousand trees."

MAYOR: "Yeah, 1,200 trees."

DAVID: "Wow, 1,200 trees, that's big." [Mayor is called away]

DAVID: "Thank you. I will contact you if I have any more questions.The conversation with the Mayor moved from thoughts about the land, the sea and the lakes to the SDG's and how they work with them in the municipality to the Mayor's personal life being an apple farmer. And, again, I just followed the story, asking to the answers from the mayor, being aware of his body language. The conversation is almost like an essay by Joan Didion, mentioned in the Introduction, as it moves between different levels.

After talking to the Mayor, I wandered around the festival and I talked to politicians who are neoliberal and socialist. I used a self-correcting storytelling method. I wanted to explore the counternarrative, and go deeper into the dialogical aspects. By self-correcting I mean I am seeking to refute the theory and abductive assumptions I have been making.

I wanted to interview a non-blue politician to get some counter-stories of The People's Gathering. I am not doing a semi-structured interview with a set of predetermined questions, nor am I trying to be neutral. Rather, I want to find a common space of co-creation, a back and forth conversation where I share my storytelling and they share theirs (Boje, 2019b; Boje, & Rosile, 2019).

Interview with Bo Mouritzen, a socialist politician

The conversation begins:

DAVID: "What is your story?"

BO: "We're the most left wing."

DAVID: "So, I'm from New Mexico, what does that mean?"

BO: "So, New Mexico is a state in the United States?"

DAVID: "So, if I am left wing what does that mean?"

BO: "What would that be? Wow. We're Bernie Sanders, then go more left."

DAVID: "I'm so happy to meet you."Compared to the conversations with the mayor this is an example where I reveal my political view. That means that *forecaring* and *together-telling* is not about being objective, it is as mentioned before to follow the energy of the storytelling being a part of it.

DAVID: "I'm just wondering. I'm a big Bernie Sanders fan, and Elizabeth Warren. Uhhh, what's your take on all this? [Pointing to the festival of The People's Gathering.]

BO: "We get to hear a lot of normal people and what do people want. I find in politics that we tell people what we want. So we hear what they want. The interesting thing in creating a society, is what the members of society want. It's not just interesting to hear the leaders, and that's what we do a lot of. The good thing about this, is we get to hear our people. The not so good thing about it is, it's so, it's very controlled from the municipality. They tell, who does what. But we can get better. And I like to think how people are driven by the ones that actually are active in it."

DAVID: "But you're opposition. Does that mean you are opposed to what they are doing?"

BO: "No, we try to say we want something different. They are very friendly to the commercial part of the city, and we would like to be more environmental. And we'd like to be strong on the environment, on the children, the welfare state, stuff like that. So that's our angle, and they're more an economic angle. They're very, you always need to see 'does it pay?' 'Is it financially [useful].' And sometimes it isn't, and so what?"

DAVID: "I'll confide in you. I just gave a presentation about the UN sustainability goals being co-opted and colonized by too much of an economic focus."

BO: "Yep, and they are. They keep talking about economic growth. And yeah, you're a critic?

DAVID: "Yes, I'm a critic."

BO: "And so are we."Here the conversation has moved into a new phase. This is not a researcher interviewing a person but two people sharing ideas and thoughts and that is what *together-telling* is about. Actually, the researcher takes over the conversation.

Soren Kjær, the head or CEO of the municipality, invited me to get the story of the Sorø Festival from its main organizer.

Interview with Nanna Kirkegaard

DAVID: "What's your story?"

NANNA: "My name is Nanna [Kirkegaard] and I started the whole idea of the, of this meeting, a gathering."

DAVID: "Oh, tell me from the beginning, the whole story."

NANNA: "Oh yeah, the story, as in storytelling [looking at my card, that says 'storytelling researcher']. Ummm, OK, I have to think about it."

SOREN: [joins the conversation] "I'll help you, just to get you [going]. So David, the Council had an idea, SDG goal number 17 and Nanna was in my administration, and she is the junior, and together with the senior, they got the responsibility. And she came up with the idea, 'why don't we call it, The People's Meeting.'"

DAVID: "Oh wow!"

SOREN: "And you can say, 'putting the gasoline on the fire'. So please (inviting Nanna to take over)

DAVID: "What did you do?"

NANNA: "So we developed the idea. So one of the things we did was to invite a bunch of people from the environment, from, and 43, how do you say 'gatherings' where people in the community gather."

DAVID: "Yes, what you say, gathering?"

NANNA: "Yes, gathering. And we had, like representatives, from them. And they had ideas, how to form this day today. For example, you have the ... horse wagons with all the ... politicians.... That's just one of the ideas. So the basic idea was to fill in the day today. It's all about dialogue and democracy. So they were about, putting in the things we are going to do today."

DAVID: "OK."

NANNA: "So they were like, forming, making this day, together, and with us.
DAVID: "Oh, wow."
NANNA: "So, that's the story, Yeah."
DAVID: "No, no, more."
NANNA: "But my job was to get the politician to talk with the water woman, who is an entrepreneur, and she started her own company, and she wants to talk with the Sorø municipality service(s), you know, us in the municipality, so she can get a ..."
DAVID: "So there is dialogue between the exhibitors?"
NANNA: "Exactly."

At this moment in the interview, we notice that the next response unpacks the commitment and energy necessary to Principle 1: You yourself must be true and prepare the energy and effort for a sustainable future.

These pieces of conversation we had with the Mayor, the left-wing politician and the organizer of the People's Gathering may seem like unstructured conversations, even a researcher losing his plan, but it is nothing like this. It's a way to do together-telling and work with the self-correcting method. To try to get not only one part of the story, but different perspectives and to use your own story to give life to other stories. It's about working with different aspects of the True Storytelling model, surfing on different boards – *rehistorizing, abstractizing, grounding* and *futurizing* – to really get a feeling of what is going on.

Wilma Dykeman and Margaret Thatcher: the falsehood of inevitability and the tina narrative of neoliberalism

To put the above into a different perspective, we could compare the ideologies of the neoliberal and those of a more green and sustainable approach with two strong women with different bets on the future Wilma Dykeman (1955) whole-storytelling masterpiece is about the "fallacy of inevitability", and it was seven years earlier that Margaret Thatcher's 'There Is No Alternative' (TINA Narrative) of neoliberalism. Thatcher's 'TINA Narrative' (TINA was a phrase coined by Norman St John-Stevas, a cabinet minister) claimed that the market economy of neoliberalism is the only system that works (Berlinski, 2011). Herbert Spencer (1851) used TINA originally in his book, *Social Statistics*. In Spencer's Social Darwinism, human progress through survival of the richest was God's plan, while the poor were always meant to be in misery. Go to the museums in Scotland and see all the industries that Thatcher's TINA Narrative ended in the name of globalism: ship building, car manufacturing, railroad locomotives, bicycles, and a whole world of entrepreneurship competency, all ended. Everything produced in Scotland went global, leaving factories empty and skilled workers unemployed.

Contrast Thatcherism with Dykemanism: the TINA narrative of neoliberalism with the fallacy of inevitability. For Margaret Thatcher, globalism is the answer to unsolvable problems. For Wilma Dykeman our problems are not unsolvable. Her solution was "Raise your voices" (1955: 291). Thatcher privatized water and everything else. Dykeman, by contrast, stressed that we shoulder all the moral answerability for 'washing the water' making any water we use fit for reuse downstream, because water is not a commodity to be privatized.

> Because just as the river belongs to no one, it belongs to everyone – and everyone is held accountable for its health and condition. (Dykeman, 1955: 291)

Dykeman begins with a theory: "water is a living thing" with a story to tell, if we know how to listen to Nature, and find our role in it (p. 282). It is a theory about the multiplicity of life in a place: "The multiplicity of the minute hidden lives around us" (p. 4) in "Natures' sponge" (p. 13). Dykeman asks, "Where does the responsibility lie for cleaning up our water?" (ibid.). Her answer: "Every city and town, and every industry is responsible for cleaning up the pollution it creates" (ibid.). Every city and industry is morally answerable to clean the water it uses for reuse downstream. Dykeman's whole storytelling of the global problem of overloading watersheds and landscapes with pollution is the watershed cannot repurify itself, cannot renew itself. She learned hydrology from her parents, how the water cycle works: "One of the miracles of water is its constant renewal" (p. 281).

"Stop killing the river's living water" (p. 290). "Hot Springs", "Little Switzerland" and "Bakersville" were all having water shortages along the French Broad River in North Carolina that was flowing by their doorstep (ibid.). They were cutting the trees, setting fire to the woodland, overgrazing on the cleared land, and then wondering why 'nature's sponge' had no water. Add to this malpractice the industries located at the headwaters of the French Broad, aptly named, the Devil's Court. The verdict came in, and the "needs for water spiraled" because there was no fresh water to be found (p. 289). This is happening in Abilene, Texas, for different reasons as the city keeps making more reservoirs, mills and miles away, laying miles of pipe, to bring freshwater to the doorsteps of the homes of an expanding population.

In 1953, along the French Broad, Dykeman recounts how a cabbage farmer had to shut down the farm because the water was so polluted the Health Department declared it hazardous to life and condemned the crop. She reports how, on mile after mile of the French Broad, the fish were dying or floating dead on the river. "Paper plants, cellophane manufacturers, tanners, canners, rayon and textile plants" (p. 286) had located at the headwaters of the French Broad, at the place called the Devil's Courthouse. This polluted everything downstream, so you had to haul water or pipe it in from miles away. Paper plants, for example, emit an odor from time to time. To the owners it is 'the smell of money' but to everyone else it is a foul smell.

Figure 1.3
Photo by Markus Spiske

Dykeman reasoned with each businessman, explaining the hidden costs of predatory capitalism (aka neoliberalism survival of the fittest). "The margin between profit and loss seemed by implication always to be just about the amount that any effective pollution – control measure would cost" (p. 287). Beside a critique of neoliberal capitalism, it is the earliest critique of the 'circular economy' and the so-called 'triple bottom line.' Both are pure 'bullshit,' the worst kind of greenwash, letting everyone pretend that economies can grow sustainably without attending to hidden costs.

Dykeman observed that industries that reduced their water load per unit of production would double the production, leaving the pollution conditions no better off than before. Industries can perform a circular economy, in their extraction of nature's harvest, and increase global heating. Dykeman asked business: why would executives and workers and customers want to locate in a place where the trees had been cut down, the water polluted, the air fouled? And why would new business want to settle here, when nature's sponge had dried up? This is an example of the quantum storytelling of biotic life.

Some notes about the concept true before we go further

The Danish philosopher Søren Kierkegaard (1843) said: "It's not about living a good life, it is about living a true life." What Kierkegaard means with 'true' is to live an ethical life where you also have a responsibility to others, to your community and, you can say, to the Earth. In the terms of Kierkegaard, the good life is the life of aesthetics, the flaneur who only has his desires and feelings to navigate from strolling through life. Kierkegaard also had the concept of a spiritual level which he connects to the concept of true. In Kierkegaard's way of thinking it is not 'either/or' but a balance. We move between the three levels.

In Aristotle's notion of moral insight, it is the balance between what is good for the community and what is good for yourself that is important (Engberg-Pederson, 1983). We will compare 'true' as an ethical and spiritual approach to the concept of 'sustainability.' You have to be true, and the method and the strategy should be true, and sustainability in economics should be concerned with humans not as 'resources' as in 'human resources,' or as 'downsizeable' or alternatives to machines. It is about real people who have a life, family and a history. The philosopher Martin Buber distinguishes between an I–Thou relationship and an I–It relationship – with the first, you care about people while with the second, people are just means to achieving a goal. This is very important when working with organizations to develop an approach within planetary limits, yet pursue a good life that is not at the expense of all life on the planet. The ethics traditions from the Greeks also stress the wise and ethical person is a happy person. Socrates talks about 'the exploring self' as the happy person. We could claim this is also a way to create happiness in society. Our French colleague Henri Savall is putting forward socially and ecologically-responsible capitalism as an alternative way to develop economies locally and globally, taming the incessant crises and catastrophes of capitalism (Savall, 2018).

How a female entrepreneur found her true story

In our work over the years as researchers and consultants we have worked with starts-up in the US and in Denmark. In this work we have observed that to be successful as a start-up you need much more than a good idea, business plan and funding. It is about finding a project you and the people you work with believe in; you have to be true, and sustain the energy for future, as Principle 1 says, which means that the business idea needs to be sustainable when it comes to production and resources, economy and wellbeing.

The CEO Anne-Marie Hall from the Danish small start-up Amazing Hall, advising the health industry, is an example of how we work with the self-correcting method, together-telling and the antenarrative method in the area of start-up:

"True storytelling totally changed my personal life and my business life," she says. It's January, late afternoon. We are walking along one of the lakes in Copenhagen, the capital of Denmark, and we can hear the sound from the cars from a distance. It's one and a half years since we started working with her; inspired by the True Storytelling principles. Anne-Marie came to us with a wish to be a better storyteller. "I have this feeling that people are not listening to me," she said. At that time, she was working for a company selling articles to the healthcare area. She was stressed, like many other people in Denmark, and not satisfied with her job or life.

Instead of teaching her how to tell a 'good' story so she could convince the colleagues and customers we did together-telling and used the self-correcting method to get close to what was true and ethical to her of 'account of oneself' (Butler, 2005). Like the essays of Joan Didion (2003) we moved between dialogue about values and concepts which matter for her (like 'caring' and 'joy' and ethical issues) to stories from her past and future about family and friends, the difference between feelings and duties and then grounding all of it through the here and now and stories of walking in the woods and getting support from the nature and the power of the flower she carried around her neck. These dialogues moved her forward not only intellectually but also as an experience of embodiment, providing her with the strength to tell her story with a very different voice, which made a difference to her career. She was headhunted by another company but she still was uneasy and had the challenge of sustaining her energy for the future and had the feeling that the company she was working for did not have the right values. She said that she had this dream of her own business, helping the healthcare industry developing a more ecological business model, reflecting her own values. But she said she was not ready to start the business yet, she needed some more years to learn more about the area.

We worked on her story with drawings and artefacts and asked her to draw her story on a piece of paper on the wall and the value or moods it should be grounded in and we asked questions and supported her with stories to give the drawing new perspective. We asked about timing.

She said: "Five years. I need to learn more."

We replied: "But why wait five years, why not now?"

And that was the kick which made the breakthrough. It was not easy, true stories seldom are, they can be hard, but because of the self-correcting process being self-reflexive about what we don't know, and have yet to learn, we experienced progress.

A few months after this conversation she started her own business, Amazing Hall, hired employees, rented an office in a Copenhagen suburb and gained big customers, helping them find their story and communicating it to their customers i.e. hospitals and doctors. She was happy and busy but suddenly after a year she lost a major customer, a project she had invested in failed. The business was going in the wrong direction.

When we met her on an afternoon in January, she said everything had gone too fast.

"I didn't listen to myself. I had to fire my employees and start up again. But the most important thing is that, although the troubles, this has been the right thing to do. It is my true story to run my own business and do it my way."

Today she and her company *Amazing Hall* has one focus-area and that is working with business development and branding within Healthcare in Europe. As charity, she is mentoring students within Healthcare how to create their own start-up and find their true storyelling (https://amazinghall.com).

This is a story about how important Principle 1 is because it creates the ground and the trust in your project which you and the people you work with can stand on when the storms get heavy. It is about doing *forecaring* and being open to antenarrative emerging.

How a Danish businessman found his true story, which combines business with charity

Another example of Principle 1 is Peter Nørgaard. He is a Danish businessman and founder of Creative Company, a company producing creative products for kindergartens and schools all over Europe. Peter is also the founder of the organization Code of Care, helping people with disabilities into work. "Companies must become better at accommodating people with mental, physical and social challenges. That's the message of the Code of Care" (https://codeofcare.dk/om-os/historie/).

"This project is so important for me. When I see how these people grow and change it touches my heart deeply," Peter Nørgaard says.

We are doing a workshop about social responsibility with Peter and the Danish professor Steen Hildebrandt, who are national experts in the UN goals, at the democracy festival Folkemødet at the island of Bornholm, East Denmark. There are 80,000 people attending to discuss the UN goals and how we can ground them into action.

In Peter Nørgaard's company a minimum of 15% of hires are disabled people and he believes that a part of his success is this philosophy. This is very important if we want to create a sustainable society in the economic and human way, because we are spending billions supporting people who do not work and who feel more and more isolated and get sicker compared to people who have work. They can therefore become a part of community and experience they have a place and create value.

You might think that it would be more logical not to hire people with disabilities and, sure, it has some challenges. Dorte Zacho Martinsen, who is a board member of Code of Care and a CEO at BmSilo, a company producing silos for farming and industries put it this way:

> In the beginning when we took people in with mental disabilities my old employees got more stress because they should use time on the new people, but we found our way to do it, inspired from some tools Code of Care has developed. If you look at the company as a circle you are shooting arrows at the new people should start working in the outskirts of the circle and then slowly be brought into the center of the company.

Peter and Dorte's stories are examples of a staying true and sustain energy for the future. These are very personal stories of how to balance business with a good life.

The Danish Police force searching for their new true story

The examples mentioned above are about individual people. But how can people such as managers who work in a political context where they have to follow the instructions from the parliament use Principle 1? An example is our good friend the former CEO for the Danish Police and now adviser for the UN in New York, Jens Henrik Højbjerg.

This is a story about how the Danish police changed their strategy. When the world changes, how can we create commitment and ownership for a new strategy and how can we work with the concept of 'true' in acts and deeds of *forecaring*? We visited Jens Henrik at Police Headquarters.

At the entrance to the headquarters of the Danish Police there is a monument to the fallen policemen created by the artist Christian Lemmerz. It is two white benches, one bearing a flag and the other a police hat, all in white marble. If you look up from the benches at the wall, there are the names of the policemen who have been killed while on duty – 25 persons over the last 50 years. On the opposite wall there is a poem by a Danish poet Søren Ulrik Thomsen.[14] The poem goes like this:

> The trees don't grow into the sky
> But they grow into the air, that we breath.
> And into the ground to the dead ones
> We miss. And that is enough.

"I like that monument. It's a place where people who lost their fathers or sons can stop for a while. Sit down and rest and remember their love ones. And it's a place for the others of us, which reminds us why we are here," said Jens Henrik Højbjerg. He was the CEO of 15,400 people of whom 10,000 are traditional policemen and the others are experts in different fields, office people, attorneys, secret agents, cyberexperts etc.

We met Jens Henrik Højbjerg in his corner office in Copenhagen, 300 meters from Tivoli and 300 meters from the harbour. On a quiet day you can hear the screaming from the rollercoasters in Tivoli. His office has a big desk and a couch and two chairs. In the corner his uniform with the medals. The room next to the office contains a ten-meter-long oak table with chairs around. This is the place he meets with his managers and this is the place where he bestows honours on colleagues on the Danish Police force. In his words:

> Around 2013–2014 the crime rate was on its lowest in many years. The Danish people had a lot of trust in the police which is crucial to our work. The more people trust us, the more willing they are to share information with us. That is very important because we need it when we investigate as well as for preventive work.... But something happened in February 2015, which was a real game changer. There was a terror attack in Copenhagen, where two people got killed and six police officers were injured. The attack was committed by a young man

> who was inspired by radical Islamism. Furthermore, six months later, in September, the big refugee and migrant crisis broke out. Hundreds of thousands of people mainly from Syria were walking through Europe. Suddenly more than 10,000 were at our borders to Germany. Within a few hours, I had to decide what to do. Should we follow the approach from some other European countries, e.g. Hungary where the police used truncheons, water cannons and police dogs to keep the foreigners from getting in and to control those who trespassed anyway? Or should we choose a more human – and probably more "Danish way" – and let the refugees through? I chose the latter.

During the next ten days, more than 10,000 people went through Denmark – some walked along the motorways, others were driven in buses. Some of them asked for asylum in Denmark, but most of them went on to Sweden. Four months later – in January 2016 – the Government decided that Denmark should implement a temporary border control with Germany under the responsibility of the police.

Højbjerg explained that the incidents challenged the police in a way that had never been seen before and put a strong pressure on resources. As a result, a lot of different initiatives were taken:

Beside the need to prioritise the tasks, the police made an agreement with the Danish defence to support the police in controlling the borders and protecting terror goals such as Jewish institutions; a new police cadet education system was established where students within six months were trained to do guarding and controlling tasks in order to ensure that police officers could concentrate on core business.

Furthermore, four new control and command centres were established to manage future serious incidents and crises. And many different experts with various educations and professional experiences were recruited.

Jens Henrik Højbjerg explained further:

> In short, within a limited period of time we had to make significant organizational changes, set a new direction and implement a new strategy. That can easily shake an organizations like ours. Even if the employees can see the rationale behind the changes it can still be challenging to implement them in practice because people in general don't like changes and specifically because the police culture and the narrative about the police is very strong.

He explained that the police made an agreement with the military about soldiers to guard some buildings in Copenhagen. It has never happened before. They educated a new police force with a shorter education time and therefore at a different level. Terror attacks were the reason for a task force which is ready to act if something happens. They recruited IT engineers and other experts "Things like that shake the organization of law and police people. Perhaps they can see the logic in the changes but it's very difficult to implement because the old story about the police is so strong," Jens Henrik explained.

How is this story about Principle 1? It's an example where a leader tries to ask "What is the story of the Danish Police right now. What kind of challenges do we have?" The police have to change to be true and sustainable in the long run. Somehow Jens Henrik is doing *forecaring* for the future because he can see the clash between the dominant narrative and the dialectical counternarrative. Something new has to emerge. Of course, as Højbjerg stressed: "We are a political organization which has to follow the politics from the government, but our job is to find the best solution in the circumstances ahead."

But Jens Henrik Højbjerg is very aware that a True Storytelling strategy is not the same as telling everything. True Storytelling puts things into a larger and ethical perspective and, in that sense, you have to do *forecaring* for the future.

The question is "How did Jens Henrik do *forecaring*?" He created ownership and commitment for new changes with a new kind of employees and a new structure. As he said

> As you can see, we had to change the strategy of the Danish Police and that is a very challenging job. Today we are a police force which can handle the big international investigations jobs, dealing with the crime gangs and also be present in the small towns.

How Lars von Triers' film producer does *forecaring*

The Danish film producer, Vibeke Windeløv, is very aware of *forecaring* although she calls it something else. She was one of the most important producers in Danish film up through the 90s and the beginning of the 20th century with the Dogme Movement and the Director Lars Von Trier and films like "Breaking the Waves", "Dancer in the Dark" with the pop icon Björk from Iceland etc.

Windeløv[15] says about *forecaring* and this part of the process:

> It's about creating an atmosphere of "home" and to build up trust. The person in charge, for example the CEO, may never be in a hurry and show she or he is busy. I invite the actors home. I spent days preparing food for them. I do this because I know it is a good investment. It's not only the actors. It's all the people on the set you should care about. Once some of the craftspeople came to me and said they were unhappy about the accommodation on the location and I told them that if they could find something for the same prize it was fine with me. They rented an old country house and were so glad they invited me and the team for dinner.

Windeløv stressed "To care about people is so important." Another example she mentions was on a production where the lead actor got ill and she had to fly home and stop shooting.

> Because we have to build trust around the actors, who are big stars, they phone their network and we got a new star for the main character – all because of time spent on building a relation to them.

So again, to create this feeling of truth and trust Windeløv knows, from her experience and history, that she has to do *forecaring* in advance. She also has to have this abstract narrative perspective, but she has to ground it through real action and she has to do all this while preparing for the future.

Very often when we work with change we don't take the time to do *forecaring*. As Donna Haraway's (2016) says: 'Staying with the Trouble'. When consulting, we often only have one or two meetings with the clients, people involved or employees. Very often we just analyze the surface. In the beginning, in the first meetings, it's important just to listen and write. They tell their story and problems and what they want to do. You just write it down, trying to be open and try to listen to everything and everybody on different levels. You have to go out there and listen and, after that, you can tell them why they lose money or why things are not going the right way. Then you can tell them about the deeper problems which are related to this. It will often take a year or more to do this *forecaring*. For example, if you work with a big company, you tell them, after your *forecaring*, that they are losing DKK 40 million and managers and employees are not doing anything.

If you take the time with the people you work with and do *forecaring*, they will be more motivated and ask you for advice; for example: "Do I have to lay off 100 people?", "No you can keep them, some have to change the way the work, but you can keep them." But the strategy has to be true and sustainable. You have to go out and listen to the stories of employees and customers and others. Then do the same with the executive. All the information you collect can help you to create a true story because it about the past, present and the future.

To be in the situation – and the art of hanging out

The American non-fiction writer Gay Talese talks about the concept of 'hanging out,' which could be a part of *forecaring*. He has written some of the best non-fiction books about American life, for example, the book *The Bridge* about the people who build the bridge between Staten Island and Brooklyn. He used years of research just hanging around people, collecting stories and observing details about how people react, how they look and their surroundings. About his method, he stresses that one of the worst things that have happened to non-fiction writing is the invention of the tape recorder. People think if they have it on record they have the truth, but that is a misunderstanding, Talese says – storytelling is a lot more than the things being said.[16]

Like Talese, we are very aware of the importance of doing observation, body language, scenography – everything which is not verbalized. We used Talese's technique in our biography about a former CEO, Harry Motor, of the Swedish car-company Volvo (Larsen, 2010). He was a great storyteller, spinning stories and living a dramatic life with great success in Palo Alto, California. He gave keynote speeches for thousands of dollars, however, over the years, he ruined his relationship to some of his children. We spent one and a half years with him, observing, hanging out and imagining the stuff he would do and say, it was also about what we thought he would do and say. After the script was finished, he could not believe he had been so open and honest. We told the untold story through the way he acted, paused, looked the other way, etc.

Principle 1 is about building up trust with all the people involved in the organization. They need to have room for their doubt and their ideas, not you telling them what their problems are and how to fix them.

Instead of being impatient and just waiting for the moment to launch our answer, we really listen to the employees, the managers, the customers or who else are involved in the process. Why listening? To really understand the challenges and problems. To explore it like archaeologists. Without trust, our job is uphill. Or as the Danish philosopher Søren Kierkegaard put it: "To meet the Other at the level where she or he is."[17] Kierkegaard talks about it in the context of the art of helping.

If I am a leader of a municipality, I would work with the first principle – you are in the middle of changes and you are going to make changes and you want your efforts to succeed and you want to sustain your energy – you need to ask is this the storytelling and the kind of change we need? You have to look at the budget. Often the budget is not well organized. Very often the people in charge won't let you see the budget but how can we advise them if we can't see the budget? The budget will give you an understanding of their priorities.

In order for managers to be able to cope with resistance in the organization, they must consider which values should characterize the process and the relationship with those involved. These values could be set as pre-conditions by which the strategy and the results may change along the way.

Preparation plays a crucial role in this principle. The manager has to step away from the daily business for a moment, in order to make the right choices and take in the strategy. What often happens at strategy meetings and seminars is, however, that this kind of preparation is neglected in favour of administrative tasks and that the manager then fails to step into character.

We can explain/illustrate "the self-correcting approach" in a more ethical way with Kierkegaard's three stages in life – the first step in the interview is the aesthetics, the next the ethical and then the spiritual/religious (embody and true) if we are to make a connection to the indigenous and quantum approach. Off course it is not a linear process – we see the Kierkegaard perspective as a way of storytelling which can embody the process for the ones who are doing the research.

When we talk about the concept 'true,' we can compare it to the picture of a hurricane. You can't control it, you need to go into it or run, you need to be in the situation, in space and time. You risk your life, but we cannot escape from climate change right now. The true is not only about yourself. No, it's about the situation you are in. It's about the society and the planet. We are part of something.

If you believe in the strategy you create a certain energy. The head of the police, Jens Henrik Højbjerg, also stressed that it is important to be true and believe in the new strategy. "I think in storytelling you need to show at all times that you believe in the strategy. Energy and power are very important." The embodiment connected to the concept of true is also important because it produces a certain personal radiation but it also creates the courage to tell the truth.[18]

Signe Jarvad, who is a development manager in the Municipality of Copenhagen, shares the same belief: "It's so important to believe in the strategy. It creates a certain energy and people around you can feel that energy." This statement is supported by Carol Dweck, professor at Stanford University and author of *Growth Mindset*. She talks about the importance of passion and trueness when we try to implement a new strategy (Dweck, 2016). In acting there is the concept of 'undertext.' You say one thing, but the audience knows that you have another agenda. Therefore, it is important to ask yourself, as we did in the beginning of this chapter: "Do we believe in the strategy?" Studies in creativity also support the importance of loving your idea if you want somebody to buy into it. Of course, there is a dark side here. History has produced many manipulators but again we should look at it from an ethical perspective.

The Danish philosopher Søren Kierkegaard talks about stepping up, or showing character, and he talks about authenticity which is connected to the above. In Kierkegaard's definition, this is the ability to reflect on an ethical level over your choice of, for example, a strategy, and then choose to follow it. Kierkegaard equates authenticity with 'identification' – a choice that is almost a feeling in the body and heart – unlike someone that only plays a role without ethical considerations. Likewise, a manager can come to perceive the strategy as true and sustainable. 'True' is therefore more than a gut feeling or a fashion or smart concept. The person in charge of the group must be able to adapt the strategy in relation to the terms and conditions given.

A production company looking for the true story when buying up new companies

We have analyzed Principle 1 in relation to public organizations and development projects in municipalities and the case with Johnny Cash which we can compare to the use of True Storytelling in coaching and mentoring. We will now focus on how a big private production company we have worked with uses the self-correcting method and is doing *forecaring*.

It is a big global and very successful production company which buys up other companies in the same field around the world. They invest a lot of time in *forecaring* – they talk to the people and visit sites around the world. They ask: "Do they have the right resources in the area?" They want to be close to the market, they look at the use of equipment. "Have they done environmental damage to the land?" The company is working fast. If they work too slow, they end up with an empty shell because all the good people will leave the company because they are insecure about the future. So it is also about timing. They do all the checks so they make sure that they don't buy something fake.

As the stories show, Principle 1 and *forecaring* is about people, environment, machines and also about the budget, the numbers and the money. The literature in this area only talks about money but we think the value proposition is a lot earlier, because it is about the relation with the people. Of course, many companies are thinking in human resource terms, but they are not taking time over it. Humans are not seen as a resource, they are treated like objects. That is what we learn in Business Schools around the world and we have a different perspective.

Again, we can analyze their process in the light of the model seeking for what is true now and what would be true for the future. They look at the history for the company from many perspectives, they have an abstract idea of what they want, they try to ground it to be out there and they think about the future.

Challenges and the dark side of Principle 1

Every principle has a dark side. For example, truth can be too abstract and forego the *rehistorizing, futurizing* and most important the *grounding* and have no connection to the real world and real actions and ideas. Anders Henriksen, associate professor at the University of Copenhagen has said:

> We are living in decades where the power of the liberal democracies are losing power. In a near future China and India will be the world's biggest economies. The answer to this is not to stand on our morals and values, but to be proactive and realistic and pragmatic in our approach to climate. If our value should be attractive we need to come up with some solutions to the problems of the future.[19]

True Storytelling is about that!

A dark side could also be jumping to conclusions too fast, before you have explored and mapped the whole story, or "Did you check it out" as we asked in the beginning of the chapter. For example, there has been a negative movement against diesel engines, and critics are right concerning the CO_2, and therefore research in diesel has got less funding. But it seems like container-ships and trucks will use these engines for years to come and the engineers who develop the engines could develop much more sustainable engines if they got the money to develop them. Not to say it's perfect but right now it's better for the Earth.

We can find many more examples where we react too fast and intuitively, before we have checked the whole story. Another example could be meat which we now know has a connection with cancer and is a big part of the CO_2 problem, but because it is such a big part of our culture, we have a tendency to deny it.

Principle 1 is therefore also about slowing down and take speed out of the decision. The Nobel prize winner Daniel Känemann (2011) wrote about the brain's two systems in the book *Thinking, Fast and Slow*. System 1 is a way of thinking where we are intuitive when it's best, and lost in prejudice when it is worst. We make quick conclusions and give answers in a hurry. In some areas of our private and working life we can make decisions this way because we have many years of experiences and praxis but very often, according to research, we make wrong decisions if we use System 1. Känemann's conclusion or main point is that we don't make decisions in a rational way but using our feelings, because we use System 1.

Principle 1 is about using System 2, the slow part where we are aware, we analyze, we talk to people and try to view the problem from different perspectives. And that is an important part of Principle 1 – to slow down and to take the time to reflect and explore.

Another example is simply denying the truth about the neoclasssic economic models we have put our faith in – we have experienced that they don't work and don't take climate change into consideration.[20]

We have now explored different stories and counterstories in relation to master narratives and counternarratives, and the six antenarrative questions and the model of the *forecaring* process. We have also looked at how to be in the situation, the art of hanging out and following the energy. We hope you have got an idea about how you can work with Principle 1.

In general, one can say that there are two approaches relating to this principle:

1 *Insight in and analysis of the story.* Is it sustainable and evident? Does it generate economical and human value? How will those involved respond? Are there any hidden stories and costs that need to be revealed resulting for instance in a slowdown of the strategy or that can help qualify it? Ask yourself: What's best for the organization, employees and society?
2 *Insight into the ethical and value aspect.* Does it make sense what we do? Is it sustainable and does it embrace the values of the manager and organization? Do we experience it as true and meaningful? What does it require from me personally? Are there any values that I can attach to and use as guidelines in the process?

Questions to ask

1 What's the story now? And how can we do *forecaring*?
2 Which strategy is true and sustainable? (human, economic and nature/earth)
3 What would the water, the air, the animals, the soil say to this strategy?
4 How does it connect to the past (*rehistoricizing*)? What is the meaning (*abstractizing*) of the strategy/concept? How can we be *grounded* in it? How does it connect to the future?
5 Do we have the knowledge?
6 Do we believe in it?

Other ways to practice our ability to search for truth

The police advisor at the UN in New York, Jens Henrik Højbjerg, recommends reading novels- novels which have what Bakhtin (1993) calls a polyphonic style with a lot of voices, for example, Russian author Dostoevsky, Jonathan Franzen, Gay Talese, Joan Didion, Wilma Dykeman and others. They can train us to be aware of the many nuances in stories. The Danish professor in literature, Dan Ringgard (2014), writes about reading: "Literature shall open our eyes to the world to show us the world in a different perspective than we are used to." In another part of the essay he writes: "Instead of clinging to one truth the readers are relieved from one truth and are put into movements between different ways of seeing the truth." So reading is an important process in this self-correcting approach. Reading can train our sensitivity to the world. The same can be said of listening to music – we recommend *American Recordings* by Johnny Cash, produced by Rich Ruben.

Notes

1 *Forecaring* (see Preface of this book) comes from Heidegger (1927/1962, 1923/1988/1999) and what in antenarrative theory is called the 'becoming' of a heart of care. Friendship is from Aristotle's (1999) Nicomachean Ethics, accessed May 31, 2019 at https://socialsciences.mcmaster.ca/econ/ugcm/3ll3/aristotle/Ethics.pdf

2 www.loudersound.com/features/johnny-cash-the-unplugged-album-that-saved-a-country-legend-s-lifehttp://performingsongwriter.com/rick-rubin/

3 Boje (2017a) develops conscious capitalism as basis for theatres of capitalism. Boje (2017b) explores quantum storytelling in relation to the upward and downward spiralling antenarrating he finds in the early work of Henri Savall. Boje, & Rosile (2003a, 2003b) interview Savall and colleagues to explore how they approach socio-economic approach as a kind of organizational theatre. It is all about finding out how garbled and fragmented the theatre script is, and then by together-telling working out the consequences of this confusion script in terms of hidden costs, and untapped human potential. Self-correcting projects (called intervention experiments) are conducted to get to a script that adapts to the situation (internal and external strategic circumstance).

4 From conversations with Top Galia and Skaerbaek. The same experiences are recalled by Danish songwriters in Jens Larsen's (2001) book.

5 Interview in the new Danish newspaper *Politiken* July 10, 2019.

6 Henri Savall (1975/2010), and work with his colleagues (Savall, Peron, Zardet, & Bonnet, 2018; Savall, & Zardet, 2008; Savall, Zardet, & Bonnet, 2008; Savall, & Zardet, 2011; Worle, Zardet, Bonnet, & Savall, 2015) gives us an important way of integrating quantitative, qualitative, and financial storytelling registers into the qualimetric storytelling. We also acknowledge their connection to the abductive-inductive-deductive semiotic method of C. S. Peirce (which we will explain later on), and there is overall an approach that combines full employment, never just laying off or firing people to achieve some bogus bottom line metric, or managing by spreadsheet that is stupidly without any understanding of 'hidden costs.' Finally, their work is about how to run finance and economics such that the cyclic crises of capitalism are contained, for not only full employment but doing capitalism within the bound of planetary limits (Rockström, Steffen, Noone, Persson, Chapin, Lambin… & Nykvist, 2009).

7 Bakhtin's (1993: 3) distinguishes between the bystander doing 'special answerability' by observing the misery and not acting at all, and the 'moral answerability' of acting

immediately to intervene, the once-occurrent eventness of Being there now and having what it takes to do something about it. Butler's (2005) giving a moral account of oneself is a 'moral accountability' beyond the limits of narrative or story coherence, but we are each obliged to do the accountability work anyway. Hannah Arendt presents a sequence of dialectical moves so that we might understand our complicity in the totality of relationships. The implication is that even if the managerial corporate hierarchy forces us into silence, we still have an answerability, a responsibility, to speak out through a True Storytelling of the whole situation. Arendt holds us all accountable as parts of the political process.

8 Gregory Cajete is a participant in the annual quantum storytelling conference (https://davidboje.com/quantum). His books (1993, 1999, 2000, 2015) are a must read for anyone trying to understand spiritual ecology, indigenous ecology, and how Native Science (how Natural Laws of interdependence with community and nature) informs our work. We will focus on a True Storytelling that is building a bridge between more abstract Western Ways of Knowing (WWOK) and the grounding ways of Indigenous Ways of Knowing (IWOK). See Rosile (2016) for ways IWOK can bring wisdom to business storytelling within Cajete's indigenous spiritual ecology.

9 Walter Benjamin (1936/1955/1986/2007) wrote the most profound work on 'storytelling.' It was written one year after Gertrude Stein's (1935, 3rd lecture) narrative lectures given at University of Chicago. Both foretell how storytelling has been coming to its end, displaced by newspaper narratives, novel narratives, and the entire informational way of telling that was happening to industrial capitalism. to recover what we call True Storytelling is to have people in organizations reclaim the ground of truth, and means speaking back to forms of power that keep one silent in the face of their own and others misery.

10 Benjamin (1928/2016) wrote 60 fragments of the future befalling a German city after WWI. It is what Boje (2001, 2011, 2014) and colleagues mentioned above, are working on as antenarrative precognitive, pre-narrative, pre-story processes and have everything to do with nevertheless giving a moral answerability, moral accountability, and a way of speaking truth to power, even when the stakes are high (see above footnotes).

11 Antenarrative began with the invention of the word (Boje, 2001) and developing the first two concepts, the 'before, and the bet.' Boje (2011) began with colleagues, to explore in an edited handbook of antenarrative, the linear, cyclical, spiral, and rhizomatic patterns of storytelling organizations. Boje (2014) expanded the antenarrative notions applying Heideggerian hermeneutics, from before (*forehaving*) and bet (foresight), to include beneath (*foreconception*), between (*forestructuring*), becoming (*foresight*). With Marita Svane, in May 2019, the beyond (*foregrasping*) was worked out as the sixth notion of antenarrative theory. There is more to antenarrative theory, and how it relates to diverse discourses, and to Indigenous ways of Knowing (IWOK) as a register of 'grounding' and to Western Ways of Knowing (WWOK) as a kind of *abstracting*.

12 The Before is for Boje (2001) an application of Paul Ricoeur's first mimesis out of which second mimesis (the emplotment) is fashioned, and then there is the third mimesis of the hermeneutic circle, and it begins again to cycle, or perhaps to form cyclic variations into a hermeneutic spiral.

13 Boje (2001: 2.3, 10–11) developed the theory of antenarrative in relation to anti-narrative. "Story resists narrative; story is antenarrative and on occasion even anti-narrative (a refusal to be coherent)" but "antenarrative is not the same as 'anti'-narrative. In anti-narrative, the person cannot narrate plot or closure, but is in the present moment". "Anti-narrative and antenarrative do share this in common: both are beyond the closure required of narrative theory' (Boje, 2001: 203). According to Riach, Rumens, & Tyle (2014, 2016) Boje's antenarrative theory is what Butler (2005) is not doing, since their reading of Butler isthat narrative and story cannot

give moral accountability, and must therefore be assigned the term anti-narrative. However, in Butler's own writing she makes the point that while moral accountability is past the limits of narrative and story, one is obligated to do it anyway. In other words, in our reading of Butler (2005) as well as of Bakhtin (1993) this is an antenarrative process.

14 Søren Ulrik Thomsen: In our own translation: "Træerne vokser ikke ind i himlen./ Men de vokser ud i luften,/ som vi ånder,/ og ned i jorden til de døde, /som vi savner. /Og det er alt nok."

15 Vibeke Windeløv gave a keynote at a Conference (Autumn 2018) which was part of a project with four Gymnasiums we did with the consulting company Navigent about how to create an environment of learning and trust instead of competition and anxiety.

16 www.randomhouse.com/kvpa/talese/interviews.html

17 Kierkegaard suggested that we become subjective toward others and objective toward ourselves. Søren Kierkegaard, *Works of Love.*

18 Different managers we have talk to have same experience, for example, Signe Jarvad, head of HR and development in the Department of Culture in the Municipality of Copenhagen. In the book *Tell to Win* the former CEO of for Sony media stresses the importance of passion if you want to get your idea through.

19 *Politiken Juni*, June 21, 2018.

20 Castle, Clements, & Hendry 2019.

2 Principle 2

True storytelling, making room by respecting the stories already there

This chapter is about surfing. It is about catching the waves and the stories and movements already there. It's about creating energy and commitment in search of a true and sustainable future for people, organizations and societies.

The second principle is about 'making room' for the stories which are already there. When we work with change and the implementation of sustainable and ethical strategies it can be hard for people to understand why they should change. Most people do their best but perhaps they don't have the time right now or the energy and they don't see the meaning of it. Or, as we often hear working with change projects, "Changes often mean we still do the same and then we just got some more to do." This principle is about being aware of which 'storytelling' that has already been going on *before* 'making room' for a new future. The principle can function as a part of the planning of a change project, it can be an important part of the implementation, and a way to spread the stories. Read more about spreading and disseminating the new story, in Principle 5 'Helping stories along.'

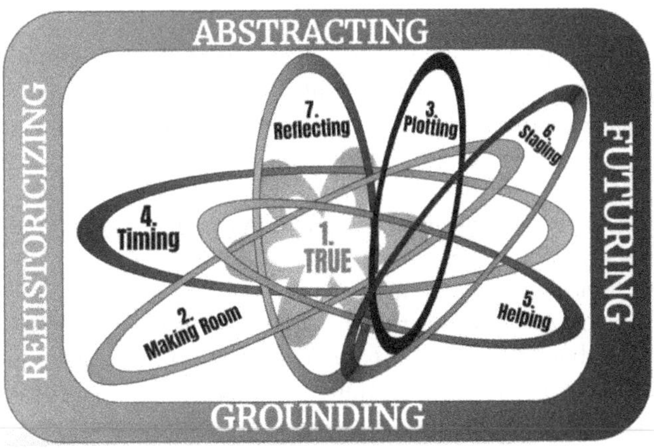

Figure 2.1

In this chapter we will answer the questions 'what does it mean to make room?' and 'how do we respect stories already there?' We will illustrate it through stories and give you and the people you work with some advice about how to work with this principle.

Leadership and change management strategies are often done quite badly, and if you don't mind our saying so, often 'quite stupidly.'[1] Managements forget to notice the 'already there.' Think of a time when you actually helped people in power respect 'what is true' now, in the already there! The people you work with are 'already there' in the 'here-and-now' bringing about one future, when management makes a decision to head into a different future. Our point is that people are already *futuring* in different directions. For example, a cabal heads off to a secret meeting with an external consultant to manage-by-spreadsheet to do cost-cutting, to make 'space' for what it is the cabal wants as a *futuring*. What they are really doing is '*Abstracting*' in the ivory tower, without actually doing the *Grounding* in the here-and-now, and without *rehistoricizing*, highs and lows of histories consonant with the newest *futuring* that is on its way into vogue.

What we recommend is some basic storytelling research to avoid the paradigm of functional stupidity that engulfs most change projects when the (new) organizational identity narrative and the myriad of living stories of people in and around the organization clash with the shifting ground (Alvesson, & Spicer 2012, 2016). Storytelling research can be as simple as getting everyone on the bus, or doing a walkabout, and having all the people, all the stakeholders experience, 'making room,' a 'reverence' for the already there. Instead of accelerating fear and evolutionary brain-reaction states of flight, fight, faint, and freeze, in a world of rumors, guessing at, perhaps misrepresenting or exaggerating the changes. With an external consultant, or with changes lead without storytelling research, everyone else's dreams of *futuring* are left out, treated as unimportant. Most large consulting firms do *abstracting* putting caricatures of people, leaving their true stories untold, and some focus instead on their own yearly bonuses and dividends in *abstracting* exercises, represented and reduced to maps of boxes and arrows. Too many change managers process by reengineering fantasies, and drink the Kool Aid of functional stupidity, eliminating valuable older workers, skilled craftspeople, and young entrepreneurs who resist the proposed changes that the cabal is fashioning, refocusing and restructuring in a vacuum of hubris saturated with ignorance. "Many of the predictions about the benefits of refocusing companies did not come true. Restructuring a company around core competencies sometimes produced superior returns, but often the financial results would be disappointing" (Alvesson, & Spicer, 2016: 150–151).

Of course, we resist the functional stupidity of leaders who ignore what is good and true about the *already there*. What the cabal of functional stupidity resists is *actual* participation, listening, heeding the lessons of history, and doing the hard work of moving from '*Abstracting*' flip chart and spreadsheet schemata and *grounding* in the 'real' and 'actual' Human-world by *preparing in advance, planning in advance, by genuine together-telling*. This is a needless waste of the human potential of people rendered voiceless, whose lives are about to be turned upside down and inside out, *othering* them, instead of *co-creating with them*. We have seen the same scenario play out again and again. It ruins universities, government municipalities, business, and international associations. And it's both arrogant and stupid to believe that one leader, or a cabal of executives and managers, have more intelligence than a hundred or a hundred thousand voiceless people. 'Making room' means caring for the history, not just losing the way, because the new 'managers,' the new 'public management,' the new 'strategy hires' are too arrogant to listen to oldtimers, and young employees, and customers. Worse, it is hubris to believe a few humans in a strategy or a board meeting, guided by a consulting firm, are smarter than Mother Nature. *Rehistoricizing* is part of evolution, because competing histories are being told, and most of the 'little people' are written out of history beyond a family album, and only the generals, CEOs, presidents, pop stars, and prime ministers, make it into the history books of society. If their place in history was based on their benefit to the planet, most would not get even a sentence. There is so much needless destruction of planetary resources, creating enterprises that need to have their charter revoked, as they cause misery for so many species left in their wake. We work with socioeconomic and Nature-world approaches that respect and cultivate by making room for the stories already there.

The Surfer Story: how to catch the waves already there

To illustrate Principle 2, making room, we look to the beaches in California, Basque Country in Northern Spain and the west coast in Denmark. All places where surfers are trying to catch waves. They are lying on their surfboards waiting for the right waves to come. "It's like you are connected to nature. You, your board and the ocean," as a young surfer, Augusta, explains it. "It makes me calm." The experienced surfers know the ocean and the different kinds of waves. They know how to catch them. It's all about timing, intuition and awareness. The French philosopher Gilles Deleuze talked about movements in the world which are already there. He compared it to surfing. When you surf, you have to wait and look out for the waves to surf on. You don't create the rules. Surfing is an act between the board, the surfer and the ocean, as Augusta says. You have to find the waves and movements which are already there to give you and your project energy. In an interview, Deleuze explains the art of surfing and similar sports like this:

> All new sports – surfing, windsurfing, hang-gliding – take the form of entering into an existing wave. There's no longer an origin as starting point, but a sort of putting-into-orbit. The key thing is how to get taken up in the motion of a big wave, a column of rising air, to 'get into something' instead of being the origin of an effort.[2]

He compares surfing with more traditional sports like football and running where you have a start and an ending.

If we compare this to working with change, we often find that it can be hard to create ownership of new changes, for example, when seeking new ways to work or implementing a more sustainable strategy. If we come up with a new concept or strategy and try to impose it on people, they will resist. Instead, we can use this idea of surfing and connections to movements or actions which are already in the organisation. Instead of setting up a new game, we just listen and try to develop the stories which are already there as they support the strategy.

A founder of a pharma company supplying developing countries with cheap medicine they can afford explains how he uses the surf metaphor in conversations with managers and employees:

> When you are in business you have this feeling about surfing on a wave when things are going your way. But sometimes you run into setback or crisis and you get the feeling that you are falling of the board and I know by experience that it is much more important to work hard to be on the board and be on the waves cause if you loose and fall into the water, you have to start all over again and it takes a lot of energy to get back on the board and in business it can take years.

Figure 2.2
Source: Photo by Jeremy Bishop

What kind of waves and stories are we looking to catch?

To nuance the picture of 'Make room for stories already there' you can use the metaphor of the different waves and surfing. If we look at the model beneath it describe different kinds of waves: small ones which you cannot catch or ride on, catchable waves which are easy to catch and catchable waves which are big and hard to catch but if you catch them you can get a great ride. Others have a C shape and are too dangerous to catch.[3]

The idea here is that there are different kinds of waveforms in the company's or society's storytelling and the skill set to recognize which waves are worth catching varies widely among people in the organization or in society. Very often we have an abstract idea about what waveform we are looking for and need to do some grounding, being open to learning more, becoming aware of the different waves, because catching a good wave can become a game changer.

We are like surfers scanning a waveform emerging at the threshold of real and imaginary storytelling accounts of the world. We don't need to catch every wave. Some waves are uncatchable, and others are best left uncaught, since the risks of getting low into the rocks or crashing too close to shore exceed the usual risk of wipe out. "Keep the board perpendicular to the wave" is good advice.

Some other good advice is: "Leap into the wave while holding your board and it will keep you from losing ground."[4] Or try turtle rolling, by flipping the board upside down with you clinging to it, and let this one roll on by. Some waveforms are small enough you can just paddle over them, while waiting for the wave that will carry you into the future.

Too many companies lack 'surfer etiquette' during the change project. The cabal does not check the direction of the breaking wave, nor protect those around them from being wiped out. They begin pearling, reaching for the pearls, and the nose of their surfboard digs into the water, abruptly raising the back of the board into the air, and launching the rider into the wave crash. Better to pivot and catch the next good wave.

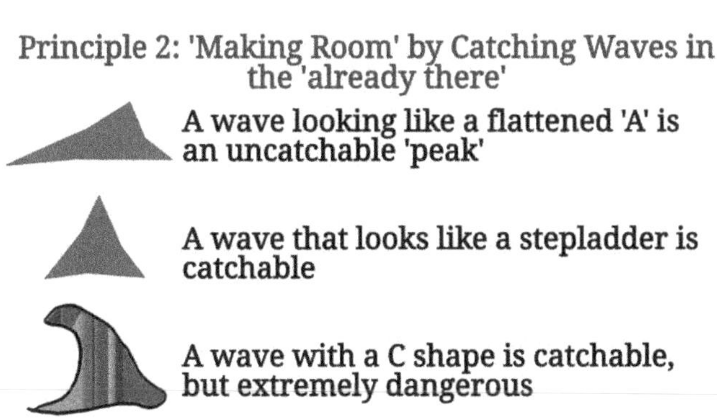

Figure 2.3 'Making room' by catching waveforms in the 'already there'

True Storytelling means taking a realistic look at the movement requirements of surfing the waveforms. It is doing functional storytelling research, rather than subscribing to the dysfunctional stupidity paradox. Too many executives try to catch a new wave to become fashionable, when they are 'weekend surfers' pretending to be advanced surfers. Often, the advanced surfers near the base of the hierarchy are practiced in catching waveforms, reading the wave movements. The executives may lack the paddling endurance and the 'water awareness' of those doing the actual day-to-day surfing. Maybe the best strategy is to send the executives to the front line, to sit it out in the back and not catch waves until they actually learn to read the subtleties and nuances of what is a catchable and an uncatchable wave, and those best avoided.

We recommend a True Storytelling 'surfer-training' bootcamp

Timing when to pop up is important. Popping up in time is better than catching the wave too late. Find your position on the board for a green wave that is smooth and stable. The green wave has an ideal shape with lower portions on tighter side of the peak. You have to paddle harder to catch the shoulders of a wave instead of riding the peak.

You can watch the waveforms, and count down the seconds between them.

Big wave surfing is dangerous, a good way to die young. It's better to study the wave sets, observe the distance left and right, of the peak, and let a few pass, until you have your bearings.

If we work with Principle 2, a way to do it could be to think about, or try to find, the untold stories about good teamwork from the Living story web and perhaps some of them could have the seed for an antenarrative story which could create this wave we could surf on together in the project. A new game changer which can give the strategy a new energy.

Gilles Deleuze could add something to this. Instead of looking for the stories in the normal places we should look around the company.

If we work with change projects which involve different stakeholders from different areas, we need to be especially aware of what kind of interests they have and consider what kind of stories we are making room for. An example could be a project which consists of companies, a municipality, the civil society, research, or education, as is illustrated in the case about the UN goals we mentioned in Chapter 1. In such a case, it is important to remember to work with *forecaring*, taking your time, listening, as explained in Principle 1, instead of moving too fast. If we cannot create ownership and build up some kind of trust the process will be hard and there will be challenges and problems.

The ThinkTanksConcerts and passionate projects in organisations and public schools

Below, we want to describe how we work with people's existing interests as waves or stories, a very effective way to create ownership in leadership programs, working with teams and running change projects in public schools and in the Municipality of Copenhagen.

We ran a change project for the Culture Department of the Municipality of Copenhagen. The history behind it (*rehistorizing*) came from a leadership-program and experiments we did with leaders from different organizations. The event took place in an old theatre, the Bremen Theatre, in Copenhagen. We called them '*ThinkTanksConcerts*.'[5] The idea was to bring leaders together around their (already present) interests; for example, American music (Johnny Cash, Bob Dylan, Bruce Springsteen, etc.), literature, arts, as well as the football team Liverpool FC. We then explored how to make room for their passion about this, "How they could use their passion as an inspiration for their leadership." For example, "How can I be inspired from Johnny Cash as a leader?" The set up was a concert we used as a metaphor for conversation. It was important for us to make the event very authentic and invite a cool band (see more in Chapter 6). Nils Lassen, who we co-produced the event with, got a band together with the singer Lars Atterman who had recorded with Bob Dylan's band in Austin, Texas. He sings his own tunes but has the voice of Johnny Cash. We also told the participants to bring their best music album. One brought Bob Dylan; Highway 61 Revisited and Johnny Cash; American Recordings and Bruce Springsteen's 'The River,' etc.

By building on their existing passion for music, we were making room, catching a wave they already were riding on, and the energy was powerful and exciting from the beginning. They worked with questions like: "How can we be inspired in our leadership by hearing the band?" "What's important in playing in a band?" and "How does a band create a certain atmosphere?" At a smaller event we invited leaders who were fans of FC Liverpool and did the same and work with questions like: "If Liverpool were my organization and company ..." "What can you learn from them, for example, creating commitment and passion around an organization?" "What can we learn about storytelling?" "What can we learn from the way Liverpool is staging the club?" etc. We took this *ThinkTanksConcerts* to other organizations, working with teams in one of the biggest Danish engineering companies COWI and the biggest Swedish bank, Swedbank. We also used the same interest networks of CEOs and managers involved in literature and art.

The former chief of the Danish Police and now adviser for UN in New York, who was a part of one of the networks, explained in the largest Danish business newspaper, *Børsen*, how he could be inspired by literature:

> When I was growing up in the town of Randers, my mom inspired us kids to read novels. I often went to the library and got a big passion for books. I have always a novel on my bedroom table. For me as a leader who works with crime, the novels and literature give me an insight in people's minds: how do they think? What is good and evil? It's a great inspiration and a big passion.

And in a conversation with us he explained:

> I read books about life and death and about evil and the good. Reading gives you a larger perspective on life and you understand that the world is not black and white. People have motives that you cannot understand. It creates a bigger tolerance to the craziness of human beings. I believe literature teaches you how to be able to understand people from different parts of the world.

One of the participants who joined the *ThinkTanksConcerts* was Signe Jarvad, the CEO for development and human resources in the Department for Culture and Spare Time in the Municipality of Copenhagen. She wanted us to do a True Storytelling project in another part of Copenhagen, Valby, where more than 50,000 people live. They wanted to create more ownership of the culture and were developing a project on how they could rearrange the libraries. The idea was that they needed to get more citizens, associations and business involved from the area and do co-creation to create commitment around the culture ideas. In Danish culture, libraries are used strategically to educate people to be responsible citizens.

After one of the *ThinkTanksConcerts* we met with Signe and discussed how the event could be made into a change project. Signe has always been open to experiment and we had this idea that perhaps the employees' passions could inspire them to create more collaboration between the libraries and the citizens of the area. We made a plan for the project and got a researcher from Aalborg University involved and we gathered a group of employees as a part of the organizers. The goal was to implement some ideas that could create the changes in culture. We combined the passion approach with design thinking and the ABCD model,[6] which is a model which helps us to plan and test prototypes

First, we asked all the employees, from the cleaning people to the culture workers and marketing, to send a picture and a small text about their interests. For example, the craftsperson who took care of the building sent a picture of himself fishing, another singing in a choir, another the theatre etc. We analyzed the different interests and came up with the four things most of the employees had in common. They were music, literature, theatre and one more. And to tie the project together we hired a crime novel writer to do a crime novel about the employees' and organisations' challenges in changing the way the libraries and houses of culture should work. Christian Dorph is one of the best Nordic noir crime writers. The story was launched in chapters, along the project, and was inspired by the locations and stories already there.

The seminar to kick off the project included a choir from a Danish prison – with the leader of the choir and three prisoners who had been in prison for many years. We sang together and they talked about how being in the choir had built up trust and energy. The employees thought about how the inspiration of the prison choir could help them in building up trust with the citizens and the associations they should work with. Their ideas were made into prototypes which they went back and tested in the organizations and worked on until they fitted. The event included the author of crime novels, Christian Dorph, with whom we did some writing exercises and he talked about how he works with the co-author of his books. And then the same process – the employees made some prototypes, went back tested and tested them and made changes or discarded their ideas.

As a consultant you know that implementation takes a lot of work and sometimes it fails, but in this project the idea was implemented when we finished the project. We somehow managed to build the train track and run the train at the same time. If we look at this project through the lenses of the model of Principle 2, *Making room for the already there*, then the *rehistorizing* goes back to the earlier events on passion and leadership, but also shows in general how people get energized and motivated and come together around their interests. An example from a company is an American start-up where they built teams around people who had the same taste in music, for example, heavy metal. Of course, the employees should have the right skills, but sharing the same passion for music made them more engaged and motivated and they found their work more meaningful. So in the area of *rehistorizing* much points to using interests in change management as being a good idea. In that sense, the *rehistorizing* also supports the idea of the wave because this is something already making a move.

Passion is a strong emotion, a desire to do amazing things. In storytelling, on an *abstracting* level, the idea of passion is a concept which is already there. On the *grounding* level we work with passions among the day-to-day, the routines and eventness of life, while making space for them to share their 'living stories' with each other, about their interest in particular places, times, and aliveness. On the *futuring* level, we encourage everyone to develop a future they are passionate about, instead of going with the flow of business-as-usual. The antenarrating level is working with the processes of emergence, how to bring about the abstracting narratives, the grounding stories, the *rehistoricizing* past, and the *futuring* of futures not yet arrived. We work with True Storytelling projects to select the wave they are ready to surf, and for which they have the energy, passion, and skill level.

In almost all our projects, we try to integrate stories and work with what is important for each participant on a personal level. Working with departments in the Danish parliament, we asked them to bring their heroes – for example musicians, grandparents, leaders etc. – and let them say why they inspire them and if they can get some ideas to put into the project or the change we are working with. In our work with doctoral students, at our three day writing boot camps,[7] we also ask them to bring heroes and role models, to explore and create energy for their field of work when they are struggling with writing their thesis.

Telling business stories which support the UN strategy in a Danish Municipality

The UN goals are a great example of a wave or a story which is already there. Global governments, NGOs and businesses connect to the sustainable development goals (SDGs), but we can also see from a research project we are doing in a Danish Municipality, as we mentioned above, that boards and civil society and businesses connect with the story of the UN goals. Although the UN goals or the SDGs have a start and an end like a football game, they are also part of a bigger story – the choice of which wave to surf.

The project we are doing is about how small and medium-size companies can use the SDG goals to create sustainable growth and value. Reports like 'Better Business Better World'[8] show that there are 380 million jobs worldwide over the next ten to 15 years in working with the SDG goals and sustainability and many of these jobs will be created among small and medium size businesses. The report also shows that many of the large companies have integrated the SDG goals into their strategy but a large number of small- and medium-sized companies are left behind.

Observations from another survey[9] among Danish companies showed that most company leaders think it is a good idea but the goals are very abstract and hard to identify with in a Danish context and they have a hard time figuring out what kind of actions they should take.

As part of planning for the project, we use Principle 2, *Making room for the already there*. For the project we needed some companies to achieve ownership and be committed to becoming part of it. Instead of choosing different or random companies, we chose companies which already worked with some kind of sustainability – it could be recycling, solutions for climate changes etc. We found that before looking for some new direction, we could support and create ownership for the stories of people already doing things. They helped us plan for the project that unfolded. You might ask: "If you only take the companies which are already working with sustainability the project would not make a difference?" Our idea is to create a strong story from the ground up, among companies and NGOs already working with sustainability, which can then inspire them to move and inspire others to catch the waves of sustainability.

When we had storytelling conversations with the company owners, which was a part of a series of articles for a local business magazine[10] about sustainability and the UN and SDG goals, we only mentioned the goals in a few words. "The Municipality has a new strategy, Vision22, which is inspired of the UN goals." Before the storytelling conversations took place, we mailed them some questions they should think about: "What's the story of your company and how do you work with sustainability?" "Is there a special moment or story about the company and sustainability?" "How does it affect you, the employee working with sustainability?" and "How does it affect the sales and the customers?"

As mentioned above, connecting to Principle 2, we tried to look at stories about sustainability – human, resources and economics – which were already a part of the company story instead of complicating things and trying to push ideas about the UN goals.

One of the companies was a company working with solutions for climate changes related to heavy showers in cities, recycling rainwater instead of using drinking water. It was a family owned company with 15 employees. The company is located in some buildings in the small village of Nyrop and a local railway track runs by. The company was founded back in the 50s by five local farmers who produced tools to drain water from the fields. We met the CEO, Rasmus Mørkenborg, in his office and later he took us for a walk around the company: "My father bought the company back in 1991 and was the first one to think about how you can recycle rainwater." Rasmus mentions his own interest in environmental issues and how they have changed the company into a sustainable company using electricity for trucks and recycle rainwater in the toilets etc.

Rasmus also told us how they invite young students into the company and share knowledge with them because they could be their new employees or a part of an important network when they get a job in a company. Although we did not ask about how he works with the UN goals, the stories he tells are examples of many of these: clean water, innovation, sustainable production, climate, partnership for the future and education. His stories are about *rehistorizing* – telling about the farmers and his dad. It's about *abstractizing* – reflecting about the importance of sustainability and climate, and *grounding* – telling about the concrete actions, using rainwater, electricity, new innovations and partnerships and *futuring* about his grandchildren.

We invited Rasmus to tell his story at a meeting about the green economy to an audience of local businesses, politicians and a big green foundation. Rasmus is surely also proof of Principle 1 because he finds this strategy true and he can sustain it for the future.

Another company in the project is Don Plast which produces plastic boxes for sushi, chocolate and different food items and pharma. They produce 50 million pieces each year and use only recycled plastic. The company has 20 employees. One of the owners, Claus Rosenfeldt, sitting in his office after he had shown us the machinery where the machines print the boxes and the big rolls of plastic from the soft water bottles, explained:

> Over the years there has been a lot of focus on products made out of recycled material. The need for these products has exploded the last couple of years. Our customers use these recycled materials in their promotion and commercials. We get recycled plastic from plastic bottles. They are not popular, but very good to use.

"We want to do something good for the environment but we are a company which looks for what the customers want in the future," says Claus Rosenfeldt.

He also explains that he thinks the discussions about plastic are narrow minded. What's most important is that we don't use too many different kinds of plastic because they are hard to use when you mix them.

As with previous examples, we searched for stories already there. We did not try to push the idea of the UN goal down their throats, we tried to create room for stories already there and try to get them to think and nuance their story.

At the end of the interview Claus Rosenfeldt said:

> We believe everyone should have a chance. We have immigrants and refugees from Iran and Afghanistan working in the production. Some of them stay and some of them leave for other jobs. One of the more funny examples, a plastic factory hired a refugee who was a plastic surgeon but because he could not use his education in Denmark he worked for us for a while until he got a different job.

Four more companies were interviewed using Principle 2 as an approach and afterwards we asked them to join the project. All of them were very positive and wanted to help in the research project and commit, depending on their resources. From that perspective Principle 2 helped us to get some insight about existing stories and how we can build on them to generate new stories of the future, but also build up trust and ownership to move a project along. Principle 2 was also why the head of the Municipality thought True Storytelling was the right way to work with their change project.

The downside of not using Principle 2 and how we can work with it

Change projects often fail, as we have mentioned many times. Perhaps they don't fail totally, but it's only a small piece of what they wanted to implement that is actually realized. A survey[11] showed 70% of all change projects fail to achieve their goals. Everybody has heard about these projects where the employees and managers just wait until the storm calms and the change project runs out.

An important reason for the failures, the survey stresses, is that people were not involved, they did not understand the reasons and the decisions were made by a few people at the top. An answer to that could be to take the time to exercise Principle 1, do *forecaring* with together-telling and try to find the truth in a way which is sustainable not only for economic reasons but also for humans and the earth and try to make room for stories already there (Principle 2) and use them to create trust and create a plan which is ethical.

Change projects in public schools

Over the last decade there has been a big reform in the public schools in Denmark. For many years, teachers used to have a lot of freedom and responsibility in how they were teaching and how many hours they spent at the school as long as they did their job of teaching the students, attending meetings etc. The government, across many of the parties, thought that teachers had too much power, and their union was inflexible. As an answer to that, they issued a reform which means that teachers should be at school from 8 am to 4 pm and at the same time they made the school day longer for the children and demanded that schools should do more projects with the surrounding society, for example, companies and sports club.

There were probably many good ideas in the reforms, including the idea that teachers should be on the grounds of the school, but the reforms and changes were decided without involving the teachers in the process and it created hard conflicts and strikes among the teachers where the schools were shut down and the kids did not get taught. Over the years many teachers have left public schools to work in private schools where they have more freedom. Of course, this created a lot of distrust between the teachers and the executives and people in charge. Five years later, nine out of ten schools are changing back to a system where the teachers have more freedom concerning their work time and schools are going back to a shorter school day. In the meantime, public schools have lost a lot of knowledge and private schools have grown. It is impossible to say with certainty, but if the people in charge had listened to the story already there, some of which could have supported some of their ideas, perhaps everything would have been different. At least they could have worked on common ground.

If we put the example into the model, the decision makers, politicians and management just made a plan and reform. They were acting on the abstract level. They did not do *rehistorizing* to be aware of the stories, they did not ground the strategy, they just left it to the teachers and school managers and their caring for the future got too abstract.

Another story and project we were a part of, from a public school perspective, is about a municipality in the northern part of Denmark where the head of public schools, Peter Larsen, wanted to implement a new way of team working called 'professional learning teams,' a concept inspired from Canada. The municipality got a lot of money from the AP Møller foundation, a part of the container shipping company Mærsk, and every teacher and school manager learned the new way of teamwork and the new 'words.' This was decided top-down. The concept was based on research and was a way to develop more learning among all students, even the students who have some challenges. There were a lot of good intentions.

Instead of *making room for stories already there* about teamwork – the Danish school system has a tradition for teamwork for many years and all teachers are a part of a team – these stories were not considered. Through the whole process there was a lot of resistance against the new way of working, both among the teachers but also among the managers who were supposed to be leading. Peter Larsen explains:

> This top-down strategy created a lot of resistance and bad storytelling about us who were in charge of the public school in the municipality. Some of the

> local leaders were very aware of not pushing the change at the local school. We did not listen to their individual stories about teamwork, everything to rush, the strategy was to create a new language about the teamwork, and we did not take the time to discuss if this was the right and true strategy.

The hipster entrepreneur trying to create a strategy

In the Bohemian part of Copenhagen, the capital of Denmark, with many students, artist and people in creative businesses, a local entrepreneur who began his career in a local grocery has, over 25 years, developed several small and very popular businesses. The grocery he began working in as a young man has now transformed into a hipster grocery, coffee house, and bookstore with its own brand of beers. Young people are hanging out, and popular events are launched in the front of the store. A bakery with excellent and very expensive bread has been established and people are lining up to buy the goods.

He invited us in to his old Volkswagen Autocamper to talk. Although business is going more than well, he is struggling to create a story which can unite all of his employees. He explained:

> I have four companies: a grocery store, a bakery, a bar and a microbrewery. I like to look at it as one company, but my employees don't feel they are connected. The bakers don't feel they should share something with the grocers. I try to write an email each Friday. I mention what's going on in the different companies. I mention my employees by name. But I haven't solved the problem.

The case is an example of how businesses and organisations, in a traditional way, try to work with storytelling and strategy as a top-down process. It is often clear and simple for the owners or the people in charge but the employees cannot connect to it. This case is different from the other examples above. The employees are not negative – they just don't care. And anyhow the entrepreneur has created a big success with his start-ups.

They lost a lot of knowledge – Bank of American

When Bank of America and Wells Fargo Bank bought 20 new banks, Bank of America fired everybody. Wells Fargo tried to change the soul of the new employees and they tried to integrate them into Wells Fargo. The bank manages central loans for houses, cars etc. They trained the employees from the banks they took over for two months but after that they were expected to flip and were not allowed to talk about the old bank. If they can't do that, they were told to leave. They lost about 80 % of their employees. These two banks were not interested in Principle 2 – if 80% leave, they lose a lot of knowledge. *Forecareing* means that you are caring in advance – good parents do *forecareing*. The managers in Wells Fargo were not allowed to do that when the employees from the old banks arrived.

Using Principle 2: Analyzing change processes

In conclusion, we will present a project we have been working on together with the organisation of craft schools in Denmark and JJKompetence. They are a part of what in Denmark we call 'The free school movement' which also includes the Danish Folk Schools. For more than a hundred years these schools have taught young girls about keeping homes and cooking and young men about farming and craft. At the beginning of the 21st century they were almost out of business. They were a fragmented group of different schools with no common story or strategy and with young students with different challenges. The organization and the school boards decided to implement a strategy which would be the answer to the demand for more young people in different crafts, for example, carpenters, plumbers, cooks but also game designers and caretakers for young and elderly people. There was a lot of resistance against this new strategy among some of the leaders and the employees. They felt their freedom was being taken away from them. We began a two-year project facilitating workshops and network meetings with the different craft teachers. We experienced a lack of energy in all the workshops on themes about learning culture, strategy network, nudging and innovation – the exceptions were the meetings where teachers from the different crafts met and shared knowledge. Instead of staying with the original plan, where we approached it as a whole, we stressed the power and the energy of the network meetings. When we had the chance, we shared our experiences from the meetings and we helped support the project. We helped them fund USD500,000 for a project about creating a pipeline from the primary public schools to the free craft schools into graduate schools of crafts. In this project we have used our experiences from the waves and the energy of the network meetings – *making room for stories already there.*

If we are aware of this it will help us to plan a strategy where the chance for creating ownership and commitment are a lot bigger in contrast to if we did not take it into consideration.

Good questions to ask in connection with Principle 2

If you are working on planning to create ownership with a certain strategy or find a way to support your start-up or movement you can ask:

1. Where are the waves we can surf which will give us the energy and when is the right moment to catch them?
2. Do you already work with something which is similar to this??
3. When did you start to work this way (*rehistorizing*)?
4. How do you actually do it? How does it affect you and others working like this (*grounding*)?
5. Are there something, any partners, trend or waves you can connect to or you have not thought about yet?
6. How would you describe this in a concept (*abstractizing*)?
7. How can this emerge into the future (*futurizing*)?

Other ways to practice our awareness of Principle 2

Go surfing! Yes, you heard right! You don't have to be a good surfer. But get the experience of paddling out into the ocean. Feel the connection between your body, the board and the ocean and think about Deleuze's idea – compare the old sports which have a beginning and an ending with surfing where you need to catch something already there and be aware of the different kinds of waves.

Then do the same in conversations. Wait, listening and being patient in conversations and wait until the right stories come along and try to surf them.

Notes

1 Alvesson and Spicer (2012) theorize that leaders and managers participate in functional stupidity by ignoring how employees mentally airbrush negative and contradictory experiences from their storytelling of the situation.
2 Deleuze, 1995.
3 We adapted this from a 'surfers' prayer' slideset, accessed August 26, 2019 at https://slideplayer.com/slide/2503330/
4 'Learning to pick a wave and tips for catching it,' Heather (no last name) March 12, 2019, accessed August 26, 2019 at https://notebookitnow.com/surfing-tips-for-beginners/
5 Jens Larsen develop the *ThinkTanksConcerts* with musicians and producer Nils Lassen.
6 ABCD model accessed August 27, 2019 at www.managingchange.org.uk/the-abcde-model.html
7 The writing boot camps were developed from a research project Jens Larsen and Mirjam Godskesen from Aalborg University did with 50 researchers over a year, developing a programme that could support researchers in their writing. More than 300 researchers have joined the programme. See more at www.writeconcept.dk
8 Better Business Better World report, accessed January 2020 http://report.businesscommission.org/reports
9 Survey VL and McKinsey at https://vl.dk/wp-content/uploads/2019/06/VL-SDG-survey-may-2019.pdf
10 We produced a business magazine together with the Municipality: Sorø Erhvervsmagasin.
11 Accessed January 2020 www.mckinsey.com/featured-insights/leadership/changing-change-management

3 Principle 3

You must create stories with a clear plot creating direction and helping people prioritize

This chapter is about *The Lord of the Rings*, TED Talks, the Folk School Movement, the SDGs and funding. It's about how we can create a plot and a story which can contain different smaller stories and provide a twist to make stories come alive and inspire change and development.

We address the essential need to keep focus on what is important and having a strategic plan to guide people as they prioritize action. We will try to answer the question: 'What is the clear plot with a *punctum*-twist which helps people to prioritize and stick to the strategy as long as it makes sense?' We will give you some advice and tools about how you can create this clear plot together with the people involved.

What is a *punctum*-twist?

The best plots have a *twist*, what Roland Barthes (1981) calls a '*punctum*.' Why? So people remember what is the thing that is most important. To create a *punctum*, select a particular object or image that jumps out at you and the

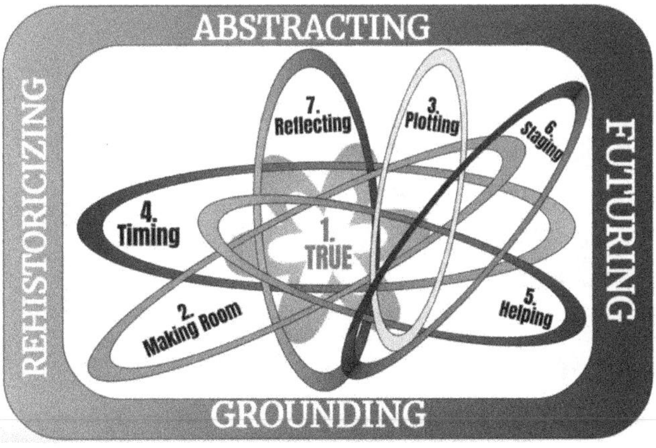

Figure 3.1

audience. The *punctum* disturbs the spectator's normal cultural way of viewing a situation as a disinterested bystander. Reverse the normal roles. Try a reversal, putting the normally voiceless person or Nature, in charge of the plot. From that new standpoint, what jumps out and attracts the attention and surprise of the spectator? A *punctum* element arises from the scene, the 'already there,' then giving them a 'new story' meaning by creating a standpoint of moral answerability. Imagine Haraway's (2014) 'multi-species storytelling' (GREEN) and the degenerating horizon of dominant plotline of carbon-capitalism (RED), and the horizon of disruptive innovations (BLACK dotted). Find the *punctums* in the already there, to nurture the values you want in True Storytelling.

This figure has a story. On August 30, 2019, David Boje, Jens Larsen and Kenneth Mølbjerg Jørgensen proposed 'Gaia Education' as an initiative to the European School of Governance (EUSG). David and Kenneth are co-directors of the #StorytellingFuturesLab and Jens is a Fellow at EUSG (https://europeanschoolofgovernance.eu/team/). We were inspired by Tanja Hichert's presentation on the 'Three Horizons Framework' and how it could be integrated with True Storytelling (see Figure 3.2). Tanja is with the Center for Complex Systems in Transition.[1] The theme of Bill Sharpe's (2013) Three Horizons book is a marvellous *punctum*-twist: 'The future is already happening in the present.'

In a start-up or a long-lived enterprise, there comes the time to plan the future, to pick out one possible future, out of many possible ones, and make your bets on the future. *Futuring* begins with the *punctum*-twist, finding little wow moments, spaces where the future is already present in the future. Some bets are safe, others quite risky, yet achievable if we work together. True Storytelling is preparing in advance that antenarrative bet on the future that is beautiful, good, just and true.

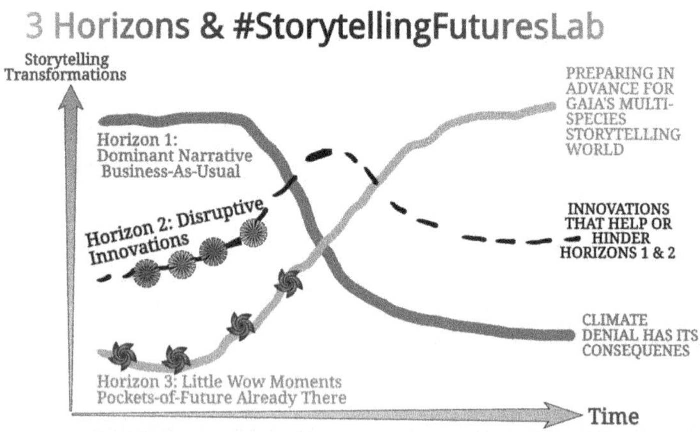

Figure 3.2 Three Horizons and Story Futures Lab of the European School of Governance

Is it RED, a future that destroys the integrity and reputation of the enterprise? Is it BLACK, a disruptive innovation? *Rehistoricizing*: are you going to be a pattern-breaker, or repeat the 'business-as-usual' status quo? Have you forgotten the lessons of history, so you must learn them all again? How to find the GREEN by *grounding*? Is this a strategy that respects planetary limits? Is it just to multi-species storytelling? Do you have the people in the planning, who are affected by this? *Abstracting*: is this 'pie in the sky' or some flipchart notes or a consultant-report, with no way of implementing it?

True Storytelling Principle 3 is about creating a plot, with a beginning, middle, and end, but not just any plot, a GREEN plot, with *punctum*-twists already there in the present, the seeds of the future that are already here-and-now. It is a clear direction, knowing full well that there are all those other directions (BLACK and RED), the other futures, gone unselected by GREEN.

It is time for Protreptic Dialogue. Why are you doing this? What are your values? What's your story, here-and-now, unfolding in the present? When we talk about Principle 3, it is important we talk a bit about the value-philosophy behind the principle. Let us return to the surfer metaphor for a moment. Deleuze's idea about fitting into waves or movement '*already there*.' We do this because we want to change something, to make a difference in the GREEN, by choosing the wave we can surf, one that does not wipe us out. We have surfed enough RED waves.

Caution about petrified strategic narratives

Long-lived companies often have done the *abstracting* to solidify a 'petrified narrative' with a clear plot, expressing core value, and a clarity of purpose, a value that is RED, and companies are stuck-in-the-past.[2] It is also important, in developing a GREEN strategic plot, to keep applying Principle 2, to make room for other stories already there that have a *punctum*-twist. In the boardroom, these RED WAVE petrified strategic narratives express the long established core values, but are they the values for a GREEN future? The problem comes in when the *grounding* shifts, and the situation calls for a de-petrification of the abstract corporate narrative of exploitative hierarchy and growth by exhausting multi-species, that has become too stuck in the past, and not recognized the shifting ground to the GREEN future. In short, some *rehistoricizing* is needed to chart a new *futuring* direction in strategy. It is easy to forget to stay grounded in what is 'True' what you are passionate about, and what gives everyone energy to sustain in the long term horizons. An organization will often struggle with being stuck in the past, for far too long, before *rehistoricizing*, breaking loose to consider different futures. In short, Principle 3 is tightly connected to Principles 1 and 2.

It is something which makes the plot, already there, fresh and noticeable. In this sense we need to draw on a more poetic language, and some techniques from movie scripts and novel writing, to create a powerful plot without losing the ethical content.

The UN goals and climate changes as some of the great plots of our time

The greatest strategic plot right now are the story of climate change and globalization put into a strategy with UN-SDGs. At the yearly People's Gathering (*Folkemødet*) in Bornholm Denmark in 2019, with more than 80,000 guests, the theme was the UN goals and I (Jens) had a debate with professor Steen Hildebrandt from Aarhus University. He is an expert who has written several books about the UN goals. Our debate was about how to navigate between this big and abstract story about the 17 UN goals and the small stories and actions on the ground which support the goals. How can we balance that UN plot about the future and here-and-now actions on a local level?

The American storyteller, and former Disney writer, Mike Bonifer puts it like this:

> In business and in change projects there needs to be a gap between fiction or the goals and real life. If the gap gets too big people think you are unrealistic and they lose their faith in you. But if it is too close to everyday and merely realistic they are hard to motivate. It is in-between you find the true story.[3]

And a good example of that is the artist and gardener Ron Finley[4] who Mike Bonifer helped with his TED talk, which got 920,000 viewers. Ron tells the story about an urban gardening project in South East LA. He has this big abstract narrative plotline about the unhealthy life of people who grew up in South East LA. He then *rehistorizes* it through images of groceries with no vegetables and wheelchairs like used cars because of people getting fat and sick. And then he *grounds* the plot through the stories of his project, he is *rehistorizing* again talking about his legacy and two sons who grew up in South East LA but rebel against the design and path made for them. And, in the end, he *futurizes* with stories of how it could be. There are probably many *punctums* in the TED talk but the stories of his legacy and the mom and daughter asking if they are allowed to take a tomato and he answers: "Yeah, that's why I planted them on the street."

For many years we have helped CEOs, managers, researchers etc. to find their own true story, helping them to prioritize, by asking them this question: "Think about an important moment in your life where you stood in front of a challenges and you either solved it or had some experiences you can use."[5] These stories often appear to have a clear plot with a *punctum*.

Using the UN and SDG goals as a frame for a plot and strategy is a good starting point

You can almost compare it with a myth or a fairy tale. There is a conflict that motivates us if we can find the balance between the more abstract goals or concepts and the small stories and actions in our own life. In the municipality working with the UN goals we have mentioned before, they are aware that the plot must be a plot everyone can fit into. They have picked nine goals to work with and have divided them into four different themes: education, health, business and a good life. They invited different groups in to tell their stories. When we talked to different people from different parties – immigrants, people working with water and waste – they experience that they are already supporting the UN goals and it gives them energy. You can identify the first three principles are in action here.

The same experience happened in one of the companies we interviewed for a local business magazine. The Danish company Simatek produces filters for environmental solutions in the farming and food industry, for example, milk powder and harvesting, filters which clean the air in the factory so the workers don't get sick and the surroundings don't pollute. There are more than 10,500 of their systems worldwide and they are present in 80 countries around the world. The company have integrated some of the UN goals into their strategy.

The CEO of the company Frank Poulsen explains the power of UN goals like this:

> We have been developing filters for many years which help workers in the factories and the surrounding society, but the UN goals has given us a common language and I believe that it does the employees more proud of their jobs. It may not be the most sexy to produce filters but if you put into the perspective of the UN goals everybody knows what we are talking about.

The quote stresses how the story or plot about the UN goals creates meaning for the employees ("I believe that it makes the employees more proud of their jobs") and it is a story they can identify with. Underneath this plot they have their own strategy but somehow in their own way it connects to a wave or a story which is already there, like the UN goals.

Again, we can see how both the municipality and the company use *rehistorizing*, we come from this, *abstractizing*, the goals give meaning, *grounding* what we deliver and *futurizing* how prepare in advance for the future we want instead of business-as-usual.

Telling the story of the Danish Folk School movement

For many years we have worked and been inspired by the Danish Folk School Movement, going back to the 18th century to the philosopher and priest Grundtvig who created the idea of a school for life for everybody. It was not only about learning skills or crafts but learning how to be a human being – what Grundtvig called *oplysning* or enlightenment or *bildung* in German. A way to reach that was through what he called 'the living word' or meaningful conversations, storytelling and being around different people

Figure 3.3
Source: @thomaskinto https://unsplash.com/photos/ECkJrSVCdIc

in a community and working with something you have a passion for. Today these Folk Schools are spread around the country and there are schools in the US inspired by Danish immigrants. The Folk Schools are an important part of the Danish soul and identity and the way we Danes approach life. And it's a great story. The former very successful CEO and owner Jørgen Mads Clausen,[6] from the Danish company Danfoss, which is a world leader in thermostats for heaters, once said that the way we do business in Denmark is rooted in the Danish Folk School movement. The cooperative movement began in the 18th century with small farmers who got together and made their own dairy, grain and feed companies which were owned by all of them. Danes have trust in people; we are good at innovation because we are not afraid of authorities or failure.

These Folk Schools spread all over Denmark and the other Scandinavian countries, and even in the US where the Danish immigrants brought the idea with them. There's a big tradition of storytelling and the heads and teachers at these schools are often very good storytellers who inspire their listeners.

We could have used the example of the head of the 150-year-old Testrup Højskole (Testrup Folk School), Jørgen Carlsen, because he is a powerful storyteller and because he took a school which was almost bankrupt and gave it new life and made it a tower in the movement. He somehow reinvented the Folk School idea.

But our example is Jens Beerman, who is the head of a school which is a Folk School for young people. This school was almost bankrupt but he and his team have made it into a success working with storytelling. When he tells the story of the school it's surely true (Principle 1), he communicates energy and he is connecting with stories already there (Principle 2). We think it's a way of creating a clear plot which helps people to prioritize and it has *punctum* or something surprising that we remember after we have heard the story.

We heard him tell the story about the school when we visited him with teachers from eleven different schools with whom we were doing a project. We were outside in the park with old oak trees, surrounded by old and new buildings, a 15-minute drive to the Danish west coast with sand dunes and kilometres of wide sandy beaches.

"We want to make a school for young people where they can learn about living instead of all these tests which make the young people stress, making them feel bad." And to strengthen his story, he makes room for stories already there.

> It has always been a part of our school since 1920 to work with young people. There has always been a lot of love for these young people. The couple who founded Halvorsminde lost their 9-year-old son to the sea. His name was Halvor. And they named the school Halvorsminde (in memory of Halvor). What we are doing now is creating a school for the future. But a school which stands on a long history.

The previous leaders of the school live close to the school and were invited to see the new school with the new design, logo, quotes on the wall by Grundtvig and the fireplace. Their response was: "This is much more Halvorsminde than it ever been." What is the *punctum*? Is it the story of Halvor who drowned or is it the response of the two former heads of the school or both? The point is, you need to have a *punctum* and these are powerful *punctums*.

We can analyze the story using our model. The *rehistorizing* is bringing the former story, diffracting it from the past through the reinvention from the quote from the former heads of the schools, *abstracting* it into a plot, a school where young people can learn about life, then *grounding* through the building and other sociomaterial ways and all the while *futurizing*, bringing it about by *forecaring* in advance to give it an edge over other futures.

To demonstrate the ideas from Kierkegaard and Jens Henrik Højbjerg, we use the example of the Craft Schools we have been working with over the last three years, where we have experienced some resistance towards creating new strategies, being a part of a wave or demand for more young people in craft and industry. In meetings with the project group, we noticed a tendency to focus on the negative side of things but if we asked the question: "If you look at the process as a story and go back three or four years, has the story developed or is it status quo?" there was no doubt. They all expressed that there has been a big change, moving from being a school movement in crisis, seeing themselves as small islands in a big sea, to being a part of a community with a strategy. And when the Head of Board, Toni Hessner, shares the story, he always starts before the project, he mentions what we have been working with and where we are now and he points into to the future. In that sense Principle 3 is both a way to plan but it is also a way to motivate and to help people to engage. In this case, teachers and people working at these schools feel they are a part of something bigger and that they are moving in the right direction.

However, it is also important to stress – especially when working with a complex project with eleven organizations in this Craft School project – we need to create a plot making room for different stories as long as we are in search of the same true and sustainable story. In that sense we can compare Principle 3 to Tolkien's story *The Lord of the Rings* which has a lot of different characters, with a lot of different ideas about how to do things, but still they manage to see themselves as a part of a task they need to solve, though not without challenges and fights.

Together-telling the strategic plot

The philosopher, Hannah Arendt, has a concept called 'action,' where people come together for a common cause.

> Action as a mode of human togetherness, Arendt is able to develop a conception of participatory democracy which stands in direct contrast to the bureaucratized and elitist forms of politics so characteristic of the modern epoch.[7]

She talks about human togetherness and participatory democracy. It is about more than rules and strategy imposed from above. It is a feeling of a deeper connection to each other and the project.

How a clear plot prevents stress

Teachers and researchers experience great pressure these years. In addition to teaching, there are meetings, student plans, etc. All these tasks create what some researchers have called 'professional dementia' (Schoenmakers, Buntinx, & DeLepeleire, 2010). We see the same pattern in researchers at universities and in higher education. To avoid it and create simplicity and direction, it is an essential part of the manager's task to focus on a clear plot.

Focusing on a clear plot also help prioritize the essential from the less significant. For example, storytelling research can reveal what Savall and Zardet (2008) call 'hidden costs' that are not being reported in the accounting information system, so managers and anyone else cannot make decisions wisely. Hidden costs keep a strategy from being effective, and people from knowing the results of their strategic involvement. Hidden costs can be converted into projects with revenue potential, and can include improving the innovation and agility of the enterprise. For example, one can ask about hidden costs in education: "Is the action I spend time on now, enhancing students' learning and well-being?" If 'yes,' we can continue to work, and if 'no' we must clarify whether it is essential to spend time and costs on it and how it ultimately affects the core tasks. Teachers spending hours and hours doing outcome assessment paperwork has a hidden cost, taking away time with students.

Staying tuned to the core task will release energy and commitment among employees, due to the fact that their effort is acknowledged as important to the organization. Their individual effort is perceived as meaning full and thereby it bridges the gap between the need for documentation and the call for passion in the organization. This can be a difficult task, especially in more complex organizations and systems.

We[8] did a two-year project and survey with 50 researchers including doctoral students, professors and associate professors. The challenges were like the example above – these people experienced a lot of stress and pressure because they were getting more and more tasks but not more time or resources. The way we developed the story was that we met with the people in charge – a professor, a manager and three employees. One of us works as a researcher at the university and knew the challenges. We developed a story with a beginning with more and more tasks and the stress and pressure; the middle was how we would focus on writing as the main task, which should create focus; and the end was about the researchers who get less stressed and more efficient. To strengthen our story – the participants would write an essay and a story about their writing praxis. At the end of the project we would ask them if the focus on the writing and research instead of teaching meeting, fundraising etc. had made them more productive and less stressed. The survey showed that although they had the same resources and time to spend as before, focus and the clear story, you can *analyze* how we create the plot through *rehistorizing*, the before and now, the *abstractizing*, ideas of stress contra focus, the grounding working with different writing tools and strategies and the futurizing, planning for the future.

The stories above are also about how to communicate complex change. Complex organizations and how to create meaning and a clear path are something former chief of the Danish Police force, Jens Henrik Højbjerg, knows a lot about. His job is to communicate with people at all levels – top politicians, the government, ordinary policemen, office clerks, experts in it, academics and experts in economics.

Jens Henrik Højbjerg stresses that it is important as a leader to be authentic and to have real trust in your strategy.

> I think true storytelling as leader is very much about having energy and power and being able to translate and handle complexity. It is about creating pictures and scenes that people can identify with and see themselves in. When I first announced that we were going to educate police cadets, the labour unions and employees in our organisation were afraid that we were going to have an A- and B-police. But when I explained to them what it was really about, then the atmosphere clearly changed. For instance, I told them that the new colleagues should relieve police officers,

> so that they could concentrate on more specialised police tasks to the benefit of Danish citizens. And also, that we could recruit new students to our Police academy among the cadettes. In other words, when people really understand the whole picture and the context in which the changes take place, they tend to be much more supportive and engaged.

If you are not able to communicate your vision, strategy, expectations and what you want, there is a risk that everything falls apart – "This is what we say. This is what we do." It is crucial to be good at communicating the big story You have to make sure that there is no doubt about the goals and the content.

Jens Henrik stressed how important it is to try to pull a red thread to make it clearer and more meaningful:

> My job has been to change the police force in a period of time when the world changed dramatically. That is why, when I tell about our new strategy, I always go back in time to some of the events which have changed the way we work. Among other things, cybercrime, gang wars, terror, the refugee crisis etc. And then I tell the story up until now and where we are heading. I try to explain what it means in the different areas of the police. Also, I always look around in the room to get a feeling of the audience in order to target my communication. What do they expect to achieve by participating? It's not because I'm changing the story. However, the use of language is important and depending on who you are talking to. Am I speaking to the Queen on behalf of the Danish police or am I talking to a group of police investigators? As I said, the basic story is the same, but the language may have different facets. It is not something I think about. I do it instinctively. The big plot must be woven together of many small stories which create the big narrative. That is also how you make the complexity simpler and more understandable to your audience.

What he mentioned here is a great tool if you are working with very complex change – going back to the 'beginning' or the part of the story where things change and trying to draw a narrative from there. The Danish philosopher Søren Kierkegaard[9] advised that if you want to step into the future with existential power you have to remember where you came from.

Principle 3 and famous brands

Looking at different management books in connection with Principle 3, a good example to be inspired by is the book *Let My People Go Surfing* by the founder of the outdoor brand Patagonia (Chouinard, 2005). He begins his story with his parents and his childhood, then tells us about his and his friends' passion for climbing and surfing and how they created quality tools for climbing and sold them to their friends. The company blossomed out of that passion, while the crisis in the 1970s caused the company to change and become more about sustainability and environmental issues. One half of the book is the story and the other half the philosophy of the company, divided into different philosophies.

Another powerful source of stories is to search for important times of the lives of organizations or important moments which become powerful myths. There is a great story told by the CEO of Starbucks, the coffee company. The story takes place in the start of the company when there was only one coffee-shop. The co-founder Jerry Baldwin tells the story:

> One day my wife's dad said he wanted to talk to me. We went for a walk in the garden and he said: "Jerry you are having a child with my daughter, you are not making any money and soon my daughter have to reduce her time at work. Can't you see it? You have to quit your coffee shop and get a real job and earn some money to your family." "I hear you," I told him. In the evening my wife asked me what we talked about in the garden. And I told her. Her answer was: "No way! This is your dream. I stand behind you and you're not quitting now."

Good stories are not only about customers or challenges to your organisations or products that have been solved. It is about a dream, about a passion; it's about will and holding together no matter what.

Creating the plot together and the Pearl Chain

The following two examples illustrate the different approaches to developing plots: one through together-telling with the users, and the other with management. The two examples are also projects for which we helped fundraise.

The first story is about how we and the people involved in a strategy created meaning on the way through the process. The story is about the development of an outstanding creative community house INSP, for citizens, entrepreneurs and NGOs in the city of Roskilde, close to the famous Roskilde Festival in Denmark.

This is a story about changing strategy, disrupting the corporate story normally used for funding and about defining business models on a large scale to be recreated in a True Storytelling context, explaining why this direction is the right one for INSP. The aim is to break the storyline up into small scale projects with respects for the historical context and 'spirit' of INSP. A project *for* the people *by* the people.

To create the future, we needed to make a pattern breaker of the past. The story of INSP is an example of an incredible sympathetic project involving thousands of volunteers and users who rejected the past story and created a new one that helped them stay true to their highly regarded INSP spirit. From a professional outlook to the Pearl Chain.

INSP had been a social economic experiment in Roskilde for eight years and was ready to go to the next level, making space for new creativity within maker spaces, creativity and electronic music. INSP has matured and is very popular among social-economic initiatives nationally and internationally.

The strength of INSP is the special method of expectations-free rooms, communities and hostels, called The INSP Way by employees and volunteers. The spirit of INSP has become much more important and respected. So how to make that move successful for management? The idea was to transform the old buildings housing INSP into a large-scale, professional, architectural, modern, co-creation project costing 90 million DKK. In order for INSP to develop new activities, the goal and idea communicated to the employees was that the new building was the answer.

In what way is the Pearl Chain a true story? The Pearl Chain story has a beginning, middle and end. We have created INSP Classic, a social room for people to restore and evolve, being united in a common sphere around food, the folk kitchen and small workshops. This is the heart of INSP we need to restore in order for the other projects, such as urban gardening, a Crea lab and an urban electronic music lab, to emerge and blossom – and shine like pearls in the community area.

The analogy of the Pearl Chain is about how buildings and spaces are placed beside each other and how they are able to nurture and help each other grow, with INSP Classic as the fundamental "greenhouse." So one building represented the history, the method, the core which was necessary to begin with. There was no large-scale construction. Keeping things simple, keeping people engaged with a clear plot we started with the foundation, then we moved forward with new initiatives, each one with a separate concept and identity, each building with its own special story told by the users of either the creative, musical or gardening spaces.

In the end, all the projects will be shining and glowing in the community area, a special part of the city of Roskilde's citizens and businesses. End of story.

The twist

Another very important aspect of a true story is the plot twist or *punctum*, as Roland Barthes says – like the movies where the murderer is the one you did not expect. You thought it was the mystic man, and it turns out to be the wife.

The Pearl Chain is a symbol of *a process, a connection*, allowing people to prioritize between which initiative they feel connected to, how engaged you are, do you feel like just to 'be' in the social space, or do you have an idea you want to test in on the Music Stage – there is room for everyone. And it is still INSP, the expectations-free room/space.

The twist is, we believed it was necessary to create a clear plot and direction through the nice drawings and architectural processes to stress that it was all for the common good, it was for the people, the volunteers, employees, co-operators etc. All the stakeholders should benefit from this amazing construction. However, in time the funding parties withdrew their interest – the employees were relieved, and a new story for the future arose. A pattern from the past, a clear strategy and direction turned out to be driven by the people – the Pearl Chain.

Power-with produces results

This story confirms the power of a clear idea and direction, accepted by the people, not *empowering* them to unfold their creativity making fancy spaces, but for them to define – *power-with* – what kind of space they need to be creative.

And the results are speaking for themselves. The first 1 million DKK was given by a fund for the basic building in order to secure the development of the rest of the Pearls. They believed in the story as true.

Many similar attempts to build large-scale projects have failed. Centers, shelters, community facilities, museums and cultural projects etc. have been implemented in good faith, as projects thought to be in the best interests of the users.

When those in charge find it best to create the plot – The Danish rock museum

When it comes to the cultural, historical museum of rock, pop and youth culture, Ragnarock in Denmark, the story is different, as their purpose is to tell a story, and we (Lena and her colleagues) helped them tell it. We were serious about the responsibility. With a story, you are allowed to reject it or it can make you say "wauw" – that's not for us to control. If we let the audience decide, the thrill or twist of the museum is gone. We wanted to make something with you, and that's how we show we take you seriously – we took responsibility of the plot. You could call that a *punctum*. People do not expect the message to be so determined. Instead of making a museum where we told the story about music, we decided to make a museum about the youth and how they express themselves through music. In 2017, National Geographic proclaimed the museum one of the 15 best museums in the world.

The story about youth culture has, similar to the story by Ron Finley, an abstract narrative plotline about how the youth made an immense impact on society after World War II. We then *rehistorized* the plot by focusing on the themes of lightning, dance, anti-society rebellion through sexuality, ethnicity and 'power of the children' (a concept arising in Denmark in the 70s, and today is more than relevant worldwide through climate action) as well as fan culture and technical development in the music industry and consumption. We then *grounded* the plot by telling people's stories, the stories out there, for each theme and then zoomed in and zoomed out on the overall plot of youth culture and what it was determined by, making room for many future stories about how youth changes society through music. Youth use music as a tool for their *together-telling* and *futurizing* stories and scenarios of how a better world could be – futures for a better world.

In a way, the museum managed to create a plot with a *punctum* people did not expect, as we took charge of the story, being true to Principle 1. Music is an individual experience, and stories only about the music would have narrowed down the room for future stories. As a cultural historical museum, the purpose was to recognize the many pasts as well as many futures. In Principle 6, the story about the construction of the museum is unfolded and related to all seven principles.

Poetic language instead of bureaucratic language

Principle 3 also includes the ability of the manager to work with language. It is about creating a poetic and living language that the target audience can identify with instead of using a scientific and monotonous language, the kind of language which often characterizes strategic interventions. The manager's task is to break free from the professional language that is still the backdrop against which the words are spoken, without losing focus. The language must come alive and be sensual. You can integrate small stories into the big plot – as we saw with the example of Ron Finley, the artist and TED talker and with the former Head of Police and Head of the Folk School. The founder of the Folk School movement, Grundtvig,[10] talked about the concept of 'heart language,' a poetic language which in the right context tells the true, keeps the wheels spinning and gives us the power to go out in the world and make a stand.

We can also use metaphors or allegories as ways to describe something very complex and create an embodied experience or the use of allegories. In our book *Protreptic: Philosophical Coaching in Management* we use the example of Abraham and Isaac from the Bible as an allegory for faith.[11] We can use, as mentioned before, *The Lord of Rings* as a way to illustrate a complex strategy with many stakeholders.

To dig more into the storytelling, we can create a scene in the story which slows the story down and make our senses comes alive. The Danish author, Christian Dorph, describes how to build a scene in a novel like this:

> When you create a scene for a novel you work with different scenes. There is the front scene, where we are or the person is; then there is a middle scene, which is nearby; and then a distance scene and then we can almost over-describe a thing in the front scene. This is what makes a great scene and lets the space or the tempo in the story slow down and get more intense.

We are now ready to develop and plan a clear plot for a new future. We are ready to plan a new future that is a pattern breaker with the past. We want a good plot, that is True Storytelling. It has a beginning, a middle and an end, giving clear direction. It has a *punctum* and it tells why we are doing this strategy.

Questions you can ask if you want to develop a clear plot which people can support and which will help them prioritize

1. What is the beginning of the story? Are there any challenges or dreams which motivate the story (*rehistorizing*)?
2. Which events did change the story (*grounding*)?
3. Who are involved? Not only people but also resources, animal, nature?
4. Which plot would create ownership and have the space for the people involve and help them prioritize (*futurizing*)?

5 How can you create a new story with a plot which break with the old one?
6 How can you translate the story and the true strategy depending on the context and audience (*abstractizing*)?
7 How can you create a simple plot although it's a complex story?

Other ways to train your ability to create clear ideas and 'heart language'

The American non-fiction writer Gay Talese (2007) stresses the importance of reading fiction novels if you want to tell a true story. He himself has read Scot Fitzgerald and Ernest Hemingway. Another American writer, Stephen King (2001), says: "If we want to write (tell good stories) you have to read." Stephen King separates his day into four hours of writing and four hours of writing. "From reading you learn the form. Your life is the content," says Theis Ørntoft (Christensen, & Larsen, 2020: 45). They all stress the important of reading.

Notes

1 Center for Complex Systems in Transition, South Africa, accessed September 3, 2019 at www0.sun.ac.za/cst/news/pushing-boundaries-to-create-positive-visions-of-the-future-for-southern-africa/
2 See work on petrified narratives in long-lived corporations by Barbara Czarniawska (2004).
3 From Mike Bonifer's conversation with the authors.
4 Ron Finley, TED talk, accessed August 29, 2019 at www.youtube.com/watch?v=EzZzZ_qpZ4w
5 The Method was inspired by developing some theatre plays together with Mette Wolf at the Betty Nansen Theatre in Copenhagen.
6 Accessed January 4, 2020 at www.mm.dk/pdffiles/bc236-33200403.pdf
7 'What did Hanna Arendt believe?' accessed August 29, 2019 at https://philosophy.stackexchange.com/questions/9897/how-does-hannah-arendt-define-freedom
8 We did the project together with Mirjam Godskesen, Associate Professor, Aalborg University. See www.writeconcept.dk
9 Accessed January 4, 2020 at https://en.wikiquote.org/wiki/S%C3%B8ren_Kierkegaard
10 Christian Dorph has written several novels, poetry, movie scripts etc. and is a legendary teacher in creative writing at Testrup Folk School
11 Kirkeby, Larsen, Dam Hede, & Mejlhede, 2008.

4 Principle 4

You must have timing

Timing is everything. Principle 1 was about finding the true and sustainable story or strategy, doing *forecaring* and *together-telling*. Principle 2 was about being aware of the stories, waves and energy already there which can support the true story and Principle 3 was about creating an inspiring and clear plot – but without the right timing, an ability to improvise and understanding complexity, everything will fall apart.

Principle 4 introduces a more complex approach to timing, which give you new perspective on how to use timing in search for your true story and strategy. *Timing* is about how we live in a multiplicity of entangled time horizons.

The STAR model is adapted from Bruno Latour's (1998) *Reassembling the Social*. It relates 'temporal interplay' with its entanglement in *spacetimemattering*. Temporal interplay unfolds in a multiplicity of 'modes of interplay' between our strategy and identity (Schultz, & Hernes, 2019). And what's true and right to do right now to prepare in advance for the multi-species future? The chapter describes considerations of the importance of the length of projects and gives examples of how flexibility versus length has been a game

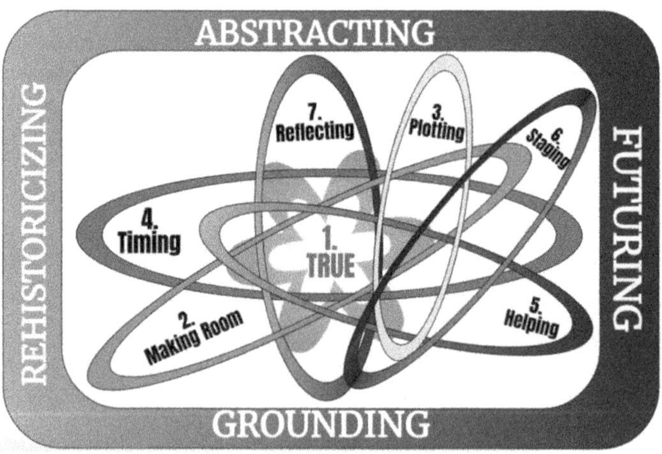

Figure 4.1

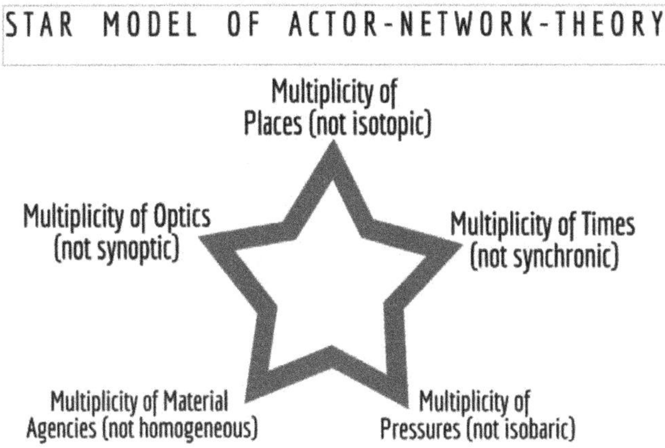

Figure 4.2 The five multiplicities of the STAR model

changer and created new engagement with entangled temporal horizons. Through conversational storytelling encounters, we address the managerial skills required to work with timing – including what we call *antenarrative-timing in the short run, to secure the long run 'bets on the future.'* This is about choosing when to keep up the pressure and when to let go and be ready to try other approaches. It is surfing the entangled waves of time:

- Clock time in the Cartesian Subject-Object Dualism wave
- *Spacetimemattering* entanglement wave (Barad)
- Ontology time, Being-in-the-World wave (Heidegger)
- Primordial existence – our birth to death time wave
- Ontic time of an entity – *existentiell* understanding of things in the world wave pattern
    - o Ready-to-hand
    - o Present-at-hand
- Existential – our being-ness in once-occurrent eventness, and moral answerability to intervene when there are no more excuses (Bakhtin)

You must have timing in the entangled time waveforms! There are many kinds of time. As nomadic peoples, our ancestors once lived by seasonal time – sunrise and sunset – in the planting and harvesting cycles. Now we know how to live in clock time, in digital time, but not how to be *grounded* in seasonal time. Time is measured in nanoseconds but approaches us in ions. There are two kinds of time we focus on: Chronos, linear time, the enforcement of beginning, middle, and end time. And there is Kairos, the timing of an action. It sounds easy enough. Then you start to look into Quantum Storytelling and all that easiness unravels.

Figure 4.3 Spiralling storytelling futures together

For example, we are planning a Storytelling Futures Lab in Berlin. We want to do 'spiralling storytelling futures together.' We believe it is important to start with 1) 'What's your story?' and move to 2) 'Connecting with other's stories,' and listen carefully to 3) 'What stories is Gaia telling?' This brings us to 4) 'Together-telling' and we can be in the spiralling time, storytelling futures together.

The *abstracting* tends to be linear, with beginning-middle-end (BME) plots, but the reality of time in its multiplicity is there are many pasts, many futures, all impacting the now, and what we do now impacting the multiplicity of pasts and futures. Instead of linear BME, we want to get to the spiralling of multiple time horizons. While we set up one timeline, others are setting up curved and cyclic, or spiralling and rhizomatic timelines. We are in our here-and-now as the *rehistoricizing*, the ongoing works of history are happening, again and again, in reply to the *futuring*. What we like to do in our workshops is some *grounding* not only of timing, but the spatializing, and the mattering, which by the way, are inseparable dynamic processes, entangled in *spacetimemattering*. To get from *abstracting* to *grounding* we are not just in time, but in *spacetime*, and that is actually in what is *mattering* in *spacetimemattering*.

Quantum Storytelling works like this. We are actually bodies with 37.2 trillion living cells, in exchange with the environment of many more trillions of living cells. We are living, walking, planetary, climate systems of colonies of living cells, and quite inseparable from Nature-world. True Storytelling Principle 4, *Timing*, is complicit in space and mattering, in *spacetimemattering*. This creates a multiplicity of patterns, some call them multifractal, so we cannot do anything without timing in the context of its embedded *spacetimemattering*.

The right timing for the UN goals

"People would not have bought into the UN goals ten years ago. I think it is the right timing," says businessman Peter Nørgaard, who for many years had emphasized social responsibility in his company, hiring people with physical and mental handicaps and running the organization Code of Care. And it is true. It is like it is the right timing for the UN goals. You see the colour logos everywhere. The kids in schools are working with them, the investors demand business to live up to the goals if they want to invest and governments make laws inspired by the goals. There is a big movement in start-ups using the SDGs as a way to create business. The report *Better Business Better World* predicted that working with the goals are a way to growth and new jobs.

As mentioned in the Introduction, timing is a very complex matter. However, if we relate timing to Principle 2, about making room for stories already there which we can connect to (for example, the growing consciousness about the climate crisis and the stories about melting ice, plastic in the ocean and the new climate movement especially among young people), we can really experience how timing connects not only to Principle 2 but also Principles 1 and 3. It is being aware of what is a true strategy for the future at this certain time in history (P1), which stories or waves to surf on and what timing is the right to catch them (P2) and when it is the right timing for the different scenes in the plot which help people prioritize and get motivated (P3).

Timing and when to make the next move

"Just take it easy until it is over" or "There's probably another boss coming soon and then he'll present a new strategy." These statements represent common reactions from employees when new strategies and efforts are to be implemented. And, in many cases, they are right. This is due to the fact that: strategy implementation is often stalled waiting for other things to get in motion, or the fact; or the manager may focus more on his or her own career than on the project; or that he or she is nervous for not being able to execute at all. Another objection may be: "How could they choose to set it up now or don't they know we need a break" or "It's stuck. What did I say." So maybe the employees are there for the long haul, but the management lacks timing in the short term and the ability to be flexible.

The former head of the Danish Police force, Jens Henrik Højbjerg stressed that timing is very important:

> I can have a very clear picture of what is needed to fight crime by criminals travelling around. But if we need the tools and we don't have the instructors and we don't have time to educate new ones you need to consider when is the right time to take action. Timing is everything in connection with your credibility. You have to take this into consideration all the time. And you need to take action when the organization has the right energy.

He believes it is good timing if "you can come out and announce that we have all the stuff we need and now we want to go all in. And it's also very important for me to keep to the strategy." Again, the example of how to approach timing can be seen in the model:

- *rehistorizing*, where do we come from and what do we have?
- *abstractizing*, what is the right timing;
- *grounding*, when do we take action and where do we start and who should we inform?
- *futurizing*, it's important to stick to the plan for a long time.

If the perspective is short, the risk of failure or resistance is much higher

As Jens Henrik Højbjerg mentioned above, it's very important to stick to the plan for a long enough time. Many change projects and efforts run for one to two years, which is often too short. For example, the implementation of a self-management or more trust-based culture takes time and often a new strategy and project is introduced to the organisation before the first has been implemented. Instead of working with a one to two year time frame, working with a five to ten year, or even 100 year time frame, increases the possibility of creating long-lasting change, especially in terms of the climate crisis.

An implemented process is like a story (beginning, middle and end) and a story is characterized by development against resistance and often through suffering and pain. But the strategy makes sense and shows results in the long run. It is important for the person implementing to focus on the process and not let preliminary results cause stress and uncertainty.

An example of this is the Finnish education system, which is said to be the best in the world, and which is characterized by the fact it has built on the same principles and values for the last 30 years. Even though they have adjusted and qualified the learning strategy continuously, it follows basically the same principles today as back then.

Another example is the project where we have working with the organization of free craft schools in Denmark, where we are still working with 12 schools. The first part of the project has been running for three years; after the first two years we helped them fund a new project which was only possible because we prepared the ground in the first one. A project with 12 organizations is complex and not all of them are engaged in the same way. When we evaluated at the office at the foundation, we asked one of the CEOs, who we knew had met resistance among her employees, how she saw the process now. Her reply was:

> In the beginning we had a lot of resistance because we had a hard time seeing how we could fit in, but it has changed and now it makes so much sense, which is because of the timing. If the project had been one or two years, we have not experienced this positive change.

We can compare this to the story of *The Lord of the Rings* again – because it is long term we can deal with failure and resistance. It gives the story or project more credibility.

Novo Nordisk's new narrative

Novo Nordisk, a global healthcare company headquartered in Denmark, has for many years worked with sustainability and had focused on how best to interact with society in an ethical and responsible way. In a world with ever more complexity in the relations between companies and communities, the need to constantly re-consider what being a sustainable business means is more important than ever.

Traditionally, global pharmaceutical companies have seen themselves as adding value to society by bringing new and better treatments to the market – innovation has been *the* key contribution. But with strained healthcare budgets all over the world (due to, for instance, the growing burden of chronic diseases such as diabetes and obesity) being innovative is no longer enough in the eyes of the public. Now, more than ever, companies need to ask themselves: "Are your profits costing everybody else?"

With this in mind, Novo Nordisk asked themselves:

> If we look at what we do from the lens of society, with an outside in instead of an inside out perspective, what truly matters is not only access to new and better treatment, as much as it is help to prevent the diseases from happening in the first place.

For a healthcare company this may sound counterintuitive – why work on preventing what your business is built on? But the fact is that, if you don't, you will be seen as someone who is only benefitting from the problem getting bigger and bigger. And that is not sustainable.

For Novo Nordisk this realization gave birth to a new corporate narrative, providing new meaning to the company's year-old purpose 'to drive change to

Figure 4.4
Source: @aronvisuals https://unsplash.com/photos/BXOXnQ26B7o

defeat diabetes and other chronic diseases.' The new narrative is built around *innovation, access* and *prevention*, and with the narrative come real actions ensuring the words are backed up with proof points.

One concrete action in the prevention arena is the Cities Changing Diabetes programme (www.citieschangingdiabetes.com/home.html). It was initiated by Novo Nordisk in 2014 as a response to the urgent challenge caused by a dramatic rise in diabetes in urban settings. The partnership initiative is designed to address the underlying social and cultural factors driving the rise in type 2 diabetes, and today the programme has grown to more than 20 cities.

Corporate Vice President, Corporate Communication, Katrine Sperling, explains about the programme:

> While only half of the world's population live in cities, two thirds of all people with diabetes today live in and around cities. This indicates that there is a link between urbanization and the risk of developing type 2 diabetes. City living is for many associated with less exercise and unhealthy food choices due to easy access to fast food, and some citizens are even faced with the challenges that come with living in the so-called 'food desserts' with simply no access to groceries with healthy food.
>
> With the Cities Changing Diabetes programme, we want to bring together all stakeholders who on a city level can have an impact on people's health weather its city planners, policy makers or community grass roots. With them we believe we can make real and impactful actions that can make a real difference. We want to convene and unite all relevant groups around a common goal: How do we build cities that are designed to and encourage people to live healthy and thereby prevent them from getting lifestyle diseases like type 2 diabetes in the first place.

Novo Nordisk has a longstanding history for being a leader in sustainable business. The renewed outside in perspective is taking this to a new level. It will be exciting to see the outcome of the Cities Changing Diabetes programme and how far the company can drive this new theme – maybe even turn prevention into a new business opportunity. Time will tell!

Waiting for the right moment

We want to end the chapter with a more personal story and reflection from a director in a Danish municipality, Marianne Hoff Andersen. She allowed local managers to spend a whole year changing practices in how to deal with children/adolescents at risk and she was under immense pressure as she had to defend this decision upwards to the politicians. Her story describes how she used timing but also the other principles, moving between *rehistorizing, abstractizing, futurizing* and *grounding*.

> I insisted on always being present at management group meetings, where one can say that the CEO really has no business. Because the center (local) manager who is their boss is the one who handles it. So I don't *have* to participate. And the center manager has often said that you do not need to be present, Marianne, but I said, yes please, I would very much like to be present. And I have participated on a regular basis. For example, regarding the children's and youth area, I have been talking a lot with the employees. I know what they are dealing with, I know the Head of the peadagogical/psychological center, the Head of health care center, etc. I insist on visiting them, listening to their problems and stories.

This statement shows that Marianne is aware of Principle 2 respecting the stories already there. As a ground rule of her leadership, she listens and makes room (Principle 4) for *together-telling*. Here employees have space to bring their stories to light on the same issues. One can say, she dares 'Staying with the Trouble,' being open to criticism or just different ways of seeing things. She is initiating a process, checking out, scanning the matter in order to be *self-correcting* and *together-correcting* with her leaders to find the right way forward. By this, she is *futuring*, caring in advance for many potential futures, being able to make the best decision, or more correctly, the most sustainable, *grounded*, decision.

Marianne continues with a concrete example:

> Then the next thing happens is, that we have to reorganize our entire preventive efforts in the (preventative) child and youth area where you go in and try to catch the vulnerable families earlier. The point is, that you make a grant that may only last for six months. Then we make agreements with the families: in half a year we'll see if you can manage it yourself (meaning the grant would stop instead of going on as the old model). This is new. This also means that social workers must have fewer cases and they must work closer with everyone. My leaders insisted on implementing this complete turnaround in ways of working and in order to do so all employees had to re-apply their positions. This was a major organisational change, and first I had to agree with the leaders on how to create this new organization, I had to believe it in myself. Next, I had to find out how to finance it, as it was politically imposed that we should find the economic space to make it happen; they would not accept extra costs. I asked the leaders if we able do that, and they gave it some thought and said "Yes, no problem. But we need a year to do it."
>
> This was a total game changer for me and I thought, wow, a year, it will never work politically and we can't wait for that at all. So I'm just trying to elaborate and explain. And then I listened – these are leaders I know so well – and then I think ok there is only one option and that is that I have to move on with this and we must leave them in peace for a year. Because I believe in them, I know who they are. And I know what they stand for. I

> have to listen to that. So, I go back to the management and politicians and announce that it's going to take a year. I put my head on the block for this, they could sense that. But it turned out so well. The leaders and employees turned the whole thing around without a single complaint to the politicians or to me. And how did they do it? I do not know. I have tried this many times before where it has "gone south" having massive troubles with the unions, the politicians etc.

In this example, Marianne complies with: Principle 1, being true to herself, believing this is the way forward convincing the politicians; Principle 2, listening to the stories already there, making room for them; as well as Principle 5, being open to experiment and taking risks.

However, the organisation succeeded, as they reflected and *abstracted* on what *timing* is and why it was important,. It was then recognized that this was so different to business-as-usual. Marianne had to address that and believe there was no other way to go forward, *rehistorizing* and *futuring*. She caught a wave, so to speak, as she saw the passion among her leaders and employees – they were already in movement towards the change, convincing her to support them and follow up. She laid out a strategy together with the leaders, securing *grounding*. Time was of the essence in this matter.

Marianne sums up:

> The benefits of the new model have been immense as the social workers are now much closer to the families and they have to manage fewer families. So they are not so stressed, they have time for these families. And besides, we changed the whole way of working together as the different professionals dealing with the families have a much closer cooperation. So it was a whole new organization, a brand new way of thinking, very different to what social workers have thought traditionally.

In presenting these cases, we have stressed how timing is important and what questions need to be asked in the process. "Are you in the beginning of you project or the end?" "Do you have to buy a new computer system?" "When and where is the right place to launch your strategy?" Timing is about taking big risks.

Questions to ask in connection with Principle 4

1 What is timing and why is it important (*abstractizing*)?
2 What has defined our timing until now in the short and long run (*rehistorizing*)?
3 What would be the right timing in the future (*futurizing*)?
4 What is your first step and what is the next step if you want to implement this strategy (*grounding*)?

5 How can you know it's the right timing and how can we create the courage to take risks?
6 How does Principle 4 support the other principles?

More inspiration to build up your ability for timing

Read biographies and longer epics. For example, *The Lord of the Rings*, which has a long perspective and contains difficulties and obstacles to overcome along the road. Read novels with many voices. Listen to great poets with great timing. Train your ability to improvise. Work with improvisation theater. Brainstorm various alternatives when you face a challenge and try to take risks. Ask others. Think about it. Ask what is best for the project. Listen to jazz and creative singers such as Frank Sinatra, Tony Bennett etc. Be aware of timing in conversations and process. Be aware of the many different times we are surrounded by old material, old people, new material etc. Think of timing as energy and as a feeling in your body.

5 Principle 5

You must be able to help stories on their way and be open to experiment

In Principle 5, we enter the very heart of True Storytelling. We may say that the four first principles are important in planning a sustainable change project or strategy. However, our self-correcting method functioning as action research and the examples show that it is about much more than planning. Anyway Principle 5 – 'You must be able to help stories along and be open to experiment' – is about being "out in the arena" as Theodore Roosevelt said.

Principle 5 will help you and the people you work with navigate through the ongoing search for your true story and strategy and to handle resistance and create commitment to the story. It's about being out where the people are. We will explore Principle 5 through cases or stories and 'conversational storytelling' interviews with people and researchers who work with storytelling and ethical changes (Boje, & Rosile, 2019). We introduce you to the concept of antenarrative, living stories, counter narratives and dominant narrative which will give you a lens you can use when you go out there in the arena and do your work.

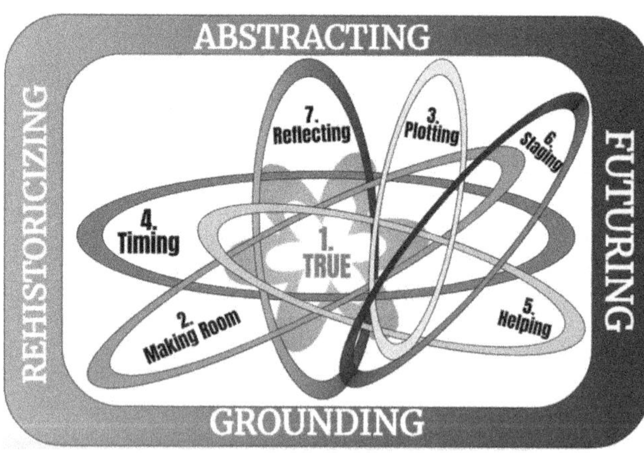

Figure 5.1

This chapter draws upon the other principles. Helping stories along and being open to experiment, you need to know how to navigate and create trust or sensemaking. You need to know what's going on in Nature, in the organisation, as well as among the people you work with. You need to know how to tell the bigger story, translate it and make it relevant for the people you talk to, and you need to know about timing – not just everyday timing but also timing on the long run.

Helping stories along is moving between helping 'living stories' (*grounding*) to be aware of why it is important on a more abstract and philosophical way (*abstracting*) asking about the past (*rehistorizing*) and the future (*futurizing*). Helping a living story along – while the petrified or master narratives are colonizing, assimilating or plain marginalizing the living stories of all the people who no longer are treated as 'mattering' – is an ongoing battle. It takes time to plan, to water, to weed and nurture a living story along, in its community, in the garden of living stories. This is a dialogical process, not just with words or texts, but in gestures, and with architecture, and all the sociomaterial ways actors and agents are interacting in any organization. To just talk about it is not enough. Design work with material things, and how those things tell a story, is part of the work. So many material things are actants, mediating how human routines are called out. Think of the apps in your cell phone, and how these little actants in digital *spacetimemattering* are affecting coordinating and influencing your human, day-to-day routines. There is more about that in Principle 6.

How to be in the event helping stories along

True Storytelling scenes of everyday life are self-organizing accomplishments of accountability "for making their affairs accountable-matters-for-all-practical-purposes" (Garfinkel, 1967: 33). People in storytelling conversations are demonstrating, detecting and co-creating "storyable" events in the achievement of everyday life (p. 34). Here, in Principle 5, we come to the very heart of True Storytelling. Self-organizing activities go unnoticed, taken for granted, in the "expected background features of everyday scenes" (p. 36) such that participants cannot tell a storytelling researcher (or observer) just what the expectancies of True Storytelling consist of. So much of it just remains unstoryable, unnarrativizable, and yet it is the untold stories, and untold narratives, that are an integral part of True Storytelling. True Storytelling is both the told telling and the untold telling, routinely produced and maintained, but any notions that True Storytelling is some sort of shared agreement remains essentially incorrect. "Common understandings cannot possible consist of a measured amount of shared agreement among persons on certain topics" (Garfinkel, 1967: 38). This is why True Storytelling cannot be researched by doing content analysis or using Grounded Theory coding to create analyzed themes by a bystander-researcher observer of a conversation among the participants. The untold story (Hitchin, 2014) is unsaid, and does not appear in the transcription for a bystander coder to register and interpret.

What is important to True Storytelling is what is left unspoken in a temporal series of utterances of a developing conversation, helping the story along (Principle 5). True Storytelling is not a string of standard linguistic terms submitted for content analysis in semi-structured interviews. In treating the actual linguistic event of a storytelling conversation, we as participants are using 'indexicals' pointing to an underlying context pattern of matters the interested parties are telling and not telling about. The 'you knows' and 'et ceteras' of a storytelling conversation are indexical examples. Helping a story along is all about anticipating, foretelling the developments of the underlying context-pattern and using the interplay of retrospective-prospective sensemaking (Boje, 2008, 2014). Indexicals also refer to the biography events-in-the-conversation each is attributing to the other conversationalist.

To help a story along, in conversation, we wait to hear what was previously talked about in the course of conversations, and what the partners might have said at a later time (Garfinkel, 1967: 41). A bystander content auditor cannot decide the sense of meaning of conversational moves to help a story along because there is an "accompanying 'fringe' of determinations that are open ... to other events, and relationships to retrospective and prospective possibilities" (41). There are no standard word meanings or phrase meanings pre-codable that are independent of the fringe that is temporally constituted. There is no "memory drum" (41), no tape recording transcript of True Storytelling that gives a definite meaning to words and phrases, in some idealized 'rational discourse' that a bystander can decipher, reconstruct or deconstruct. Helping stories along is attending to the retrospective-prospective sense of present conversational occurrence that is contextual, historical, futural, grounded in the mattering of patterns of events, all of which lack any standardized truth.

"Tell-a-story-aboutable, analyzable, in short *accountable*" (33) is the individual's methods of making True Storytelling "storyable" and "accountable" in the everyday ongoing achievement of everyday life "in the open fringe" (33–34). Meaning depends upon context and where the indexicals to context appear to help a story along in spatiotemporal, 'you know' calls to the 'et ceteras' of intersubjective reflexivities. As Bell and Willmott (2019) put it, there are entanglements of three reflexivities: epistemological, constitutive and disruptive. Helping stories along is about the *glossing*, and answering these questions posed by Garfinkel (1967: 16):

1 How much do you gloss?
2 How much can you conceal?
3 How much can you hold as none of the business of some important persons?

Glossing is the common work of 'storytelling organizations' (Boje, 1991, 1995, 2008) and is all about the "*ad-hocing*" (Garfinkel, 1967: 21) done by organizational participants who play with the rules of the game, helping the story along. Researchers also do *ad-hocing*, to make truth claims intelligible without as Butler (2005) puts it, giving a [moral] account of oneself. True Storytelling occurs in the scenes of conversations in an intersubjective world where there is glossing, 'you knows' (indexicals), and retrospective-prospective sensemaking that no tape recorder or transcriptionist, or bystander researcher, can decode. They cannot decode the accompanying fringe of untold stories left unspoken, yet so decisive, unnoticed background expectancies conversationalists are telling about in the lives of organizationally situated conduct (34–37). There is no clock time coordinating "events-in-a-conversation" into "standard time" so we can decipher the "matter talked about" without addressing the course of action of True Storytelling.

An example of this could be from our work with a small company which is creating commitment for a more sustainable future inspired by the SDG/UN goals. We were sitting in the kitchen with a company owner talking about sustainable production, listening to the stories, moving from the traditional "question and answers" approach to a conversation about life and challenges in life. Jens shared his story about his stutter and showing vulnerability and the company owner opened up and shared his story about a personal challenge and how it has changed his perspective on life and changed the culture in the company. "Before I experienced this challenge, I was much more focused on money and work. Now we have created a culture which is healthy and we take care of our colleagues. Work is not everything, we are like a family." This story also relates to our model with *rehistorizing, abstractizing, grounding* and *futurizing* illustrating how conversations from a bottom-up perspective emerge to be stories about SDG goals.

This example is also about the ability to be in the situation when we work with helping stories along. The dialogue philosopher Martin Buber (1923) introduced as mention earlier two different approaches about how to meet another human being: either as "I and it" or as "I and you." In the first approach you see the other one as an object you perhaps want to manipulate and get something from and in the "I and you" you see the person as a human being you have respect for. The approach you chose will create the conversation or meeting in a positive or negative way. The Greek dialogue concept, protreptic, which we have been working with for years with leaders, employees and students of all ages, also gives some advice about how to be in a situation or event. In our book[1] with the Danish philosopher Ole Fogh Kirkeby, who took this concept and transformed it for modern times, we call the ability to be in the situation 'eventuals,' joining together the words 'event' and 'situation.'

The first eventual is *Heteroteles*: "To be there for the other one," the second is *Synkatathesis*: "To be open and critical at the same time." The next one is *Lepsis*: "How being there with your body creates answers and questions," then *Katafygé*: "The feeling for dramaturgi," and *Prosoché*: "To be aware and the ability to surprise" and the last one *Ergon*: "The ability to finish and take responsibility." A part of working with eventuals is to be aware of different attunements when we approach an event or situation. Attunements are like two sides of a coin – you can choose how you approach a situation. You can do it in an anxious way or an open-minded way. Heidegger (1927) writes also about attunements and describes 11 different attunements. Stories and storytelling are also about dealing with attunements. We can almost feel the connection to the indigenous way of knowing and the concept of energy between things of Cajete (2000).

This approach also fits with Kierkegaard's statement about being objective to yourself and subjective to others. Principle 5 means that by creating rapport with your bystander, you will be able to help stories along. People feeling equality and trust are unconsciously telling the stories not told.

Power with instead of empowerment

You do not create stories in a vacuum; there are always stories going on. It's about understanding what's already there. Everyone has their different stories, but it is the difference that *matters*, thus differentiations, need a process to work through it. An example could be Mary Parker Follett's work with big companies and unions in the 1920–1930s where there were big challenges in working together (Metcalf, & Urwick, 2004). She said, we are going to sit down and focus on the situation and this situation is going to be our invisible guide, almost like Donna Haraway's (2016) 'Staying with the Trouble' does with the climate perspective as mentioned above. The union said the situation is this way and the manager said it is this, now you have to get numbers, lawyers and accounts. But what do we have in common is that while working through the differences we will understand each other better. The difference between empowering somebody and 'powering with' someone is that you can't empower anybody. You can give them space, responsibilities and you can coach them. Again, we need to work more intuitively and be aware of the energy and attunements.

Figure 5.2
Source: @emotional_discord https://unsplash.com/photos/Ju-ITc1CcOw

To add another perspective on the 'power with' concept compared to 'empowerment,' we want to mention the Danish theatre group CONTACT which we have been working with and which is famous all over the world for their plays where they use real people who tell their own stories. The theatre was created by one of Danish Theatre's grand old men, Henrik Hartmann, and has involved plays about homelessness, friendship etc. One of their recent plays is about anger and the actors were a former president for a right, ultra, Nazi organization and a Muslim gang leader who just got out of prison. The setup was a tattoo shop with young people telling personal stories about anger. The reason we mention this play and this group is because this is True Storytelling and through sharing stories these stories help both the actors and the audience along. As one of the actors who used to be a rightwing Nazi said: "This play has saved my life. It has helped me to see others peoples' perspective on life. And I feel I am a part of a community." It's not about getting the actors to feel naked but tell the stories which have a bigger purpose for people and humanity. We have been working with this method for years with managers and employees – telling and sharing stories about their lives and what is important for them. To share these stories is about helping stories along, being open to experiment and trying to discover resistance and hidden costs, so long as it supports a true and sustainable future.

This is also an organization where we can move from top-down management on the macro level to talk about *ensemble leadership* (Rosile, Boje, & Claw, 2018), where the manager's role becomes more of a facilitator and where the micro level is also addressed. You cannot just impose a concept; people have to accept and understand it. In ensemble storytelling everyone is part of leader ship and the creation and implementation of strategies for change.

An organization and its employees, customers and collaborators contain a myriad of stories, both stories that can slow down the implementation of the strategy you want to implement and stories that can expedite implementation. The key to success is to identify the stories that create commitment, deliver innovation and become crucial game changers. They can be real and lived stories, but they can also be parts of stories that can be developed and bring new power into the implementation process and strengthen the relationship between those involved.

US author Stephen King (2000) talks about the author as an archaeologist who uncovers and propagates stories that are already out there. The Danish philosopher, Søren Kierkegaard (1941), writes that one has to have faith that the good is found in the individual – as opposed to being distrustful. Collectively, one can say that it is essential for the manager who works to implement a strategy and create change to believe that the stories are out there both as living stories and pre-stories which just need light shone upon them.

Being aware of different kinds of stories – Quantum Storytelling

An excellent and creative method approach to how everyday storytelling works is the Quantum Storytelling framework (Boje) which contains of three parts:

the Living Story Web; dominant and counter stories; and ante-narrative. A way to explain the categories on an oral level (stories can also be material) could be the very famous Danish radio program *Mads and Monopolet* which has been running for years. There is the host and a panel of different people known to the public. The host presents a dilemma from a listener, for example: "I am happily married, we have two children, but have met the love of my life. Should I get divorce or stay in my marriage?" At the beginning of the panel discussion you could say that it's the dominant and counter narrative that are fighting. "You should stay because ..." "You should leave because..." Then the host asks for a different perspective and says he has more information about the dilemma. The host, the listener and the panel uncover some untold stories and very often, after a longer discussion, new possibilities emerge which surprise the participants. In the framework of Boje's Quantum Storytelling, you could say that the radio host, together with the participants on the panel and the listeners, create ante-narratives which are new solutions and perspectives or bets on the future, as Boje calls them.

In the role of the radio host above, you could almost say that managers must be scriptwriters. Not like the ones who sit alone in towers, but like those who have the responsibility of developing a screenplay with a group of screenwriters. To fill that role, the manager, NGO or consultant should dare to let go of control and authority and experiment with the employees or citizens to create the 'true' tale that makes sense for the team and the community, and that they can act upon. That is the ability to pay attention to oneself, to the other and to the process while at the same time being able to surprise and improvise.

Often, there are no 'fully-fledged' and finished stories, but instead ante-narratives or pre-narratives. An example may be a manager who has become aware of a customer who is not thriving. Thus, attention has been drawn to the challenge. The manager must be able to take this pre-story and, together with the staff and the team, help it on its way and unfold it so that it becomes a story that the team can act upon and experience as meaningful. It may be that the recognition of this pre-narrative and its unfolding, becomes what we call a "game-changer" for the company, and can eventually become a story that, through knowledge sharing, can dissolve innovation.

Working with storytelling in Greenland

Jens Henrik Højbjerg, the former chief of the Danish Police and Police counselor at the UN says:

> When I am out talking, I strive to involve the audience in a way so that their experiences, insights and stories come into play and become part of the great narrative. For example, I can ask in the room: "What is your experience in solving the problem we are talking about? What kind of new and innovative solutions have you chosen in your area?" I use their experiences and stories as a contribution to the great narrative, which

should bring us forward and continuously ensure that we make the right decisions.

A great inspiration about storytelling and sharing stories is from my time in Greenland. Many people up there are storytellers. It is a very old tradition that goes back to the time when they didn't communicate in writing and had to verbally pass on important stories about hunting methods, dangers etc. in order to survive. That tradition has been maintained and because of that they still use stories a lot to tell about everyday problems and experiences. That is why, when I meet and communicate with people from Greenland, we always share stories.

Jens Henrik Højbjerg gives an example:

> Not so long ago I got a mail from a former colleague in Greenland. Without any particular reason he shared a long and wonderful story about a practical joke with some stolen falcon eggs. Even though I was not a part of the story back then, it was obvious that my friend was eager to share the story with me because it said something about our relationship and cooperation many years ago.
>
> The first time I worked in Greenland, in the beginning of the 80s, it was hard to recruit new police prosecutors and police officers because knowledge about what it was like working there was very limited. I then went to the annual meeting for prosecutors in Denmark and told them how a fantastic an adventure it is working there but also how hard and challenging it can be with child abuse cases, illegal fishing involving millions of Danish kroner, murder cases etc. In other words, I used True Storytelling in order to recruit the right new personnel. I also used my ability to tell stories and my insight from Greenland when I was invited to a conference on Nordic Justice Society in Sietka, Alaska. Among the audience were a lot of indigenous peoples inhabiting the Arctic. I was invited to talk about our work in Greenland and the Greenlandic legal tradition.
>
> So, in my presentations and conversations I used stories as an example to show how Greenland could be compared to the North West Territories, Nunavut and Alaska, but also that in Greenland there was a different approach to crime and punishment. For instance, in many cases people were allowed to go to work in civil society in the daytime even though they were imprisoned. It is a tradition that originates from a time when a good hunter could be crucial to the existence of a small settlement.
>
> I could feel these stories were relevant for them. They could feel my energy and enthusiasm towards the lives of indigenous peoples. They sensed that I understood their conditions even though I am not a Greenlander myself. It was True Storytelling. It has always been in my DNA to be concrete and talk in pictures. To relate practice to theory.

In the above, Jens Henrik moved from the abstract to grounding, to the past and on into the future. He also moved on the continuum between monologue and co-construction. In a monologue the storyteller holds the floor and in the co-construction he or she invites people to create the story together (Van Hulst, et al., 2020: 369). Each of the people engaged in the storytelling brings different knowledge and perspectives to the story. Research from the police in the Netherlands showed how storytelling helped police recruits share challenges they have not experienced themselves as a way to develop "a sensibility for policing" (370). And storytelling can help to bond people at the station. If we ask how stories work, you could say that the work is done by the storyteller, the story itself and the context where the story occurs (369).

Resistance and helping stories along

In this part of the process, where the person in charge also works as a kind of archaeologist and anthropologist, she or he must also be open to relate to the suppressed tales and have the ability to see them as possible potentials to support implementation and create engagement. Suppressed stories can contain hidden costs or hidden values.

At the business university in Lyon, France, professor Henri Savall has, for more than 35 years, been working on what he calls the hidden costs in companies and organizations. The hidden cost can be stories which block the way for the strategy to move along even though it may be true and sustainable. So how can we work in this field where we navigate between different resistances, moving stories along and experimenting.

How to help stories along in a complex project

Another example of helping stories along is the project with the 12 crafts schools we have mentioned earlier. Three years ago, when we started working with them, they saw themselves as independent schools but to survive, get more students and get support from the government they needed a stronger common story. The board of the schools decided that the schools as a movement should have a clearer plot which could help them and their customers – that is, young people and parents – to understand what value they were creating. They decided to focus and brand four lines: 1) Craftsmanship and industry; 2) Food and tourism; 3) Health; and 4) Game design. The *punctum* could be that these schools have a 100-year-long tradition of practical teaching compare to primary schools. Concerning Principle 2 and the surfer metaphor, everyone is longing for practical teaching and companies are in need of young people with craft skills and people who want to work in the healthcare system. So the wave to surf on was already there for these craft schools.

But many of these schools have a hard time seeing themselves in this new story. Some of the schools have young people with challenges and some of them did not have a link with a particular theme. They were feeling very uncomfortable compared to the schools which supported the new strategy. Concerning timing, we were aware of the different levels of commitment and resistance. If we look at the process in the model, some of resistance was due to *abstractizing* – people were insecure and had a hard time understanding the project. We work with *rehistorizing* all the time – where are they coming from – using the project as pattern breaker and creating a new future.

When you help stories along, it is about working with the negative and positive stories, or the dominant and the counternarrative, and being aware of the untold stories in the living story web and being open to antenarratives, which can become small or big gamechangers. For example, in the first part of the two-year project, we conducted workshops where, through teaching and storysharing, we educated the employees to give them some skills they could use in the new strategy – for example, how to network and involve companies, method in innovation and teaching. We also brought teachers from the different disciplines – for example, craftmanship and industry – together to share knowledge about how they work and to develop teaching projects in their fields. We experienced, as mentioned before, quite a lot resistance in the workshop which had more abstract themes like networking, learning culture etc. Some said they felt like they were wasting time. We believe the workshop was important because they developed the teacher skills which were necessary for the new strategy. Compared to the workshops, the network meetings were very popular. The energy from the network became a kind of ante-narrative for the project and we started to focus on that. We stressed the work of the network and it's became an important way to helping stories along; the most important driver for the project now is the network. In our newsletters we have tried to balance the dominant and counternarrative but have always tried to stress where things are actually moving in a positive direction. We use stories from the teachers which show we are going in the right direction.

Create commitment to a sustainable strategy in a municipality

It is one thing is to work with Principle 5 in one to one coaching sessions, in teams, organizations and even in a project with twelve organisations. Another way is to use it in a community, for example, in a municipality.

Above we have mentioned the project about implementing the SDGs in a Danish municipality and explained how we talked with companies and different people at the People's Gathering. If we look at this case in a broader perspective, this contains ideas about using the SDGs as a part of the strategy for the municipality. It began as an idea from the head of the municipality who used to work in parliament with environmental issues and water. Before the board of the municipality adopted the strategy, they created meeting for citizens and invited them in for a dialogue.

The first meeting was quite top-down, led by Connie Hedegaard, a former Danish environmental commissioner from the EU and now CEO for a green thinktank. The next event was more bottom-up. Although there was a presentation from the financial minister of the Danish Government Kristian Jensen about the UN goals, people sat around tables and got the chance to bring their ideas and reflections to the table. The above may seem quite controlled, but somehow it moved the process. People had the chance to say what they meant. We all know that people who come to these events are engaged people but it still got the story or wave moving.

After that they created groups for citizens around the different UN goals, helping the ideas and story along: the education and school systems got involved; there have been events about the strategy and goals; the People's Gathering; politicians have been talking about the project; we produced a magazine where we interviewed business owners etc. The balance is always to have a feeling about how to approach these conversations. Of course, this is also about the self-correcting method but it can also be helpful to remember John Dewey's idea about democracy not as goal but an ongoing dialogue among citizens and a willingness to be open to different perspectives and accept that there always will be conflict and disagreement.

Some critics claim that in Dewey's approach "there is nothing wrong or right" but that is not true. Dewey's aesthetic ethics were inspired by Aristotle's notion that poets know what is right. And he took the best from Jefferson but was also aware of dark side of America. In relation to the municipality, Dewey was inspired by the little town where he grew up, where the tradition for everyday political dialogue among the citizens was strong.

Creating commitment to an overall strategy in the municipality

This case is about the implementation of a national school reform in Denmark (made law in 2013) which required more Mathematics and Danish language classes, more physical activities, more activities with local museums etc. It called for a much longer school day for children and teachers should be physically present at the school for longer hours. In each municipality, everything had to be politically planned and decided by 2014 – just one year to plan the implementation of something very complex. It was a huge process. Marianne Hoff Andersen was CEO in Elsinore Municipality at that time.

> We had to find out what kind of school we wanted according to the new overall narrative – in our case a day-school (previously not common to the Danish school system) – then we had to choose a strategy to involve the unions and school leaders and set up working groups that should return with suggestions on how to implement the many new things. However, it was crucial to stick to the overall story of the political goals set for our school and to remember the core of the story of why we should do this. Things got out of hand. There was a strong protest from the teachers and a national lockout. It was really complicated. But my aim was to stick to the core story; what is the goal, the overall narrative for our schools. Then we can start *together-telling* as to how we do it; what is important, how do we proceed.

The strategy began with the training of all the school leaders. This was set up immediately due to the difficult situation that the school leaders had caused. You can say that 'Staying with the Trouble' was a way to acknowledge there was a conflict, however the school leaders were key to this issue and they had to assume leadership much more than they used to do. Marianne says:

> The leaders had a bunch of teachers bored of it all. Angry or sad. And, at the same time, quite a number of concrete things to implement. The parents were uneasy. How would the leaders handle it?

The leaders' own histories and counter-narratives (and therefore their personal leadership) were the focal point of whether they would succeed with the reform. A year later, timing being an issue again, Marianne gathered all the leaders to share stories and their perception of the overall political narrative and they met with their school teams, *together-telling* on the burning issues of: How should they get this reform implemented at their own school? Will the name of the schools be changed?

Marianne continues:

> And they hadn't tried that before. Working so closely together in their team with something that was so concrete. And then they could unload their frustrations on each other, at a venue outside school. Plus, there were other school leaders present. How do you really do in your school? And there were lots of dilemmas, some ethical. I participated regularly, constantly looking and adjusting, addressing their concerns, clarifying, for example, the change of school names etc. I helped them move on.

By this long process, they managed to *rehistorize*, addressing the reform story up until now with the teacher conflict and the importance of the story (*abstractizing* – we have to stick to the core story, the reform is decided and we have to deal with it no matter what) and they expressed their individual stories for how it could be (*futurizing*). Finally, they agreed on what was the sustainable story or stories on how the reform should be implemented at their school; grounding.

For Marianne as CEO, listening to the stories, being challenged herself to keep telling the core story so that the reform did not disappear, made her able to adjust and help them proceed with their stories. In this she was also self-correcting and reflecting on the process she had initiated and was responsible for. In 2020, an evaluation report of the reform was released criticising lack of results, especially of the pupils' Maths and Danish skills. However, any major working change like this would cause an effect on something; it would be interesting to measure the working environment in Elsinore.

Be open to experiment

You could say that coaching and conversations contain a large amount of experiment and are about helping stories along. You are working with particular challenges and you are trying to create new perspectives and solutions with people through stories and questions. Experimenting is an important part of the self-correcting method, moving forth and back while trying to get closer to the truth. This process can be a part of the coaching process, where we encourage the people we coach to test new ideas we have invented together and see if they works or they have to adjust them. We do that when we work with researchers, start-ups and leaders and also in our own projects where we try to create ownership of a strategy and adjust the way we move forward, balancing between *rehistorizing, abstracting, grounding* and *futurizing.*

Start-ups and the importance of listening

An example of adjusting strategies and ownership and how things can go wrong occurred with a start-up business named PING PONG, a table tennis hipster concept in CPH and Berlin in 2004. They applied to be tested as a start-up business in a board member excellence programme. We used a 360° programme for developing corporations, testing products, branding, finances, budgets, manpower, logistic etc. This is an excellent tool for developing responsible board members, however this start-up business needed their story straight and aligned. Two young men had successfully built light-blue table tennis tables out of concrete. Art, performances, music and communities blossomed from these odd tables, placed in public spaces. To extend their business, we suggested moving to mass production but in light-weight materials, made in shipyards, and calculated ROIs, etc. This was a mistake, as the young men were selling experiences or, more correctly, SDG goals before they were invented/formulated. They sold hope and well-being. More importantly, they would never succeed if they did not believe in the story themselves, their story and vision about creating a *together-telling* community.

We did not ask the most crucial question: Did they still believe in their story long-term, was it true and sustainable – for them and their families and partners? We did not dare, ourselves, to be open to experiment, helping these creative minds to develop their PING PONG story, listening to the untold telling. What did they actually tell us and each other? We needed to see the meta-messages but did not succeed in establishing rapport. Instead, we only had our eyes fixed on them as objective individuals, on data in order to make a business-as-usual plan and strategy that they were not happy and passionate about. If we had made them *rehistoricize* their personal and professional (often the same) experiences, their living stories, we might have discovered the concept was already *grounded.* And we might have found some hidden cost in their current strategy, helping them articulate *future* scenarios.

Using the participants' passions and heroes as a way of helping stories along

An example of using experiments to create commitment to a change was a project, mentioned earlier, we did for the Department of Culture in the municipality of Copenhagen. It was inspired by an event we conducted with groups of leaders in a theatre in Copenhagen, where we worked with their passions for, for example, music, heroes, football. One of the leaders who attended, and who we have worked with in different projects, was Signe Jarvad, the head of libraries and community houses in an area of Copenhagen. The challenge in a change project is always to get people committed. Signe saw an idea in working with employees' passions in a project which should bring out new ideas about how to work more closely with local companies and organisations.

We used the employees' passion for theatre and movies. The group worked with a theatre instructor and afterwards they reflected and created some ideas about how they could be better at inspiring and inviting companies and NGOs in. We will come back to this example in Chapter 6 but it was a great success and Signe stressed that we should see it as an experiment and not a compromise.

The idea of using passions we have brought into coaching but also into network meetings with CEOs from private and public organizations. One of the network meetings involved five CEOs. To each meeting they brought a book, a record or a concert which had inspired them and we discussed how it could inspire them at the moment of dealing with a challenge. We did the same with researchers to help them get inspiration for their writing from their heroes. We also held workshops with employees, for example, working with Folketingets Ombudsmand, which is an independent department in the Danish Parliament which looks after the citizens of Denmark and ensures their rights are observed correctly.

When we do this in coaching or meetings, we have to be sure it is the right timing. Sometimes we just take a chance and bring in an idea, metaphor or story which might become an ante-narrative and move the process along in a new and productive way. You can say that the example above is also about using metaphors and allegories in working with change. In our book about Ancient Greece dialogue concepts (Kirkeby, Larsen, Dam Hede, & Mejlhede 2008), we write about the use of metaphor and allegory and use the example of "Abraham and Isaac" from the Bible as an allegory about how leaders sometimes have to keep secrets if they know it will upset employees but have faith in the strategy. The Danish philosopher Søren Kierkegaard used it as the main allegory in his book about faith, *Fear and Trembling*. Experiments are about taking risks and having faith in yourself. To quote Bob Iger, CEO at Disney: "Take risks. Don't listen to data but to experience and your gut feeling." Brain research stresses that we understand the world through experiments; we create pictures of the world which we then test. This is also the experience of Niels Bohr in relation to Quantum Physics and the idea that we can't explain and plan everything. Some things are coincidence; the important thing is to be open to experiment (Nortrander, 2017).

We hope the above have giving you some ideas about how you can work with Principle 5. It is crucial to stress that Principle 5 is so much more than words and narratives, it's about being in the situations and the event. Being aware of the different kind of stories inspired by Boje's Quantum Storytelling and have faith in your own experiences and dare to take risks. Principle 5 is about being aware of the energy, as in indigenous knowing and native science.

Questions to ask in connection with Principle 5

1 What is the story until now (*rehistorizing*)? Share stories together. Don't give advice.
2 What would be the best stories for the future (*futurizing*)?
3 What is the stories about and why is it important (*abstractizing*)?
4 How can we ground the true and sustainable stories (*grounding*)?
5 Which stories of your own would challenge the story you hear? And which one would help them along?
6 What are the dominant narratives and the counternarratives?
7 What are the untold stories? Share stories together. Don't give advice.
8 What could become the ante-narratives – bets on the future and experiments? Share stories together. Don't give advice.

More inspiration to train your ability to help stories along and be open to experiment

If you are trained in coaching, then use your coaching skills but invest yourself in the conversation. Listen and try to be open and not judgemental. Use the art of hanging out and create a good atmosphere, as mentioned in some of the earlier principles. Listen to conversations in trains and dinner parties. Be aware of how bands play together. How do they connect? How do they create attunements? Be aware of how the different stories or words you put into the conversation move it forward or create resistance or thoughtful moments. Be aware of how you feel and react in conversations. Be aware of your body and the attunements. Are you stiff and suspicious or open and curious? Try to connect to the energy and be inspired in your conversation by native science and quantum mechanics. Read books and watch movies, reality shows and talk shows with different dialogues to get a feeling for the flow.

Note

1 Kirkeby, Larsen, Dam Hede, & Mejlhede, 2008.

6 Principle 6

You must consider staging including scenography and artefacts

This chapter is about a prize-winning Rock Museum, it's about hiking in the mountains, coming together in a theatre and sharing passion for music and your heroes. It's about how space, room, nature and bodies affect us.

Staging will help you and the people you work with in your search for a true story and help you to succeed with your new strategy, start-up or project. When we work with strategies we often forget the importance of *staging* and how we can use our own appearance, the body, the artistic space, material and natured surroundings, artefacts etc. to move the process on. This chapter describes, through conversational storytelling interviews, examples of different kinds of material *staging* and how you can work with it. It also describes the importance of *spacetimemattering*. Finally, we draw on native science (Cajete, 2000) and indigenous work with ceremonial rituals as part of the staging.

Staging is an important way to move from *abstracting* ideas into narratives and counternarratives to *grounding* in the 'living story web' in the sociomaterial *staging*, in the material artefacts and material-actants that Principle 6 is all

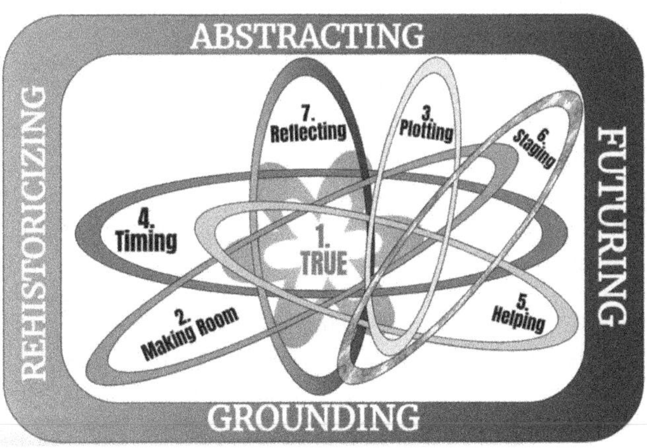

Figure 6.1

about. It is part of moving from retrospective *rehistoricizing* into the prospective sensemaking '*scenography*' that allows the constituting of *futuring* manifesting one possible future into being in its *spacetimemattering* instead of business-as-usual. What do we mean when we say *spacetimemattering?*

How global crises are staged matters

We live in a world increasingly defined by global crises often staged in today's 'negatively globalized planet.' How global crises are staged intensifies their impact. Extinction Rebellion stages die-ins to draw attention to the role of fashion in global warming. Municipalities stage UN SDG festivals to bring community awareness to both problems and potential solutions. These ways of staging are interdependent. Claims-makers design the staging of the dark side of the "negatively globalized planet" where "there cannot be local solutions to globally originated and globally invigorated problems" (Bauman, 2007: 25–26). An alternative to top-down UN SDG is to stage an 'en-light-ened,' local bottom-up approach to global crises that express the potentiality to create well-being for the multispecies, in a 'multispecies storytelling' (Haraway, 2016).

By en-light-ened storytelling, we do not mean the Age of Enlightenment where modernity was going to civilize and colonize the forces of premodernity. It is time to reclaim and rekindle indigenous ways of knowing (IWOK) about how to revere Nature (Rosile, 2016) and listen to Nature in what Cajete (2000) calls 'Native Science.' Western ways of knowing (WWOK) have been about putting economics and profit ahead of equity and the ecosystem, *abstracting* to neoliberal economic market universal claims, such as how market forces will bring about solutions to global crises. WWOK keeps *abstracting* ways of staging the underlying globalizing dynamics into growth and more economic growth. IWOK, by contrast, is about listening to what Nature is saying, learning to be *grounded* in harmony and balance with Nature. WWOK is about competition and domination, whereas IWOK is about cooperation and coexistence. WWOK is disembodying what Giddens (1990) calls 'action at a distance' where reflexivity turns humancentric, global communications are centric, reinforcing business-as-usual. WWOK is still colonizing IWOK, but native peoples are seeking to re-indigenize, to reclaim their Native Science, Native language, and Native ways of staging ceremonies focused on *living with* Nature, *being part of her spiritual ecology*. WWOK is still about the "evinced enlightenment" of the "risk society" and global insecurities, staging gatherings in the risk society (Cottle, 2009: 498)

Gaia-dialogues (or Gaialogue) is a way to desever (Heidegger's term means to de-distance), so human kind has 'Being-in-the-world' instead of in separation from Gaia.[1] A Native Science way of staging the global crises and solutions includes the appreciation of the spirit in all things: rocks, rivers, forests, mountains, stones, oceans, and so on.

As global crises and catastrophes materially unfold in the world today, we can learn from indigenous ways of staging, a reflexivity that is multispecies storytelling (Haraway, 2016; Cajete, 2000). This is a contrast to the media staging of global crises, showing the same images of apocalypse or greenwashing to make crises disappear from visual imagery.

Regimes of truth make claims and counter-claims about global crises, each seeking funding and support for their goals and methods. Bearing witness to multispecies suffering, and doing collective problem solving through Haraway's (2016) 'Staying with the Trouble' in order to do *forecaring*, to come up with solutions by *together-telling*, is a viable alternative to the staging of greenwashing. Staging needs to embed the large-scale threat to life in order to scale up the change efforts done with ensemble storytelling where everyone is responsible in leading changes in lifestyles and working practices.

The wars of the 70s, 80s and 90s were about the end of peak oil. The wars of today are about water. An alternative to water wars is to change the staging of water storytelling of anthropogenic climate change, which is dewatering rivers and lakes, acidifying oceans, polluting waterways, and resulting in water scarcity, The deliberate staging of ways communities can be in harmony with planetary water sources is a way to change the global thinking of water capitalism into water responsibility. Water is how people feel climate change. People's lives, the lives of plants and animals in shared life space are affected, and become noticeable.

How do we stage community ceremonies that focus on potential opportunities to avert extinction (Boje, 2019a)? Legitimating the power of the 1% seems a risky approach. Gaia-conversations – that include listening to Gaia, learning from the weather how anthropogenic actions change weather patterns, and how we are affected – means learning about our relationship to weather, not just creating weather disasters, but creating better weather in the long horizon of centuries by recharging aquifers, taking less water from Nature than she is able to put back in from her water cycle.

The US is staging its own rebellion by refusing to sign the Kyoto accords, withdrawing from the Paris emissions agreement, and so on. Extinction Rebellion is staging die-ins, and stopping traffic, in order to get politicians talking with climate scientists about the reality of problems and potential solutions. Are there other ways to stage rebellion? Other ways to enact support for the International Panel on Climate Change (IPCC) reports about rising world atmospheric temperatures and impacts on health and well-being of all?

The theatrics of staging

Staging involves the foregrounding of oppression, and the backgrounding of the pretence of positivity, what Augusto Boal (2000) calls *Theater of the Oppressed*. Foregrounding is dramatizing the future being brought into Being, and backgrounding the business-as-usual scenarios. People in workshops can act this out with Augusto Boal's *Image Theater*, putting the future into image sculptures without words, adding artefacts to the foreground, doing so without words, if they choose. Stop action allows the audience to interpret the images, making sense of the actor and actant configurations in each scene. A second mode of *Theater, Invisibility Theater*, can add improvisation with words that come out of the situation being dramatized, to bring the backstage power and oppression, foregrounded, to the front stage. The third mode of *Theater* is *Forum Theater*, a special event of training. It allows spectators to come onto the stage and become *spect-actors*, who attempt to try out their problem solving in the situation being staged as the actors maintain the problem dynamics. In all three kinds of theatre, the audience gets involved by suggesting changes to the scene, scenography, and how the problem could be solved.

Why staging?

After the above more philosophical reflections we want to explain this through some examples. We all know how surroundings, space and people's bodily appearances affect us, and create motivation or drain us of energy. For example, compare sitting in a nice living room with art on the walls, flowers at the table etc. with a cold white office in a public building. Or walking along the beach or through a forest compared to the stress of a busy downtown street park with people, loud noises, cars, smoke, cheap fast food shops etc. It may not be a bad experience but it is surely different. Or to be around people who are open and relaxed compared to people who are stressed and upset.

Figure 6.2
Source: @yiranding https://unsplash.com/photos/OfdewINkVdQ

Art calms or aggravates the soul of hospital patients. Some visually abstract art is so ambiguous, it can actually be emotionally and even physiologically harmful to psychiatric patients, a threat to their well-being (Hathorn, & Nanda, 2008).

On the other hand, art with natural images positively affects the outcomes of heart-surgery patients in intensive care units. A PhD research project by Stine Maria Louring Nielsen and Michael Mullins from Aalborg University studied hospitals using figurative and abstract art. Observations showed how it helps the patients to heal faster and view themselves in a more holistic way, be calmer and less stressed than patients who stayed in rooms without art.

There is another research project about how different approaches to light affects the patients at the hospital. A research project from University of Southern Denmark showed how nature heals people with stress and mental illness and helps people with heart problems to recover and learn how to ground and breath.

The French philosopher Maurice Merleau-Ponty (2003: 12) stressed, as mentioned in the beginning of this chapter, how we interact with the world around us:

> The world is ... the natural setting of, and field for, all my thoughts and all my explicit perceptions. Truth does not inhabit only the inner man, or more accurately, there is no inner man, man is in the world, and only in the world does he know himself.

The research project from a police station in the Netherlands (Van Hulst, Merlijn, Yberma, & Sierk, 2020), concluded about staging: “If the lunchroom and the desk is the backstage region of the police station, the patrol car would be an even confidential or intimate space.” And later in the same article: “Apart from colleagues’ queries in the car, the landscape also often triggered stories.”

To use surroundings and design to create changes in behaviour has become popular through the concept of nudging (Thaler, & Sunstein, 2009), for example, with food waste using smaller plates in the canteen, footprints on the street leading to the garbage can or garbage can with a sound as deep as a well when you throw garbage into it which inspires people to keep the streets and parks clean. Stairs in a railway station decorated as a piano with sounds inspiring people to use the stairs instead of the elevator as a way to prevent obesity. Or the Danish supermarket brand Netto which changed how vegetables and fruit were placed in the shop which resulted in customers buying more fruit and vegetables creating better health and lower CO_2. There is no doubt that it is powerful to use surroundings, artefacts or your body and be aware of the power of staging when we search for our true story or strategy.

However, we would like to stress the danger of using concepts like nudging and using the theory of system 1 and system 2 without utilising Principle 1 and critical and ethical thinking and dialogue. If we use only nudging or staging as a way to promote a certain action, we use the way of the salesmen and the algorithm we know from our smartphones and computers, which make us numb and open to manipulation and, in the worst case, has lead us to where we are now with problems with stress and the climate crisis and plastic pollution. That's why one principle cannot stand alone. True Storytelling is about the whole story.

Mountain leadership, Native Science and CEOs

An example using surroundings in the search for a true story is the leadership bootcamp, Mountain Leadership. We take leaders and people who want to reflect on their life and career up a mountain. We have done this in the Pyrenees in Spain and in the Dolomites in northern Italy. It was a good colleague of ours, Jakob Aagaard, who first invited us to teach at his concept Walk to Explore in 2015, where we hiked in the mountains and had meaningful conversations inspired by Greek philosophy. In the article "The Break: Work–Life Balance and Leadership"[2] we try to connect walking, philosophical dialogue and the surroundings.

This is similar to the founder of the outdoor brand Patagonia, Yvon Chouinard (2016), who wrote about how he took his leaders down to Patagonia in Argentina to hike and discuss the meaning and philosophy of the company.

In our Mountain Leadership programmes we combine hiking and philosophical dialogue (*protreptic*)[3] with the True Storytelling principles and indigenous people storytelling and science. The goal is to use the surroundings to support the search for a true story. The staging is illustrated by the walking instead of more traditional teaching and we use the mountains as a scenography which can inspire conversations and add some new perspectives to them. Walking was an important part of the teaching of Aristotle in his academy in Ancient Greece. They called his students 'columns' because they were standing up or walking around and discussing concepts and ideas. New research from Stanford University stresses the merits of walking – it has shown how walking can have an enormous effect on our creative thinking.[4]

In the essayistic book, *A Philosophy of Walking*, Frédéric Gros shares how philosophers and thinkers like Nietzsche, Thoreau and Kierkegaard use walking as a way of thinking. He quotes Nietzsche saying: "To evaluate a book, a man or a piece of music it's important to ask ourself, Can this man wander?"

For indigenous peoples, the surroundings and the places and how they affect us has always been an important part of their science and philosophy. The Native American researcher, Gregory Cajete (2000), writes about the importance of surroundings and places of spiritual ecology: he invites us to understand how indigenous stories "relate the experience of life lived in time and place" (Cajete, 2015: 96). Cajete goes on to write that we humans are "storied and storying being" and it's time to change the "story line"; "changing storylines of dysfunctional to ones of functionality, moving towards health" (ibid.). The indigenous stories he writes "have deep roots" in the very "heart of the human psyche" and "the geography of the human soul" (96).

In our three books about famous Danish fiction writers and poets and how they write we asked them about the connection between the place they grew up in and how they write.[5] For example, the author Naja Marie Aidt, who grew up in Greenland, explained it this way: "If you are brought up in Greenland as I am you don't have the same taboos about your body, sex and death. Nature and society are very rough and the border between life and death is little." In an interview with the poet, Theis Ørntoft, he drew a line between his anxiety and his feeling of the brutality of nature.

Ringgaard (2010) also explored how different writers throughout history have been connected a place and how it has inspired their thinking and writing, for example, the German philosopher Martin Heidegger, who had cabins in the mountains in the south of Germany.

ThinkTanksConcert and events for start-ups and investors

In Principle 2 and Principle 5 we told the stories of the *ThinkTanksConcert*,[6] where leaders, CEOs and teachers worked with their passions as part of their personal leadership development. The staging was in an old theatre in downtown Copenhagen. The idea was inspired by working with the songwriter and producer Nils Lassen and by a visit we made to Olympia, the Capital of Washington State, where we heard about the *backstages concert* and when we visited the independent record company K-records whose logo Kurt Cobain from Nirvana has tattooed on his upper arm (tattoos are another staging statement).

At the backstage concerts, the band had their backs to an empty theatre and the audience were standing backstage looking at the band and empty theatre. We did the same at the *ThinkTankConcerts*. The leaders and CEOs came through the back entrance and up on stage, sat at the chairs which were placed in a semicircle and listened to the Americana band standing with their backs to the empty theatre. The band and Lars Atterman, who have recorded with Bob Dylan's band in Austin, Texas, was totally acoustic. After playing half an hour, the participants discussed how the concert could inspire them in their leadership and later reflected on how their musical heroes could inspired them as leaders and as human beings.

After the event we interviewed some of them and there was no doubt that the scenography had moved them and given them embodied experiences in working with the different approaches to leadership. One of them, a CEO from an advertising company, said: "I need to go home and change my life."

Later, we did a different event about heroes and leadership, together with the CEO for the sports brand Hummel, Christian Stadil, and how the American beat poet Allen Ginsberg had inspired him. Before Stadil reflected about Allen Ginsberg, his poems were read out loud with a band. Stadil was inspired in four different ways by Ginsberg:

1 Support and connect with your employees.
2 Have the courage to be grounded and authentic under pressure.

3 Create a brand and stories people like to tell to others.
4 Be upbeat in your approach then you have nothing to lose.

As we wrote earlier, these events inspired the big project about using our passion for music, theatre and literature to change cultures in organizations and create a creative and innovative mindset.

These *ThinkTankConcerts* were also inspired by our work with metaphors[7] and artefacts. The concerts and the events were examples of taking the metaphor all the way. We started working with artefacts back in the mid-90s, at a creative writing event at the Testrup Folk School. We used them as an inspiration for essay writing and later in companies, for example, an innovation workshop with researchers from the company Novozymes in 2001 which at that time was a part of Novo Nordisk. As a way of generating ideas, we used artefacts, toys etc. and a big raw redfish and creative writing. We did the same for a one-year project called 'The innovative human being' back in 2002 (nobody knew the word innovation at that time). We used artefacts as a way to create ideas and stories for teachers to create better workspaces. Later on, from 2004, we worked with artefacts as part of protreptic dialogue, in one by one dialogues and coaching and in workshops with companies and organizations. In 2015 we got in contact with a research project at Aalborg University led by associate professor, Anete Strand, worked with a method called material storytelling which also uses artefacts when working with different challenges.

Another project we are part of is the investor network, Baxters, founded by Mikael Bak,[8] who is a CEO for a Danish shareholder organization. In his job working with investors, he has always stressed the importance of investment with meaning and not just money. The Baxters network has investors and business angels and creative people. Each meeting is staged in a different place and each time the meeting has three start-ups who pitch their business case. An example of staging was an event in the studio of the legendary Danish punk and rock band, Sort Sol, starting with a tour around the studio given by the guitarist Top Gailia, telling the stories about the instruments, the guitar pedals and the bands who have been recording in the studio. Another example is the Roskilde Festival which is a music festival with 100,000 participants which has been going on for 50 years. The meeting at the Festival was held in a backstage area, with conversations with two Danes who shared their stories of working with Dropbox, WhatsApp, Uber and the football team Manchester United.

Each time at these Baxters meetings we have pitches from three start-ups and the staging is an important part of it – both how the entrepreneurs make their pitches and how they are in the room, how passionate they are and their ability to improvise. And for the Baxters investors, they often argue that they invest in people who are passionate and true. An important part of these start-ups is how they are stage their product.

An example which illustrates this is the start-up Matchboard with their product, Yoli. This is a learning tool for children in kindergarten. The idea (*abstractizing*) is that employees in kindergartens are challenged by the amount of time where they can teach and educate the children and live up to the goals and demands of the government. In a busy day, they often don't have the time and it creates stress among the parents and arguments when they have meetings with parents or their manager.

Another idea behind the Yoli board is that parents and employees resist using iPads too much (*rehistorizing*) but they like the idea of the elements of gaming which motivate the children to learning and prepare them for school (*futurizing*). The Yoli board has some of the same abilities as an iPad but it is staged (*grounded*) or designed differently. It looks like an old wooden toy where you can put five wooden cards on top. Each game has 30 cards and the children can choose which card they put on the top. The algorithm in the board changes and we are able to draw data which can help the employees working with the children. The material is sustainable and the used boards go to the charity where they go on the global market.

The Ragnarock Museum – staging the story of music

In 2017, Ragnarock was honoured as one of the top 15 museums in the world by National Geographic, especially for its excellence in the use of interactivity, storytelling and historical dissemination. Ragnarock is close to the world-famous Roskilde Festival of music. This is a story about how to use staging and artefacts as tools for a successful process with buildings and exhibitions in creating a museum. Across a 12-year period, the other six principles – plotting, reflecting, making room for people's stories, timing and not least the importance that you yourself believed in the story as sustainable – supported the conception, fundraising, construction and exhibitions of the museum up to the opening in 2016. Compared to the other examples mentioned above this was a much more complex project.

This case is, surprisingly, not about how to stage the story of rock and pop music – the voice of up and coming youth culture, a totally new phenomenon after World War Two but which is still here today and will be in the future. You have to visit the museum to discover what it is truly about. It is instead the story of how to manage construction, stakeholders, employees, consultants, processes, buildings, communities and more, etc. leading to innovation and excellence.

Staging an exhibition and building

To create a prize-winning museum is a tough nut to break for almost every organisation as it is easy to fall into traps. Here are some of the challenges:

- The money comes too fast and you do not know what kind of museum you, the employees or the audience want – you just want to hurry and please the stakeholders and yourselves. As an example of that is the amazing rock museum in Seattle, Experience Music Project, which was built in the beginning of the 2000s based on the story of Jimi Hendrix, leaving the grunge scene story and the story of the city Seattle untold and Kurt Cobain's smashed guitar in the storage room. Today, the museum has changed all that and they have used the time and *forecaring* to renew the museum.

- The design team – staging – takes over the experience, leaving the audience in a cool, designed gallery or store or architectural dome with no clue as to what the exhibition is about, but it looks nice or fancy. These kinds of museum often get the highest rates, as they are staged according to WWOK, in a bottom-up approach. Management hires an external firm to stage the museum, often leaving employees' stories suppressed in order to meet deadlines for openings.
- The historians dominate the exhibition with the (mis)use of historical materials/artefacts – staging what they believe is the true story. They insist on having more artefacts – guitars, clothes, records etc. – displayed in the exhibition. However, the many artefacts overflood the area, leaving no room or space for reflection or pause, making no statement in terms of *why* this artefact is so necessary. The stories are not helped on their way and there is no clear plot.
- The communication team takes over and keep posting the audience with over-explanations, materials and manipulating, storytelling messages leaving the audience with no mystery or individual thought about what their own story could be, related to the museum. In an airport you need guidance and no misunderstandings about where to go or what to do. In a museum, you need to direct people without them knowing it, risking that they might reject your storyline or premise.

In the above list, we have not even mentioned the star-architects of the building, who are not designers of the exhibitions and therefore not in control of the overall staging, and what trouble that can end in. Staging the museum can, at several levels, become one big power struggle among the central actors or partners.

Staging a process – the sweat hut

Using staging as a *method* or approach to gather – or more correctly, *balance* – the three individually important bodies of the exhibitions – design, artefacts and communication – made Ragnarock a success. Actually, this process was the toughest of them all. It was much more difficult than fundraising or construction (which it must be stated, is horrendously hard as well).

Many approaches, companies, processes and clever people were consulted and hired but in the end we gathered together a few people we thought could make it. We called all their sessions 'Sweat Hut,; like the Indians. They met, they worked, they produced. However, while time was of the essence, we agreed that the museum would not be opened until we were satisfied – we had to be true to ourselves and the story we believed in all the way.

The key here is to insist on balance and use the approach *spacetimematters* instead of business-as-usual. In order to help your employees, designers and communication team absorb your triangular concept 'design, artefacts, message,' you need to make room for stories and counter narratives, you have to be clear about your own plot/story, you have to make timing your friend and not your enemy (as long as the direction is right or true, time is no problem – that was what we said all along, mostly to calm our nerves).

Staging staff and stakeholders – the museum without walls

Staging was used in a particularly important period of the development of the museum – in the beginning. Offices and employees were moved from the municipality, corporate-like surroundings to a completely empty area – the area where the museum would be built. The area, named Musicon, was an old concrete factory and a former cesspool. It contained a dance theatre, a skating hall, an E-sport company (before nobody even knew what that was) and now a rock museum was on its way. The administrative municipal employees were assembled in this former industrial workers' place – you could still smell the sweat from the rough workers having a small break from a hard day's work.

The only activities on the site were stoned teenagers from nearby schools, racing cars and smoking weed. There were number plates from cars fleeing from nearby gas stations, stealing gasoline, lying all over the floor. It was dusty and windy and the only noises were those coming from the nearby interstate.

This atmosphere reflected *spacetimematters* – not being forced into business-as-usual at the City Hall or the main museum gave us room to use scenography, *futuring* the museum to be. As an example of living scenography, we hired some young people with interest in music to do some museum-based activities on the ground, at their own expense, without us controlling them or telling them what to do. We did not even tell them what the museum was all about. We slowly became a museum without walls, starting to do exhibitions and events in the local city and in Copenhagen, then in the other Nordic countries and finally in Paris and Spain. The museum was not yet built – like a snail it had a body, however no roof or floor. A CEO from a foundation once said: "Be aware that when you finally get your physical building, you will find yourself in business-as-usual, not able to open yourself for other narratives and scenographies. Innovation will decrease."

Staging the SDG goals and our research project about them

As we have done though out the book, we want to share some ideas about staging and Principle 6 concerning our research project about working with the SDGs in a Danish municipality. The project was about how to create sustainable growth among business and well-being among employees. In Principle 1 we mentioned how the municipality created events and *together-telling* to do *fore-caring* before the new strategy was decided in the city council and we have mentioned how they put on a People's Gathering for the SDGs with all the stakeholders. We have shared how we through the self-correcting method, creating commitment to our project. We want to explore a little bit more about how staging come in to action in this project.

The organizers of the People's Gathering, the local SDG festival, got 51 different organizations and stakeholders involved and built up the event near the lake and the old academy in the city of Sorø. We did one of the talks, together with Professor Kenneth Mølbjerg Jørgensen, where we invited people up on stage to share their stories about how they work with the SDGs.

The organisers used the perspectives of the four different approaches of *rehistorizing, abstractizing, grounding* and *futuring*. They were inspired by the people catering at Bornholm, which is a big democracy festival with more than 100,000 people and thousands of events on a special rocky island near the Swedish coast (*rehistorizing*). They had this idea or concept about creating a scenography where they would bring committed people and organizations together and create networks and relations which could create commitment (*abstractizing*). As one of organizers, Nanna, said: "Our success lay in having brought all these good people together and to give them a space and time to talk." It was a totally different approach to just focussing on how many participants or citizens could have joined the event. The staging was *grounded* in the place, in the tents, the events and people and in the history of the place going back to the Middle Ages. There is the famous monastery, in the 18th century Hans Christian Andersen visited Sorø and the founder of the Folk School movement, Grundtvig, wanted to start the first University for the People here. Concerning *futurizing* the event, this feeling of embodiment and good experience, the *together-telling* among the people and stakeholders, surely created a story and relationships for the future.

In developing the project with the stakeholders, it has grown and they want it to cover a broader area, not just the municipality but the whole region, and we have discussed how we use staging and artefacts. One idea is the construction of a very long bridge from northern Germany to the southern coast of Denmark – if this ran through the area it could be an important artefact or symbol which could *ground* the story about a sustainable future. We cannot stress enough how important Principle 6 and staging is if we want to create commitment to, and ownership of, changes.

In our pre-project for the research project we wrote six stories with local company owners about how they work with the SDGs. The magazine has since been an important artefact in the story of Sorø Municipality's work with green growth and we have been out doing keynotes with some of the business owners from the companies as an example of being out there, staging and telling the story.

This led us to how the UN has staged the 17 goals:

"I'm almost sure that people wouldn't have bought into the UN goals 10 years ago or perhaps 10 months ago," said the businessman and founder of Code of Care, Peter Nørgaard, when we discussed with him and Professor

Steen Hildebrandt why everybody knows about the UN goals today and how they have become one of the big narratives. Of course, it is complex, with the stories about ice melting, the powerful storytelling of Greta Thunberg, demonstrations, with many scientists pushing the agenda. We agree that they make sense for everyone and cross political borders but a part of it is also the way they are staged. Everybody knows the colourful squares of the SDGs with the goals and drawings. And they are not just two-dimensional – they are like Lego bricks. They are colourful and you can build and play with them and make simple drawings which are easy to recognize. They talk to something more than rational thinking – they talk to our body and imagination. Or as the Danish professor Steen Hildebrandt said in a debate we had at the Danish People's Gathering which celebrated democracy, politics and the UN goals: "Yes, you play with these squares and that means we can create some new ideas."

How CEOs work with staging

In this part of the chapter we want to show how two CEOs worked with staging in their approach to leadership, how they used frames and rituals and their own appearance in order to let the abstract ideas and narratives and themselves become materialized, staged, and thereby grounded.

According to Marianne Hoff Andersen, director of Faxe Municipality, she is constantly aware of how she enters teachers' rooms, showing the teachers they are all on the same team, playing on the same side. She has the power, but she has no intention of frightening them or signifying power. Instead, she wants to show she is genuinely interested in teachers' stories.

She also talks about singing at the beginnings of meetings/assemblies as something she is insisting on doing, as well as simply saying hello and goodbye to co-workers as an important ritual.

> I am very conscious about the basic things; I think a lot about it. What are the values and frames I want for this workplace? Greeting and singing creates a sense of community. Perhaps that is part of my inspiration from the Danish Folk School where singing and shaping a community is very important. And I have to be a good example. I am aware of being where I need to be; it can be a staff meeting or celebrations. I am also thinking about how I dress and being neutral. I must be prepared to shift role, both being able to take the podium but also go along with the co-workers. I am the same person, just more subdued. This is very difficult today. Many leaders are expected to be extroverts. And you have to have an opinion about everything in order to offer clear leadership. And that is also important. But I just want to say, "Shut up and relax. Listen."

Marianne reflects on how staging is a process she controls or something the employees have an impact on and how they react.

> One must not make everything informal because it becomes difficult for the employees. You must not intimidate the employees either. It is a balancing act. Especially if you have to announce budget cuts – no soft chairs and cake. We do not need to have fun. The framework – physically – has to make space for the employees to reflect, they must be allowed to be in peace when they receive such a messages as budget cuts. I think a lot about that.

If using scenography is transforming the process from *abstractizing* to *grounding*, this statement gives the opposite point – if you use staging and narratives in a thoughtless way, things can go very wrong.

Marianne is also aware of her appearance when helping employees share their stories with her. Because when she sits down at the table

> [t]he conversation focuses quickly around me and my children. They have to ask each other about that. So I have practiced getting into a room and preparing myself to make the conversation about them, in order for them to hear about themselves and their lives and children. Then I can enter into a relationship where I can be equal and can ask and not be in the centre. However, it is never a powerless room.

The former Chief of the Danish Police Force and Police Adviser to the UN in New York also stresses the importance of being in the room:

> I am a very physical person and it means a lot to policemen and others that they can feel your presence and that you walk the talk. I put a lot of energy into my job and it is very important to me that I am able to engage and inspire people and create enthusiasm wherever I go. I try to visualize things. I say: "I can clearly imagine the ideas." People might not agree with me, but at least they can feel that I mean what I am saying and that I know what I am talking about. For me True Storytelling is about being authentic and real. Otherwise it is not a professional performance but entertainment, and our job is not entertainment.

The uniform, the handshake, the way you look at people and the fact that they know you are focused and never giving up is very important. It's similar with the military. The uniform is a symbol of authority and strength. In True Storytelling, artefacts like that can be a way of establishing a certain relation between you and the people you communicate with.

Wrap up

We have previously stressed that storytelling is more than words; it is also about staging and materiality. The manager's physical presence and authenticity is important for implementation. As in the choice of narrative, the space or scene you choose to use also has an effect on how the target audience receives it and is thus also significant to the implementation.

We have described Principle 6 and argued that there is a correlation between the story, the body and the scenography that will be in play to support the implementation of strategies and change management.

Materiality, embodiment, emotion

Materiality is a substantial element in True Storytelling, due to the fact it is contextual and makes the target audience embodied and emotional. Using of the artefacts method produces significantly positive results as words are expressed through objects.

This method provides:

- an overview in a situation of complexity
- new knowledge instead of individual knowledge
- co-creation and friendship.

Proven results include: the implementation of strategy, co-creation and prototype development, team development and conversations.

Space and rooms

Another effective and meaningful element in the use of scenography is the room and space where employees, middle leadership teams or executive teams are gathered physically – meeting rooms, conference rooms etc. Changing the scene to, for instance, a walk and talk session outside, a non-formal venue at the company or an external place, will all have an impact on the way company strategies are expressed and perceived. People are more open minded and, in a way, they are able to rise above business and everyday life in order to act on a value-based basis.

A new scene will open up the improvement of dialogue, embracing all the other six principles, thereby supporting change management and the implementation of company strategies.

The dark side of staging

Earlier in the chapter we mentioned how the concept of nudging has a dark side which may lead us along a way without critical thinking. This book is all about *not* being manipulative. However, staging and using artefacts is a difficult balance. As Municipality CEO, Marianne Hoff Andersen, says, "No soft chairs and cakes." You cannot gather staff to receive an announcement on budget cuts in a super cosy environment, it just does not add up – this is hard stuff and it is not nice. Management should be aware of how they use rooms or settings creatively – making people feel uncomfortable, even though it is with good intentions, can make them feel hijacked or manipulated.

Have in mind the minds

Another negative thing, or something to be aware of when using scenographies and artefacts, is the diversity of people's minds and behaviours. People have different personalities and, therefore, different perceptions of what is true and authentic, what feels convenient or not. We all react differently to social, well-staged meetings in concert or festival environments, or even in a simple social bowling activity at work: some people love aesthetics; some of us are less socially minded; some of us are focused on how our leader are doing; some on logistics such as is there enough coffee for everyone; some people do not like the scene to change unexpectedly, they need to be prepared.

There are as many nuances to this as there are different personalities. Therefore, we should not take for granted that people will sense the same thing in the same way. People do not feel inspired or open to share stories in the same way. This is not rocket science, but more an indication for us be careful when planning spaces, rooms, activities and scenographies.

According to Kierkegaard's advice we should have in mind that

> when we judge the actions of others, we should put ourselves in their place, trying to understand how they see themselves and their world. And when we judge ourselves, we should see ourselves as other sees us, overcoming the ease with which we find extenuating circumstances for ourselves. (Riso, & Hudson, 1996)

However hard to live by, True Storytelling is all about that – trying not to narrow down space, time or matter in order to find *futuring* scenarios to follow. When we use artefacts, symbols and designs etc. to support our strategy we cannot be sure if it will work as it depends on people and their perceptions. However, because staging is often tactile and physical, something you do with your body, it is ten times stronger perception-wise. Things can go wrong faster than we can imagine!

Questions to ask in connection with Principle 6

1 How have we used staging and artefacts in the past to support the true story (*rehistorizing*)?
2 What should the staging illustrate or symbolize in terms of concept and meaning (*abstractizing*)?
3 How should staging look like in the future if it is to support and create commitment to the true story (*futurizing*)?
4 How can we stage and use artefacts now, which will support and create commitment to the true story (*grounding*)?
5 How can we use our appearance?
6 How can we stage *together-telling*?
7 How can we invent new staging over time?

Other ways to be inspired to work with staging

Go to cafes and theatres and feel the scenography. Be aware when visiting people, private or professional, of which staging inspires you. Use the healing of nature. Be aware of good handcraft and art. Be aware of people you love being around – are they open or closed? How are their faces? There is a Norwegian psychiatric research project which showed that faces affected how patients healed – an open face moved the healing along, but a closed and untrusting face had a negative effect on the healing of persons.

Be aware of how your heroes act and look. We can mention how the American beat poet Allen Ginsberg, with his big black glasses, tall Stars and Stripes hat and poetry, created a whole movement. This movement inspired the Danish businessman CEO, Cristian Stadil,[9] who is the owner of the sports brand Hummel and 200 other companies. We worked together with Christian on some chapters about leadership and how he was inspired by Ginsberg.

Notes

1 See our call for Gaia Storytelling, ways of staging, accessed September 18, 2019 at https://docs.google.com/document/d/1utIvL1Rsqlp4MskRyomv3aiv4upcgLhSvJb9PIwXFGo/edit?ts=5d6c2351#
2 Larsen, Strand, & Aagaard, 2018.
3 Kirkeby, et al., 2008.
4 Oppezzo, & Schwartz, 2014.
5 Christensen, & Larsen, 2014, 2016, 2020.
6 It was co-produced with Nils Lassen and Kristian Riis. When Jens was a partner in the coaching company CCC he did 'Stand-up leadership' at the theatre working with how stand-up comedians could inspire leaders.
7 Kirkeby, et al., 2008. We have a chapter about how to use metaphors in dialogues.
8 The co-founders of Baxter are Christian Honore and Thomas Juhl.
9 Hein, et al., 2012.

7 Principle 7

You must reflect on the stories and how they create value

The last principle is about the importance of *reflecting* on True Storytelling. Reflect on the question: "What's the story now?" It's time for evaluation, not to get people stressed but to have an idea about if we are moving in the direction of the future people want and how it fits the situation-at-hand. You could say that all the principles in True Storytelling are about reflection but Principle 7 is about looking at the project or the concept in the bigger picture, like an eagle flying above looking down. The Greeks talked about 'being master in your own house' and to be that you need to reflect.

This chapter explores why it is essential for people to reflect together, on a strategic and value level, on implementing strategies and changes, it explores what it means to reflect on values and strategies and how we can do it in practise. This chapter will contain cases from our own work and interviews and discussions with managers on the benefits and challenges of dealing with this principle.

We propose four directions for this reflection: *futuring*, reflecting upon the relative merits of the future the *together-telling* is brining into being;

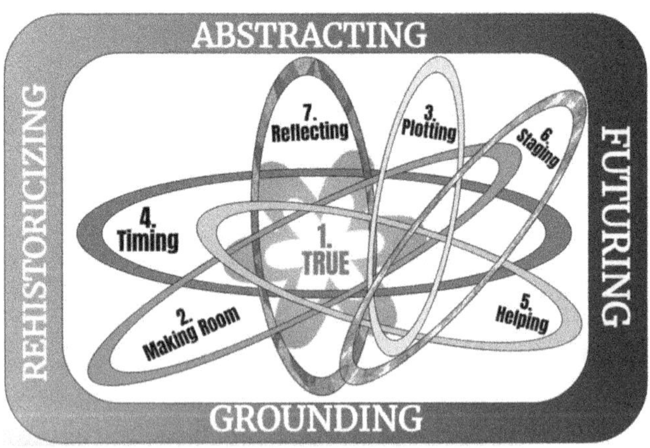

Figure 7.1

rehistoricizing, a reflecting on the diverse pasts that are related to that *futuring; abstracting* on the value propositions, the core values that are constituted in the narratives-counternarratives people in the workshop have been working on; and *grounding*, reflecting on the sociomaterial situation, the relationship of Human-World to the planetary limits of Nature-World. Is this grounding sustainable?

In classes and seminars, we ask people to reflect on their valuations of the 17 United Nations Sustainable Development Goals (SDGs). Value propositions typically skip over being a *grounding* in planetary limits. Typically, it is reduced to combinations of products and services of value to the customer. We are seeking a business model that is ecologically *grounding*. This means *grounding* the value proposition from more than a humancentric standpoint, and including the full employment of people and the planetary limits of Mother Earth in the valuing. The *grounding* of the value chain includes *reflecting* on the *forestructuring* of the logistics coming in from the supply chain, the operations, and what are the logistics going out of the project or enterprise to the customer and any after-purchase services. Every aspect of production and distribution in a supply chain has planetary implications (water, energy, forests for paper, and so on). Ecological business modelling of the value chain includes sociomaterial, socioecological, and terrestrially *grounding* ethics. The complexity of the systems that are entangled need *reflecting* upon: political systems, ecological systems, industry systems, legal systems, sociomaterial systems, biological systems, and so on. Critical accounting and qualimetrics are ways to generate interrelated metrics that are qualitative, quantitative and financial. Critical accounts, for example, are accounts constructed in Critical Theory Accounting (CAT) for the voiceless, such as people in the organization, the ecology planetary limits, and so on. Qualimetrics stresses the interdependencies among quantitative, qualitative and financial metrics.

Reflecting and existential storytelling

True Storytelling is all about the existential relationships between the planet's living systems – the elements of life (air, water, earth and fire) – and what is necessary for the continued existence of our multispecies. Existential storytelling takes living story relationships of place, time, and value to the level of True Storytelling's ethical answerability for environmentally responsible behaviours in lifestyles of consumption and in activities of production and distribution. Existential storytelling (including True Storytelling) is more than sociomaterial analysis. Existential storytelling (including True Storytelling) is more than what Jane Bennett (2010a: 3–4) calls the "onto-story" of materiality – how human activities and (non-human) thinghood overlap, becoming vital players, Being-in-the-world (ontologically):

> The strangely vital things – a dead rat, a plastic cap, a spool of thread – are characters in a speculative onto-story. The tale hazards an account of

materiality, even though it is both too alien and too close to see clearly and even though linguistic means prove inadequate to the task. The story will highlight the extent to which human being and thinghood overlap, the extent to which the use and the slip-slide into each other. One side of the story is that we are also nonhuman and the things, too, are vital players in the world.

Existential storytelling is also more than positivist empiricism, such as the 97% consensus that human activities have caused a rise in average global temperatures since the Industrial Revolution. It is more than epistemological (ways of knowing), or ontology (ways of Being). Rather it is about the critical ways of doing, of intervening to bring about a value: environmentally responsible behaviours in the situation of global heating of the atmosphere. Boje's (2014: 89) GOPE model of four pragmatisms can apply to 'True Storytelling' as its nexus.

Our first point is that *reflecting* in Principle 7 is all about the values of caring for people and the planet, not just maximizing profit in short-termism. Our second point is that True Storytelling is a kind of 'existential storytelling' a caring-in-advance (Critical pragmatism), 'grounding' (Ontological pragmatism, preparing-in-advance that is *grounding* and *futuring* in planetary systems (Positivistic pragmatism), and ways of knowing (Epistemic pragmatism). Our final point, before getting into our cases, is that 'self-correcting' involves a

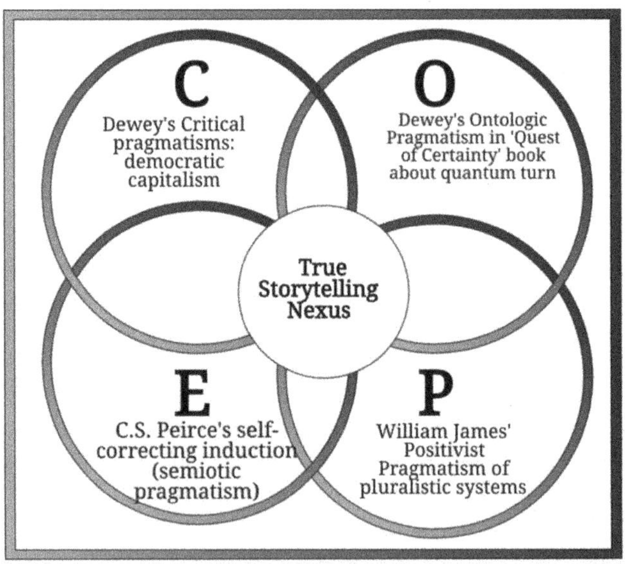

Figure 7.2 True Storytelling as the nexus of four pragmatisms
Source: E = Charles Sanders Peirce's (1930/1960) *self-correcting induction* approach that is incorporated with abduction and deduction that we have referred to throughout our current book.

mode of getting closer and closer to the truth, by eliminating the fake, doing more COPE pragmatism studies to get you closer to True Storytelling, knowing full well that one keeps striving for true but one never arrives. That said, *reflecting* as one's reflexive praxis, as a way of doing storytelling conversations with others, or by looking to the positivistic science, or even doing interventions and experiments, is a way to test the argumentation (Principle 7).

Make the tales even stronger through dialogue and reflection

> We need to put the project into a broader perspective so that we get beyond our operations and everyday lives. This can be done in the dialogue with the managers and employees. But it's hard.

The words come from a top-level manager in a public institution and describe very well the way that successful change is the ability to make sense of the edge of stories and the dialogue about the stories. *Reflection* must make sense for the individual, but also redeem innovation and give new ideas, because the tales are incorporated into a broader context.

Therefore, it is important for managers to be in dialogue with management and employees about the key stories and ask: "What is this story or situation about?" "Is it important to our organization?" "Which values and concepts does it contain?" Then unfold the values and concepts. It's not about agreeing how to interpret the values, but about mirroring them and keeping them alive as the glue that can bind us together along the way to the goal.

"It's fine enough with stories, but how are they related to our values and the general company strategy and goals?" Or "It's hard to see how there is a link between the story and our values and that makes me and my colleagues insecure." Such expressions often come from middle managers and from the employees of the organization who are driven by values and passion and who have a need for coherence.

There may be similarities between Principle 5 (helping stories on the way and experimenting) and Principle 7. But the crucial difference is that Principle 5 focuses more on the narrative and concrete plan – that is, the stories that are out there or that are being developed – where Principle 7 focuses on the values and the conceptual and strategic plan. It is, in fact, an ethical plan which relates to a larger context, the organization, the community. In the following we look at the ability to reflect on a value plan and a strategic plan.

How a rock band drew upon reflection tools from the Ancient Greeks

The art of reflection is very important when we are working with the self-correcting method we introduced at the beginning of this book, but reflection can take place on different levels, depending on the project or task. It can be reflection on important values or concepts for the people involved or the organisation both to align with these values or to get some new understanding. It can be reflection on how the project connects to some ethic values or reflection on the strategies and goals of the project. To illustrate this, we will give some examples.

In Chapter 1 we told the story about Johnny Cash searching for his true story. Here we start with a story from a famous Danish rock band, Nephew. Kristian Riis, the guitar player and founder of NordicLA, who we have been working with on a different project, described how he and the other musicians in the band reflect on the things about which they disagree:

> Everyone has their own ideas about what would be best. One wants some more guitar, another some more bass. Very often we have asked the question: "What would be best for Nephew instead for each of us as individuals?" Very often this has helped us to rise above our disagreement and personal views and see what is the best for project.

This approach is about pulling yourself up from the personal level and asking what is best for yourself and for the project. To analyze the case of the rock band with our model, you could say that the discussion about how each member wants to deal with it is the *rehistorizing*; the *abstracting* is to ask "what is best for Nephew," the *grounding* is the decision they make about making a record, going on tour or a break and *futurizing* is what will come.

Why do we even put values and ethics in play with stories?

Because True Storytelling is ethical storytelling and the stories we deal with are linked to the ethics and values we see as true in relation to our strategy and organization. Because values enable us to stand in the hurricane's eye, where there is peace, even if the storm is raging outside; values are stepping stones in a changing world. Values contain power because they speak to something deeper in us, something basically human, which is beyond daily operations and our stomach sensations and mental state of mind. There are also values behind every action we take, just like there are stories everywhere. Our choice is whether we use values and stories ethically and strategically or ignore them. We want to follow the path of the value in the next examples which are also about reflection.

To go up in the mountains and reflect

As mentioned in Chapter 6, each year we take people up into the mountains in the Pyrenees in Spain or in the Dolomites in Northern Italy as part of our program Mountain Leadership to reflect about which concepts and values are important for them, but also to reflect about where they are in their lives. In reflecting about concepts, we combine the True Storytelling principles with the Greek dialogue concept of *protreptic* which we have been working with for years. This is an approach exploring and implementing personal values and important values for the participants, organization or company. In the *protreptic* approach you are not supposed to use examples and stories from the participants' personal and working lives but to explore in more philosophical and abstract ways.

We use all the principles in the programme, but inspire by Principle 7 we ask "How do you know you live the value or concept?" and "How can you adjust it?" On the last trip to the Dolomites, one of the dialogues was with a CEO of a construction company. He wanted to explore the concept of 'holistic' and the dialogue went into reflections about sustainability, how he saw it in his life and work and how he could develop it in the future. The conversation went from *abstractizing* to *rehistorizing*, to *futurizing* to *grounding* as he explained how the company could use more sustainable materials and how he could take more care about himself and people around him.

When we reflect on our lives on the Mountain Leadership programmes we are inspired by indigenous wisdom about how we connect to the community. One more important way of reflecting on these hikes, inspired by indigenous ways of knowing, is to ask questions of the mountains and nature because it is an important part of True Storytelling to always be connected with nature and try to fit into nature instead of controlling and occupying it.

Over the years we have been coaching start-ups, researchers from Universities and leaders at all levels. An important part of this has been to reflect not only about the challenges and goals, but also to give time to reflect on the bigger picture: "Where are they coming from?" "Where are they now?" and "How do they see their story of the future?" It gives people the way to ground and

Figure 7.3
Source: Tyler Lastovich fromPexels

embody their own story and gives them pleasure in realizing how it has emerged. When they reflect on their story, going back and forth and reflecting on a more abstract level, they realize that a meaningful or true story is not only a happy story but a story with some challenges and perhaps painful situations where you need to take care of yourself.

The importance of reflecting together on complex projects

The art of reflecting is also very important in more complex projects. The museum of rock, pop and youth culture, Ragnarock, in Roskilde took a long time in coming. From the first ideas of the late 90s, to the grand opening in 2016, many thoughts, people and processes have been shared, told and innovated.

This ongoing process mirrors the True Storytelling approach, as we believe the museum would never have succeeded if we had not (however, unaware at that time) been following the five entangled processes, moving from *abstracting* (the philanthropic idea), to *grounding* (who are we really; and do people support our perception; do they want to work for us), to *futurizing* (what is the museum going to be, with far too many opinions on that issue) and *rehistorizing* (new counter stories and time challenges constantly made impacts on how to proceed).

During the entire process, all seven Principles were activated, however Principle 7, Reflecting, stands out as the one essential for progress. In a 12-year, circular process, one tends to fall asleep, zombieing through time, constantly 'one step forwards, two steps back,' and the easy way would have been to turn to a business-as-usual approach in order to make it all end. Instead we began to ask ourselves: "What is the story now?" "Does anyone believe in it?" "Does anyone support the story?" "What are the ante-narratives?" "Are we including the right people in the project?" "Are we open for counter stories?" "Are we heading in the same direction?" "If timing is an issue, why and for whom is this important?" "Does the project contribute to a greater good or value – and how?"

The worst question to deal with kept popping up from time to time: "Why should we have a rock museum at all?" I don't know, but I am going to find out starting with Principle 1.

By checking each principle, we started to wake up, finding either a passion or a narrative or counter narrative helping the story and project on its way. By reflecting and evaluating the situation over and over, we managed to secure a *grounding* at a both qualitative, quantitative and financial level. We reflected upon how the project contributed to the SDG's goals, as well-being and education are core values in a museum business, both at national museums and in a community-based museum in Roskilde. Is it economically sustainable? Maybe not, as it is expensive to keep running. However, more taxpayers will move to the city and the museum is a driver for urban development in a low social area of the city.

Fundraising: a reflection

This is a reflection on funding, an occupation requiring an ethical approach, reflecting on how the story can create value for the common good.

In dealing with funding assignments for schools, museums and urban projects, we have experienced the same method being useful. Finding funding is same as writing a manuscript – first you gather the people to be involved, then you find out what is the true story you and they can share, then you explore what angles to tune your story to in order to obtain finance (however, do not crash your own core values as it is no longer true to yourself), then reflect on the value of the story to the World and solutions to problems. Then you have a proposition, a manuscript, to forward to investors, to test if it is seen as you think and hope it will be. As with publishers, they reflect and get back with feedback, often very valuable and constructive. And now you must test yourself to see if you are open to critique, and if you are willing to accept changes. Somehow, we find this phase the most difficult, because criticism always makes people think they are rejected.

If the funding application is rejected, it is usually due to the fact that it is not true in the sense it is lacking vision: who believes in this story, can we feel the people behind it, is it grounded in the organisation, the partners, the municipality/who supports this project, is it financially sustainable, etc.?

We are aware, of course, that external circumstances in the foundation can be the reason why an application or a preliminary query is rejected. While this is not the focus of this reflection, it is, however, often the reason why it happens.

To reflect through the lens of sustainability

True Storytelling is, as mentioned many times before, related to nature and planetary ethics. Therefore, we want to go into how we can reflect on sustainability and, more precisely, about 'water.' We do this with the Tamara-Land theory of storytelling developed in Boje (1995), which can be used at the 'organizational storytelling' level or at a global level (Boje, 2019b). We want to reflect on the situation at hand through the perspective of water, a basic need for all living beings.

Boje and Rosile (in press, 2019) apply Steven Toulmin's approach to ethical argumentation to self-correcting in a 'storytelling science' that has implications for True Storytelling *reflecting*. In other words, (as depicted above), *grounding* the 'data' develops ideas with verification (backing) which can promote the initial claims (abductive hypotheses) which then get refuted by rebuttals and qualifiers to generate final conclusions.

Here we summarize Boje and Rosile (in press, 2019). The above figure is a way to graphically integrate a Tamara-Land (Boje, 1995) scaled to the level of global water capitalism (Boje, 2017a) that we are all within, and the ways of doing argumentation based on Steven Toulmin's (1972) and his colleagues' work (Toulmin,

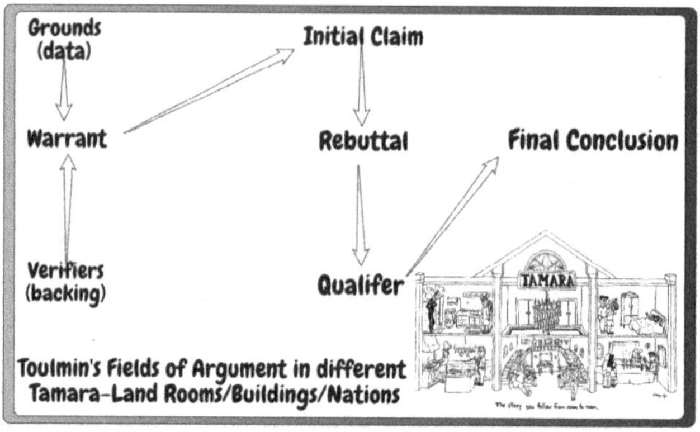

Figure 7.4 Toulmin's fields of argumentation as a mode of self-correcting, in global Tamara-Land storytelling

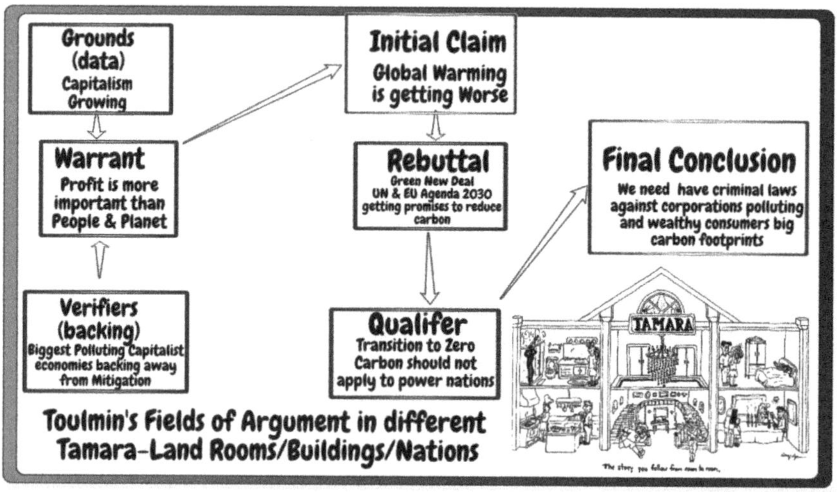

Figure 7.5 Example of argumentation applied to True Storytelling Principle 7
Source: Boje, & Rosile, in press, 2019

Rieke, & Janik, 1980). We cannot escape capitalist approaches to the privatization and commodification of water, even if we have our own rainwater collection system, reuse it, use greywater and so on. Every product and service of capitalism uses water not just directly, but also through the virtual water of energy, machines, supply chains, transport, etc. We have gone past peak oil and peak carbon, and are now past peak water as it too becomes scarce and scarcer with global warming. Water capitalism is growing despite the efforts of the United Nations sustainable development goals (SDGs) and the European Union's Agenda 2030 which aim to keep average the global temperature from rising more than 1.5°C since the

Industrial Revolution. The UN and EU initiatives around water, carbon and temperature, to control desertification, deforestation, and so on, have been colonized by two corporate narratives of denial and delay: triple bottom line (3BL) and circular economy (CE) (Boje, 2016). The two are not independent or mutually exclusive. CE is a kind of 3BL logic, where continued capitalism growth is storied as possible by turning to technologies such as renewable energy for electricity, electric transport, carbon capture and attempts to 'Reduce Emissions from Deforestation and Degradation' (REDD) have failed.

A personal story about water

Talking about water, we want to finish our discussion of Principle 7 with a story about working with the SDGs and sustainability in a municipality in Denmark.

It is the story of Ramus and his company, Nyrop Plast, which we have mentioned before. It's a small family-owned company with 15 employees, located in the small village of Nyrop, east of Sorø. The company worked with solutions for climate change related to heavy showers in cities and recycling rainwater instead of using drinking water. The company was founded back in the 50s by five local farmers who produced tools to drain the fields of water.

> "My father bought the company back in 1991 and was the first one to think about how you can recycle rainwater." Rasmus mentioned his own passion for environmental issues and how they have changed the company into a sustainable company using electricity for trucks, recycling rainwater in the toilets etc.

As he goes along, he reflects on his stories: going back, *rehistorizing*, telling about the farmers and his dad and his reflections on rainwater and sustainability. It's about his own reflection, *abstractizing*, reflecting about the importance of sustainability, rainwater and climate, and *grounding*, telling others about the concrete actions, recycling rainwater and reflecting on the future, *futuring,* when he says: "It's our grandchildren who will take over an Earth we did not take care of. That is an issue I often think about."

Questions to ask in connection with Principle 7

1 What is the true story now compared to the past (*rehistorizing*)?
2 Which goals have you achieved (*grounding*)?
3 Have you recognized any side benefits which are important to share in stories (*grounding*)?
4 How do the smaller stories fit into the bigger picture (*abstractizing*)?
5 Do you need to add or change anything (*futurizing*)?
6 Which concepts or values illustrate the stories (*abstractizing*)?
7 Questions to reflect on values and concept's inspired from the 7 principles

- a Which values or concepts are important for moving the story along and creating commitment to it?
- b Why are these concepts important for nature, well-being and a sustainable economy?
- c Where do you see this concept in action?
- d How would you tell the story about the concept?
- e What is the right timing and how does it depend on time and culture?
- f How can you help it along and rethink it?
- g How can you stage the concept?
- h How do you know you live the concept?

Other ways to train in the art of reflection

Listen to narratives on an everyday level and try to analyze which values or concepts they are about. Read books about philosophy and ethics and sustainability (for example, Rosile, 2016), but also novels and short stories written in a more essayistic way, like those by Joan Didion. Philosophy expands our mind so we can look at life in different ways. And remember to take breaks, go hiking in the mountains, walk along the ocean and talk to friends.

8 Anti tools for working with the True Storytelling principles

The reading of the chapters above about the principles should have given you ideas about how to work with the principles and how to approach them. True Storytelling is not a tool box – we hate this demand for tools which we have experienced over the years – as it is not about tools but about energy, complexity and caring and the ability to connect to all living beings. If it was only about tools, or nudging without critical thinking or embodiedness, it would be like if you gave a racket to a guy who had never played tennis before and believed he could play the game. A bad joke perhaps, but the demand for tools come only from people who need somebody to blame if they fail and selling tools is a large part of the consulting industry.

So please look at True Storytelling as a practical philosophy in the same way as Gilles Deleuze defined philosophy as a concept to approach the world or Hannah Arendt's concept of 'action' or John Dewey's 'pragmatism': True Storytelling is like Native Science – it is action researching, becoming in the now, it is a *self-correcting* method and it is about standing in the arena and daring to be vulnerable. To quote Theodore Roosevelt again:

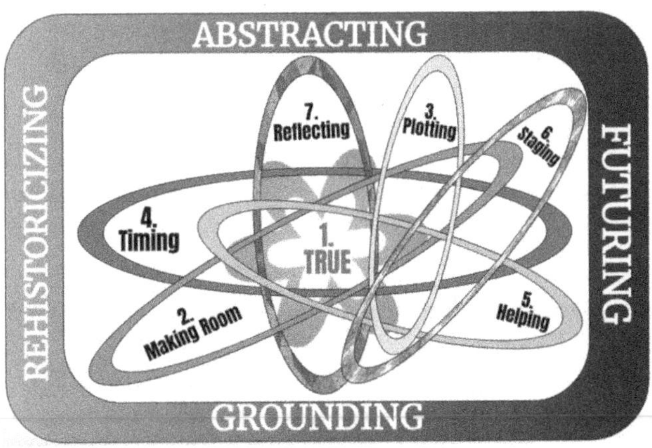

Figure 8.1

> The credit belongs to the man who is actually in the arena, whose face is marred by dust and sweat and blood; who strives valiantly; who errs, who comes short again and again, because there is no effort without error and shortcoming; but who does actually strive to do the deeds; who knows great enthusiasms, the great devotions; who spends himself in a worthy cause; who at the best knows in the end the triumph of high achievement, and who at the worst, if he fails, at least fails while daring greatly, so that his place shall never be with those cold and timid souls who neither know victory nor defeat.[1]

With this in mind, we want to share some of the manuals and working papers we have used with the people we worked with. We call them anti tools. What is an anti tool? We don't know.

Tools for ethical change management

True Storytelling is a dialogue which creates sustainable growth in companies working with sustainability and the UN Goals – the SDGs.

The working questions below were designed for the business department of the municipality in Denmark, which we worked with. Some of the same questions were also used in working with students at Aalborg University Denmark.

Principle 1: True: You yourself must be true and prepare the energy and effort for a sustainable future

Companies need to experience working with the UN goals as true and sustainable.

Questions which create commitment:

1 What is your company story until now in working with sustainability?
2 What is the best strategy for your company in connection with sustainability and the UN goals?
3 Do you believe in the strategy?
4 Do you have the knowledge to implement the strategy or do you need help?
5 Is the strategy sustainable when it comes to nature, well-being and the economy?

Principle 2: Making room: True storytelling makes spaces respecting the stories already there

We need to find stories and actions in each company which already support the work with sustainability and the UN goals because they create energy and innovation.

Questions which create commitment:

1 What is your company, you as a manager, your employees, partners and customers already doing which supports sustainability and the UN goals?
2 How can you use it as an advantage? And can you do more of it?
3 Is there a challenge if your company is already working with sustainability and the UN goals?
4 Which events can shed light on how you already work with sustainability and the goals? Meetings, stories on the web etc.

Principle 3: Plotting: You must create stories with a clear plot creating direction and help people prioritize

We need to create a clear plot in the municipality which all the companies can identify with and which can help them prioritize working with sustainability and the UN goals.

Questions which create commitment:

1 How can we and the companies create a clear plot which will break with the old one?
2 What can we do to help every company identify with the plot?
3 How can we make the story clear, while remaining complex?
4 What could be new and surprising about the new plot?

Principle 4: Timing: You must have timing

To keep the motivation and energy in the companies working with the UN goals we need to consider timing in the long- and short-term.

Questions which create commitment:

1 When is the right time for working with sustainability and the UN goals?
2 Which activities should we put into action now and which ones later?
3 What is the right time to involve people, for example, employees, partners, customers etc.?
4 What is the right length for the activity? One year, five, ten?
5 When should we communicate the activity?

Principle 5: Helping stories along: You must be able to help stories on their way and be open to experiment

We need to support the companies in developing powerful, new stories which can help them work with the UN goals and encourage them to create new and innovative stories.

Questions which create commitment:

1 What are your best stories about working with sustainability and the UN goals? Are they able to inspire you in the future?
2 What is the dominant story about sustainability and the UN goals? What are the narratives which are in opposition and do you need to take them seriously?
3 Are there untold stories or stories we are not aware of about sustainability and the UN goals which are important for strategy?
4 Which stories could become game changers in the future?

Principle 6: Staging: You must consider staging including scenography and artefacts

We and the companies need to support the UN goals and sustainability with scenography, artefacts, design and passionate body language?

Questions which create commitment:

1 Does your company do anything to show how you work with sustainability which helps your employees or customers to change how they act?
2 Could we in the Municipality be better at staging the work with the UN goals and sustainability? E.g. posters, t-shirts, magazines, our water tower, festivals etc.
3 Can we and the company become better at creating small actions (nudges) to change how people act?

Principle 7: Reflecting: You must reflect on the stories and how they create value

We must reflect on and evaluate how the companies work with the UN goals and sustainability.

Questions which create commitment:

1 How does the work on sustainability today compare with earlier?
2 Which goals have you achieved?
3 Are there any side effects of working with the UN goals which it is important to share inside and outside the company?
4 How do you celebrate what you have achieved?
5 If you need to adjust, how and where will you do this?

True Storytelling as a philosophical coaching approach

Values are important for both leaders, organizations and countries. To shed light on these values is a way of integrating them into everyday life. It's an approach which has its roots in the *protreptic* philosophical approach which we have mentioned above and co-written a book about. The following paper was used in our leadership programme, Mountain Leadership, which combined dialogue with walking and Indigenous knowing. We held the five-day programme in the Pyrenees in Spain and the Dolomites of Northern Italy and one-day programme in the mountains outside Las Cruses in New Mexico, USA – the land of Pat Garett and Billy the Kid and the Apache tribe.

The questions in the paper are inspired by the seven principles of True Storytelling and *protreptic* dialogue concept of Aristotle.

In the dialogue you are not allowed to ask for personal experiences or examples but must ask questions on a more general level. Use the questions below for inspiration.

Questions

1 True

Why is this concept/value true and important?
What is the meaning of the concept and the word? Which other concepts are a part of it?
What is the opposite?
What do you need to live the concept?
Is it sustainable: ecological, human and economic?

2 Make room

Where do you see the concept/value living and can we surf on these waves?
Is there a challenge that it is already alive?

3 Plot

What is the powerful, new story of the concept/value which will help us break with the old one?
Can we make a story about the concept/value which invites other people in and helps them to prioritize?
How can we make the story clear although it is complex?
What is the *punctum* or the surprise in the story?

4 Timing

What is the right timing for the concept/value?
How does it unfold in different times and cultures?
What kind of different times do you experience right inow connecting to the concept?
How should we time the concept in presenting it to different people?

5 Helping stories along

Which stories can we use to help the concept/value along?

What are the positive stories about the concept?
What are the dominant stories about the concept?
What are the counter stories?
What are the hidden stories?
How can we be open to experiment and which could be antenarratives?

6 Staging

How can we stage and embody the concept/value?
Does the concept belong to a certain place and what does this place say about the concept?
What kind of the metaphor could we put on the concept?
How does the concept connect to the body?

7 Reflect

What is the story of the concept now?
How do we know when the concept/value is alive?
When is the concept best for the whole organization?
Are there side gifts we need to celebrate?
Do we need to adjust anything?

True Storytelling in fundraising

We have developed a model for fundraising based on the 7 Principles:

- Conception phase – Principle 1

  a The prospectus checklist (see below) plus which funds are giving to what?
  b What is the story and do we believe in it ourselves?
  c Is it sustainable?

- Test phase – Principle 2

  a Which funds are included?
  b Initial response to the project – and strategies for the next step.
  c What are the stories out there – what are being told and not told, which should we listen to?

- Adaption phase – Principles 7 and 3

  a Do we need to change something?
  b If foundations are our project partners and it is OK to review the concept but not the idea – the true story *you* believe in yourselves, being supported by partners or maybe *grounded* already.
  c Think visionary.
  d This is the self-correcting phase. Are we on the right track? How must we adjust the project?

e Clear plot and direction: "OK to change the concept, but never the core idea."
f This phase is repeated over and over again during a fundraising process.

- Timing – Principle 4

a When to put what into action – advisory board, companies, partnerships, feasibility studies, architectural competition.
b Time is not an issue as long as the direction is right in the sense of being true and we believe in it ourselves. There is no quick fix in fundraising. It is all about maintaining the trust of your partners, waiting for the finance to complete, holding on to the dominant narrative.
c Finance is the balance between time and money.

- Formalities

a How to secure fund commitments – law, fund construction, ministry, construction, international affairs.
b This is not referring to any specific principle, however *grounding* is dependent on the framework being solid and legally supported.

- Actions – Principles 5 and 6
- How to help the project along, what to prioritize – alliances, co-creation, partnerships, dissemination, pilot projects, communication, event, activities using scenography, materiality, artefacts.
- How do we help stories along, *grounding* the narratives, creating scenarios which *futurize* the idea of what the project should solve or contribute to.
- How do we stage the process and product in order to help our narratives turn from *abstractizing* to becoming *grounded* and thereby achieve our goal. "Not all will do, but we have to try."

Checklist when fundraising

1 Common understanding of history and direction – do the board and management agree?
2 Project description/prospectus must include:

a Concept/idea

- Clear purpose – for example, a beacon for future education – we want to change the world!
- Unique, relevant, new, social/SDG – for example, young people, workplaces, health, well-being, education.
- The involvement of i.e young people – food as an entrance to their own history, the family, better transitions. Informal bridge building.
- For the benefit of whom? Schools, businesses, citizens?

- Functions? Workshops etc.?
- The place? Is it open to others, the public, volunteers, neighbourhoods?
- Corporate social responsibility – local, regional, national, international
- History – what is the history of the building, constructions site, the people?
- What do others do – and how unique are you?

b The building – content, activities, outdoor/surroundings, do we need a building?
c How are you organized – who are co-partners, municipality, companies, university, actors, etc.?
d The economy – is it sustainable to ask for 100 mio, do you finance yourself, is the daily cost budget sustainable, business case, etc.?

3 Strategy – Partners, endorsements, ambassadors, outreach, branding, networking, communication plan?
4 Time and money for development – it takes money to get money.

Note

1 Theodore Roosevelt quotes, accessed August 19, 2019 at www.goodreads.com/quotes/7-it-is-not-the-critic-who-counts-not-the-man

Links about True Storytelling (tools, articles, seminars, certificate program etc.):
true-storytelling.com
truestorytelling.blog
truestorytelling.org

Appendix I: About the authors

David is Professor Emeritus and Regents Professor at New Mexico State University (NMSU) in Las Cruces. He is also Professor of Management and Business at Alborg University. He has published over 140 journal articles and 24 books, including *Narrative Methods for Organization and Communication Research* (Sage, 2001), *Storytelling Organizations* (2008), and *Critical Theory Ethics in Business and Public Administration* (2008). His recent books are listed at http://davidboje.com/vita . He is known for his 1991 *Administrative Science Quarterly* and 1995 *Academy of Management Journal* articles on 'storytelling organization' in relation to the currency of sensemaking in organisations such as Tamara-Land. He is also founder of the *Tamara Journal for Critical Organization Inquiry*. In 2012 David was awarded an Honorary Doctorate from Aalborg University, Denmark.

Jens is a storyteller researcher, executive coach, master in literature and media and the founding partner of the Danish consulting company Old Friends Industries. Jens has worked with managers from brands like IKEA, Novo, Microsoft, Mærsk and public organizations and NGOs like Red Cross. He has conducted complex change projects with many partners. He has written and co-written eight books about storytelling, coaching, leadership, strategy, culture and philosophy. He teaches at Aalborg University, Denmark, conducting research into storytelling and sustainability. He is the co-founder of the concept 'New Nordic Leadership,' a Scandinavian approach to leadership, and the concept True Storytelling. See true-storytelling.com; www.oldfriendsindustries.com ; www.linkedin.com/in/jens-larsen-6220136/

Lena has 24 years of professional experience as a manager, advisor and consultant within the public and private sector; including Roskilde Municipality, The Rock Museum RAGNAROCK and a communication consultancy. Lena is partner in Old Friends Industries, helping public organizations create innovation and implement strategies and development initiatives of importance to employees and organizations alike. She holds a position as examiner at the Department of Communication, Business and Information Technologies (CBIT), Roskilde University and at the Business Economics, Copenhagen Business School. She is co-founder of the concept of True Storytelling. See www.oldfriendsindustries.com; https://www.linkedin.com/in/lena-bruun-832b374/

Appendix II: Full interview/*together-telling* from Chapter 1, Principle 1

Example of a True Storytelling self-correcting interview about the SDGs (UN goals)

Interview with the Mayor

DAVID: "What is your story about?" [We think that's a powerful question because it is very open.]

MAYOR OF SORØ: "It is amazing to me that we have taken this initiative to have this vision in 2022. We have chosen nine out of the 17 goals. We are actually on an island. The lakes surround the island. And of course, a lot about the sea is not appropriate to us. But something could be similar with our sewage or wastewater. If that is going to float over and into the lake"

DAVID: "Yeah, that would be a big problem. You might get some complaints."

MAYOR: "Yes, in Denmark we've got a green flag. We've got a blue flag. It's ok to go there and swim. There's no problem about that. So the problem is similar. We have to transfer the 17 goals to Sorø."

DAVID: "Right."

MAYOR: "OK, so that has been a very interesting process, involving all the population of Sorø, and so forth. So it was a good experience for us to invite people, to invite Connie Hedegaard, the earlier European Commissioner for [Climate Action 2011–2014] and so forth. So I am glad we have so many people even though we have bad weather."

DAVID: "Rain is a good thing. So how do you explain this municipality Sorø has done more. It is not just talk, talk, talk. You actually have programs and implementation."

MAYOR: "All the heating in Sorø, you have a central distribution center, where we make all the elating and electricity. Before we had these sustainable goals, it was used by natural gas."

DAVID: "Natural gas, Yeah."

MAYOR: "Afterwards we said we have to make some new things. We'll have it with biofuel. We have to make a partnership, goal number 17, with all the collectors of garbage cans, and they also collect, we have a lot of trees, a lot of forest. And then the people are going to cut trees in the gardens, we collect it in one place. And we use it for the biomass to make the heat. It's

CO_2 zero. Before we did natural gas with a lot of CO_2 emissions. So that is an example of where we said 'we have to be CO_2 neutral in 2030.' We have changed this kind of fueling. That's one thing. And, of course, in our elderly help."

DAVID: "Yeah."

MAYOR: "We have the normal gasoline and diesel cars, when we have money enough we will go to hybrid cars."

DAVID: "Yeah, I just bought one. I'm so happy."

MAYOR: "So that's another way where we have changed our attitude to showing people which kinds of initiatives we are taking. Goal number 13, climate: Bring down the CO_2 emissions."

DAVID: "Yeah that's so wonderful."

MAYOR: "So we have a very specific plan. So it is necessary for us it also be economically sustainable because we don't have, we can't pull up money for everything. So, it has to be step-by-step, we are promising a small community with 30,000 inhabitants, will not save all the world. We will make and we will be clear in which kinds of initiatives we are taking to do."

The conversation began with an open question: "What's your story about this?". The Mayor told the story about the land, the water, moving into how the citizens got involved and the different actions they have been taking. Somehow the Mayor's story unfolded by itself with a few comments from me, but almost no questions. I knew the Mayor has an apple farm, so I took the Mayor's answer and used it as a personal question, just going with the energy of the conversation:

DAVID: "You have an apple farm, and do you practice these things with your farm?"

MAYOR: "Actually, two years ago we don't make it as a commercial thing. No NPK [Nitrogen (N), Phosphorus (P), and Potassium (K) fertilizer] and so forth.... And in Denmark if you don't change the trees, to be effective, every ten years."

DAVID: "Ahh, I didn't know you have to change the apple trees every ten years."

MAYOR: "If you do it commercially, because in Denmark if you are growing the trees, the leaves is growing such a way [motioning with his hands] and you do it, actually like grapes. And you have a line, and you put up..."

DAVID: "How do you know the apples are going to taste good. Because there are so many, like 4,000 different kinds of apples."

MAYOR: "Yeah, but no, you have normally one sort." [Both of us laugh]

MAYOR: "For a thousand trees."

DAVID: "Wow, you have a thousand trees."

MAYOR: "Yeah, 1,200 trees."

DAVID: "Wow, 1,200 trees, that's big." [Mayor is called away]

DAVID: "Thank you. I will contact you if I have any more questions.

The conversation with the Mayor moved from thoughts about the land, the sea and the lakes to the SDG's and how they work with them in the municipality to the Mayor's personal life being an apple farmer. And, again, I just followed the story, asking to the answers from the mayor, being aware of his body language. The conversation is almost like an essay by Joan Didion, mentioned in the Introduction, as it moves between different levels.

After talking to the Mayor, I wandered around the festival and I talked to politicians who are neoliberal and socialist. I used a self-correcting storytelling method. I wanted to explore the counternarrative, and go deeper into the dialogical aspects. By self-correcting I mean I am seeking to refute the theory and abductive assumptions I have been making.

I wanted to interview a non-blue politician to get some counter-stories of 'The People's Gathering.' I am not doing a semi-structured interview with a set of predetermined questions, nor am I trying to be neutral. Rather, I want to find a common space of co-creation, a back and forth conversation where I share my storytelling and they share theirs (Boje, 2019b; Boje & Rosile, 2019).

Interview with Bo Mouritzen, a socialist politician

The conversation begins:

DAVID: "What is your story?"
BO: "We're the most left wing."
DAVID: "So, I'm from New Mexico, what does that mean?"
BO: "So, New Mexico is a state in the United States?"
DAVID: "So, if I am left wing what does that mean?"
BO: "What would that be? Wow. We're Bernie Sanders, then go more left."
DAVID: "I'm so happy to meet you."

Compared to the conversations with the mayor this is an example where I reveal my political view. That means that *forecaring* and *together-telling* is not about being objective, it is as mentioned before to follow the energy of the storytelling being a part of it.

DAVID: "I'm just wondering. I'm a big Bernie Sanders fan, and Elizabeth Warren. Uhhh, what's your take on all this? [Pointing to the Festival of The People's Gathering.]

BO: "We get to hear a lot of normal people and what do people want. I find in politics that we tell people what we want. So we hear what they want. The interesting thing in creating a society, is what the members of society want. It's not just interesting to hear the leaders, and that's what we do a lot of. The good thing about this, is we get to hear our people. The not so good thing about it is, it's so, it's very controlled from the municipality. They tell, who does what. But we can get better. And I like to think how people are driven by the ones that actually are active in it."

DAVID: "But you're opposition. Does that mean you are opposed to what they are doing?"

BO: "No, we try to say we want something different. They are very friendly to the commercial part of the city, and we would like to be more environmental. And we'd like to be strong on the environment, on the children, the welfare state, stuff like that. So that's our angle, and they're more an economic angle. They're very, you always need to see 'does it pay?' 'Is it financially [useful].' And sometimes it isn't, and so what?"

DAVID: "I'll confide in you. I just gave a presentation about the UN sustainability goals being co-opted and colonized by too much of an economic focus."

BO: "Yep, and they are. They keep talking about economic growth. And yeah, you're a critic?

DAVID: "Yes, I'm a critic."

BO: "And so are we."

Here the conversation has moved into a new phase. This is not a researcher interviewing a person but two people sharing ideas and thoughts and that is what *together-telling* is about. Actually, the researcher takes over the conversation.

DAVID: "I look at it like the circular economy model, you know. Okay, 'it's a circle' so it [still] uses resources, and you are going to keep growing, and you're going to use more resources. So, I don't quite buy it."

BO: "No. No at some stage we have to stop thinking. On March 29 2019, [the overshoot day in Denmark][1] we used up all the resources for the entire year. And that means we can't keep on going like that because they'll be no future for the kids or anybody else."

DAVID: "Just so I'm clear, that's in Denmark by [March 29] what the Earth would provide."

BO: "No that's another thing. That's the United Nations. Now it's called Earth Day" [April 22 2019 when one billion people turn out, in the largest day of civic action in the world][2]

BO: "And we come to that point, now we've reached the point of what the Earth can actually regenerate in the next year.... What you are using now, you cannot regenerate that. And everybody is still talking about economic growth, and growth, and growth. And it's like, just any kind of growth. It's not like, we like to grow this because we know, it is relevant. No. No. No. We just want to grow. We just want financial growth. OK, who is going to benefit from this?"

DAVID: "Schumacher [1973] and others have been writing about this since the 1970s. You have to stop the growth model and get o, uhh, no growth."

BO: "Yeah."

DAVID: "To zero growth."

BO: "Yes."

DAVID: "So you would agree."

BO: "Yes, the financially strong, the developed countries, are the ones that need to stop first."

DAVID: "Yeah. Yeah, like the United States of America."

BO: "We use an enormous amount of coal, and then we are like; *No, no, we don't use that much. It's not produced here.* But we use it. It may be produced in China, but we use it. It may be produced in all other countries. But it's on our behalf because ... we're going to buy new things all the time."[3]

DAVID: "The UN wants to hold the global temperature from CO_2 with the other gasses, to 1.5° C by 2030. But, if you look at their four pathways in their Agenda 2030, they're all about growth, growing the economy and you look at I think it's the third one, a little bit of changing the consumer habits today, but still grow."

BO: "Yeah, like just the consumer still consuming. We are talking here about the United Nations, the goals and stuff like that, and we're making a policy called growth."

DAVID: "To me its co-opted and colonized by the growth model. If we don't meet, containing that temperature, and I told this to the audience the other day, if the temperature by 2030, jumps to 4 or even 6 degrees by 2100, you won't have an economy."

BO: "It's like with the old saying by the [indigenous] Indians: 'After you've removed everything, you can't eat the money!'"

DAVID: [laughing]

BO: "When the grass is gone, when everything is polluted, you can't eat the money you made out of it. And that's the problem here. We really need to get people to understand, we can't eat money. We need to do something else. We need to change our way of living. And I find right now, there's a competition, an ideological battle between the neoliberals and people wanting sustainability." [background noise]

The conversation has moved from talking about the challenge with the temperature and what needed to change into a story or a quote from native Americans. That engages David even more and starts some reflection about ideology.

Soren Kjær the head or CEO of the municipality invited me to get the story of the Sorø Festival from its main organizer.

Interview with Nanna Kirkegaard

DAVID: "What's your story?"

NANNA: "My name is Nanna [Kirkegaard] and I started the whole idea of the, of this meeting, a gathering."

DAVID: "Oh, tell me from the beginning, the whole story."

NANNA: "Oh yeah, the story, as in storytelling [looking at my card, that says 'storytelling researcher']. Ummm, OK, I have to think about it."

SOREN: [joins the conversation] "I'll help you, just to get you [going]. So David, the Council had an idea, SDG goal number 17 and Nanna was in my administration, and she is the junior, and together with the senior, they got the responsibility. And she came up with the idea, 'why don't we call it, The People's Meeting.'"

DAVID: "Oh wow!"

SOREN: "And you can say, 'putting the gasoline on the fire'. So please (inviting Nanna to take over)

DAVID: "What did you do?"

NANNA: "So we developed the idea. So one of the things we did was to invite a bunch of people from the environment, from, and 43, how do you say 'gatherings' where people in the community gather."

DAVID: "Yes, what you say, gathering?"

NANNA: "Yes, gathering. And we had, like representatives, from them. And they had ideas, how to form this day today. For example, you have the ... horse wagons with all the ... politicians.... That's just one of the ideas. So the basic idea was to fill in the day today. It's all about dialogue and democracy. So they were about, putting in the things we are going to do today."

DAVID: "OK."

NANNA: "So they were like, forming, making this day, together, and with us."

DAVID: "Oh, wow."

NANNA: "So, that's the story, Yeah."

DAVID: "No, no, more."

NANNA: "But my job was to get the politician to talk with the water woman, who is an entrepreneur, and she started her own company, and she wants to talk with the Sorø municipality service(s), you know, us in the municipality, so she can get a ..."

DAVID: "So there is dialogue between the exhibitors?"

NANNA: "Exactly."

DAVID: "Not just with the people coming to visit?"

NANNA: "No."

DAVID: "But between these."

NANNA: "Yes."

DAVID: "So this is a dialogue between the 56. Is that right?"

NANNA: "Yes, that's right. And especially the politicians, as you say. Because we want them to get in eye contact with the citizens, in these gatherings. That's also the goal for today."

DAVID: "Very nice. Wow. You must be tired."

NANNA: "I am a bit tired." [laughing]

DAVID: "Are you going to do it again?"

NANNA: "If we can, and if we show, that's up to the politicians, and my advice, if we are going to do it again ... first of all it should be in June, second of all the organization of this should be different. We should have the local adviser to help us.... If you do this co-creation with people." [Jens joins us in the conversation]

DAVID: "She is saying this is a dialogue among the 56, not just the people coming, she wants the dialogue between them to happen."

JENS: "That make sense."

NANNA: "Yes."

DAVID: "That's her goal."

JENS: "That's a good idea. People are coming, and then bring these people together."

At this moment of the interview, we notice that the next response unpacked the commitment and energy necessary for Principle 1: You yourself must be true and prepare the energy and effort for a sustainable future.

NANNA: "Yes, these people have something in their hearts, and they're really engaged in society, and maybe people who visit, are just visitors. I mean these are really exciting people. Right. They organize a whole stand. They plan for it. They could really make a partnership. That's part of our partnership for development."

DAVID: "Right, right."

NANNA: "So umm ..."

DAVID: "A question. So, you went and did 30 interviews with people, was that so they should say, you should have this one, this one, and this one?"

NANNA: "No, I made it with leaders and with just co-workers, and some from outside the municipality, and the public-thing. And they pointed out, 'we co-work with these' and I made a list and its network, all the time."

This long piece of conversation we (David and Jens) had with the Mayor, the left-wing politicians and the organizer of the People's Gathering may seem like an unstructured conversation, even a researcher losing his plan, but it is nothing like that. It's a way of doing *together-telling* and work with the self-correcting method: to try to get not only one part of the story, but different perspectives and to use your own story to give life to other stories. It's about working with different aspects of the True Storytelling model, surfing on different boards *rehistorizing, abstractizing, grounding* and *futurizing*, to really get at what is going on.

Notes

1 Accessed August 22 2019 at www.overshootday.org/newsroom/country-overshoot-days/
2 Accessed August 22 2019 at www.earthday.org/earthday/
3 Denmark announced it will phase out coal production by 2023 https://poweringpastcoal.org/members/denmark

References

Allen, R., Packer, J., Eccles, J. C., Parton, H. N., Forder, H. G., & Popper, K. R. (1945). *Research and the University: A Statement by a Group of Teachers in the University of New Zealand*. A two-page pamphlet. Christchurch, NZ.

Allbon, C. (2012). "Down the rabbit hole" – "curiouser and curiouser." Using autoethnography as a mode of writing to re-call, re-tell and re-veal bodily embodiment as self-reflexive inquiry. *Journal of Organizational Ethnography*, 1(1), 62–71. Accessed March 28, 2019 at www-emeraldinsight-com.ezproxy.canterbury.ac.nz/doi/full/10.1108/20466741211220660.

Alvesson, M., & Kärreman, D. (2000). Varieties of discourse: On the study of organizations through discourse analysis. *Human Relations* 53(9): 1125–1149.

Alvesson, M., & Kärreman, D. (2011). Decolonializing discourse: Critical reflections on organizational discourse analysis. *Human Relations*, 64(9), 1121–1146.

Alvesson, M., & Spicer, A. (2012). A stupidity-based theory of organizations. *Journal of Management Studies*, 49(7), 1194–1220.

Alvesson, M., & Spicer, A. (2016). *The Stupidity Paradox: The Power and Pitfalls of Functional Stupidity at Work*. Profile Books.

Arendt, H. (1958). *The Human Condition*. University of Chicago Press.

Arendt, H. (1977). *The Life of the Mind: Thinking*. London/NY: Harcourt Brace Javanovich.

Arendt, H. (1978). *The Life of the Mind: Willing*. London/NY: Harcourt Brace Javanovich.

Arendt, H. (2001). *The Human Condition. Philosophy and the Problems of Work*. University of Chicago Press.

Aristotle (1954). *Aristotle: Rhetoric and Poetics*. Written 350 BCE, intro by Friedrich Solmsen; Rhetoric translated by W. Rhys Roberts; Poetics translated by Ingram Bywater. New York: The Modern Library (Random House). Accessed March 11, 2019 Rhetoric at www.bocc.ubi.pt/pag/Aristotle-rhetoric.pdf and Poetics at www.gutenberg.org/files/1974/1974-h/1974-h.htm.

Bakhtin, M. M. (1973/1929). *Problem on the Work of Dostoevsky*. University of Minnesota Press.

Bakhtin, M. M. (1981). *The Dialogic Imagination: Four Essays*. Edited by Michael Holquist; Translated by Caryl Emerson and Michael Holquist. Austin, TX: University of Texas Press.

Bakhtin, M. M. (1990). *Art and Answerability: Early Philosophical Essays*, vol. 9. Foreword by Michael Holquist, and translated with Vadim Liapunov. Austin, TX: University of Texas Press.

Bakhtin, M. M. (1993). *Toward a Philosophy of the Act*. Austin, TX: University of Texas Press.

Bamberg, M., & M. Andrews (eds) (2004). *Considering Counter-Narratives. Narrating, Resisting, Making Sense*. Amsterdam and Philadelphia: John Benjamins.

Barad, K. (2003). Posthumanist performativity: Toward an understanding of how matter comes to matter. *Signs: Journal of Women in Culture and Society*, 28(3), 801–831. Available online at www.kiraoreilly.com/blog/wp-content/uploads/2009/06/signsbarad.pdf

Barad, K. (2007). *Meeting the Universe Halfway: Quantum Physics and the Entanglement of Matter and Meaning*. Durham/London: Duke University Press.

Barad, K. (2008). Queer causation and the ethics of mattering. In Noreen Giffney, & Myra J. Hird (eds) *Queering the Non/Human* (pp. 311–338). Hampshire, England/Burlington VT: Ashgate Publishing.

Barthes, R. (1981). *Camera Lucida: Reflections on Photography*. Macmillan.

Bell, E., & Willmott, H. (2019). Ethics, politics and embodied imagination in crafting scientific knowledge. *Human Relations*. Draft accessed August 15, 2019.

Benjamin, W. (1928/2016). *One-way Street*. Translated by Edmund Jephcott, edited with intro by Michael W. Jennings, and preface by Greil Marcus. Cambridge, MA/London: The Belknap Press of Harvard University Press and Penguin UK.

Benjamin, W. ([1936]/1955/1986/2007). The storyteller: Reflections on the works of Nikolai Leskov. In H. Arendt (ed.) *Illuminations* (pp. 361–378). NY: Harcourt, Brace & World, Inc.

Bennett, J. (2001). *The Enchantment of Modern Life: Attachments, Crossings, and Ethics*. Princeton University Press.

Bennett, J. (2004). The force of things steps toward an ecology of matter. *Political Theory*, 32(3), 347–372.

Bennett, J. (2010a). *Vibrant Matter: A Political Ecology of Things*. London/Durham, NC: Duke University Press.

Bennett, J. (2010b). A vitalist stopover on the way to a new materialism. In D. Coole & S. Frost (eds) *New Materialisms: Ontology, Agency, and Politics* (pp. 47–69). Durham: Duke University Press.

Berger, P. L., & Luckmann, T. (1967). *The Social Construction of Reality: Everything that Passes for Knowledge in Society*. London: Allen Lane.

Bergson, H. (1960). *Time and Free-Will: An Essay on the Immediate Data of Consciousness*. Translation by F.L. Pogson. New York: Harper & Row.

Bergson, H. (1988). *Matter and Memory*. Translation by Nancy Margaret Paul and W. Scott Palmer. New York: Zone Books.

Berlinski, C. (2011). *There Is No Alternative: Why Margaret Thatcher Matters* (2nd edn). Basic Books.

Bloc, V. (2019). Nothing else matters: Towards an ontological concept of the materiality of the earth in the age of global warming. *Research in Phenomenology*, 49, 65–87. Accessed March 11, 2019 at www.academia.edu/keypass/SnZwL1F6TjFzaVN2akNDT1lxQ2dDMEVkVE51bjBSNFQrZlA5YmlacnF2TT0tLXkxd2VpM2c1R3A2bWswVk9OaVFHQXc9PQ==–871e9faae2dc8c65e099bff573292b5c7d20ce5e/t/KAxn-MYnLVd4-bmWBki/attachments/58580093/download_file

Bloomfield, E. F., & Tillery, D. (2019). The circulation of climate change denial online: Rhetorical and networking strategies on Facebook. *Environmental Communication,13* (1), 23–34. Accessed August 7, 2019 at www.researchgate.net/profile/Emma_Frances_Bloomfield/publication/

Boal, A. (2000). *Theater of the Oppressed*. Pluto Press.

Boje, D. M. (1991). The storytelling organization: A study of story performance in an office-supply firm. *Administrative Science Quarterly*, 106–126.

Boje, D. M. (1995). Stories of the storytelling organization: A postmodern analysis of Disney as "Tamara-Land". *Academy of Management Journal*, 38(4), 997–1035.

Boje, D. M. (2001). *Narrative Methods for Organizational & Communication Research.* Thousand Oaks, CA: Sage.

Boje, D. M. (2008). *Storytelling Organizations.* Thousand Oaks, CA: Sage.

Boje, D. M. (2010a). Side shadowing appreciative inquiry: One storyteller's commentary. *Journal of Management Inquiry*, 19(3), 238–241.

Boje, D. M. (2010b). Narrative analysis. In A. J. Mills, G. Durepos, & E. Wiebe (eds) *Sage Encyclopedia of Case Study Research* (Vol. II, pp. 591–594). Thousand Oaks, CA: Sage.

Boje, D. M. (2011a). Introduction to agential antenarratives that shape the future of organizations. In D. M. Boje (ed.) *Storytelling and the Future of Organizations* (pp. 19–38). Routledge.

Boje, D. M. (2011b). Reflections: What does quantum physics of storytelling mean for change management? *Journal of Change Management*, 12(3): 253–271. Accessed March 11, 2019 at https://davidboje.com/vita/paper_pdfs/JCM_BojeReflections_July 21 2011.pdf

Boje, D. M. (2012). Reflections: What does quantum physics of storytelling mean for change management? *Journal of Change Management*, 12(3), 253–271.

Boje, D. M. (2014). *Storytelling Organizational Practices: Managing in the Quantum Age.* London: Routledge.

Boje, D. M. (2016a). *Organizational Change and Global Standardization: Solutions to the Standards and Norms Overwhelming Organizations.* London/NY: Routledge.

Boje, D. M. (2016b). *SEAM's 'Storytelling Dialectical Method' and the Failure of Appreciative Inquiry as a Scientific Method of Organizational Development and Change.* Conference presentation to The "Organization Development and Change" Division and the "Management Consulting" Division of the Academy of Management (USA), 9–10 June, 2016, Lyon, France.

Boje, D. M. (2016c). But that's not a story! Antenarrative dialectics between and beneath Indigenous living story and western narratives. In Grace Ann Rosile (ed.) *Tribal Wisdom for Business Ethics* (pp. 69–72). Bingley, UK: Emerald Group Publishing Limited.

Boje, D. M. (2016d). Critique of the triple bottom line. In Grace Ann Rosile (ed.) *Tribal Wisdom for Business Ethics* (pp. 181–198). Bingley, UK: Emerald Group Publishing Limited.

Boje, D. M. (2017a). *Theaters of Capitalism: Creating Conscious Capitalism.* Las Cruces, NM: TamaraLand Publishing.

Boje, D. M. (2017b). *How does quantum storytelling relate to Savall's socioeconomic double spiral?* Proceedings Paper for the 7th annual Quantum Storytelling Conference, December 14–16, 2017. Available at http://davidboje.com/quantum/pdfs_quantum_2017/Boje_SEAM_DOUBLE_SPIRALS_and_STORYTELLING.htm.

Boje, D. M. (2018a). Preface: "Global capitalism is unsustainable". In H. Savall, M. Peron, V. Zardet, & M. Bonnet, *Socially Responsible Capitalism.* London: Routledge.

Boje, D. M. (2018b, in press). The interplay of philosophy of science, statistics, and storytelling. *Nova International Handbook of Psychology.*

Boje, D. (2018c, in press). Risky double spiral sensemaking of academic capitalism. *Routledge Companion to Risk, Crisis and Emergency Management.* London: Routledge.

Boje, D. M. (2018d). *Seven true storytelling solutions to the global water crisis*. Proceeding paper for 8th Annual Quantum Storytelling Conference, December 13. Accessed February 9, 2019 at http://davidboje.com/388/2018%20storytelling%20conference%20BOJE%20__%20True%20Storytelling%20of%20New%20Mexico%20Water.docx.

Boje, D. M. (2019a). *Global Storytelling: There is No Planet B*. Singapore/London/NY: World Scientific.

Boje, D. M. (2019b). *Organizational Research: Storytelling in Action*. London/NY: Routledge.

Boje, D. M. (2019c). *Storytelling Interventions in Global Water Crisis*. Singapore/London/NY: World Scientific.

Boje, D. M. (2019d). *The dark side of water storytelling and sixth extinction denial*. Keynote address to Dark Side of Communication Conference (2nd International and Interdisciplinary Conference on Discourse and Communication in Professional Contexts), 14–16 August, Aalborg University, Denmark. Accessed August 20, 2019 at https://davidboje.com/Aalborg/Dark%20Side%20of%20Water%20Storytelling%20for%20Aalborg%20Conference.pptx

Boje, D. M., & Cai-Hillon, Yue. (2017). The fifth epoch: Socio-economic approach to sustainable capitalism. *Markets, Globalization & Development Review*, 2(2). Online at http://digitalcommons.uri.edu/mgdr/vol2/iss1/2.

Boje, D. M., & Dennehy, Robert F. (1993). *Managing in the Postmodern World: America's Revolution against Exploitation*. IAP.

Boje, D. M., & Henderson, T. L. (eds) (2014). *Being Quantum: Ontological Storytelling in the Age of Antenarrative*. UK: Cambridge Scholars Publishing.

Boje, D. M., & Mølbjerg Jørgensen, K. (2018). Making the future: The antenarrative challenge of sustainability for problem-based learning. *Learning Organization Handbook*. Palgrave MacMillan.

Boje, D., & Rosile, G. A. (2003). Theatrics of SEAM. *Journal of Organizational Change Management*, 16(1), 21–32.

Boje, D., & Rosile, G. A. (2003). Comparison of socio-economic and other transorganizational development methods. *Journal of Organizational Change Management*, 16 (1), 10–20.

Boje, D. M., & Rosile, G.A. (2015, March). *Equine-assisted restorying for veterans and their loved ones*. Presentation at the Annual conference of the Equine Assisted Growth and Learning Association (EAGALA), Utah.

Boje, D. M., & Rosile, G. A. (2019, in press). An antenarrative amendment to learning organization theories to avert sixth extinction. Accessed February 1, 2019 at https://davidboje.com/vita/paper_pdfs/Antenarrative%20Amend%20LearningOrg%202019.pdf

Boje, D. M., & Sanchez, M. (2019a). *The Emerald of Handbook of Quantum Storytelling Consulting*. UK: Emerald Press.

Boje, D. M., & Sanchez, M. (2019b). *The Emerald of Handbook of Management and Organizational Inquiry*. UK: Emerald Press.

Boje, D. M., & Saylors, R. (2013). Q4 Virtuality and materiality in the ethics of storytelling. In Rune Todnem By, & Bernard Burnes (eds) *Organizational Change, Leadership and Ethics: Leading Organizations towards Sustainability* (pp. 75–96). London: Routledge.

Boje, D. M., & Saylors, R. (in review). Contributions of social entrepreneurship to narrative reconstructing United Nations' goal 14: Life below water. *Strategic Briefings in Entrepreneurial Finance*.

Boje, D. M., & Strevel, H. (2016). Feature choice: Using quantum storytelling to bridge appreciative inquiry to socio-economic approach to intervention research. *AI Practitioner: International Journal of Appreciative Inquiry*, 18(3), 79–89.

Boje, D. M., & Winsor, R. D. (1993). The resurrection of Taylorism: Total quality management's hidden agenda. *Journal of Organizational Change Management*, 6(4), 57–70.

Boje, D. M., Gephart, R. P., & Thatchenkery, T. J. (1996). *Postmodern Management and Organization Theory*. Thousand Oaks, CA: Sage.

Boje, D. M., Gergerich, E., & Svane, M. (2016). Fractal change management and counter-narrative in cross-cultural change. In *Counter-narratives and Organization* (pp. 137–162). Routledge.

Boje, D. M., Haley, U. C., & Saylors, R. (2016). Antenarratives of organizational change: The microstoria of Burger King's storytelling in space, time and strategic context. *Human Relations*, 69(2), 391–418.

Boje, D. M., Larsen, Jens, & Brunn, Lena. (2017). True Storytelling: How to succeed with your implementation. Working paper at http://oldfriendsindustries.com/?page_id=1048

Boje, D. M., Oswick, C., & Ford, J. D. (2004). Language and organization: The doing of discourse. *Academy of Management Review*, 29(4), 571–577.

Boje, D. M., Svane, M., & Gergerich, E. (2016). Counternarrative and antenarrative inquiry in two cross-cultural contexts. *European Journal of Cross-Cultural Competence and Management*, 4(1), 55–84.

Boje, D. M., Baca-Greif, H., Intindola, M., & Elias, S. (2017). The episodic spiral model: A new approach to organizational processes. *Journal of Organizational Change Management*, 30(5), 683–709.

Bookchin, Murray (1982). *The Ecology of Freedom*. Palo Alto, CA: Cheshire Books.

Buber, Martin (1923). *I and Thou*. Bloomsbury Academic.

Boundas, Constantin V. (2010). Virtual/virtuality. In Adrian Parr (ed.) *The Deleuze Dictionary Revised Edition* (pp. 300–302). UK: Edinburgh University Press.

Burke, K. (1969). *A Grammar of Motives*. CA: University of California Press.

Burrell, Gibson., & Morgan, Gareth (1979). *Sociological Paradigms and Organizational Analysis Elements of the Sociology of Corporate Life*. Aldershot, UK/Burlington, VT: Heinemann Educational Books. Accessed March 8, 2019 at http://sonify.psych.gatech.edu/~ben/references/burrell_sociological_paradigms_and_organisational_analysis.pdf

Butler, J. (1988). Performative acts and gender constitution: An essay in phenomenology and feminist theory. *Theater Journal*, 40(4), 519–531.

Butler, J. (1990). *Gender Trouble*. London: Routledge.

Butler, J. (1993). *Bodies That Matter*. London: Routledge.

Butler, J. (2000). *Gender Trouble: 10th Anniversary Edition*. London: Routledge.

Butler, J. (2004). *Undoing Gender*. London: Routledge.

Butler, J. (2005). *Giving an Account of Oneself*. New York: Fordham University Press.

Cajete, G. (1993). An enchanted land: Spiritual ecology and a theology of place. *Winds of Change*, 8(2), 50–53.

Cajete, G. (1994). *Look to the Mountain: An Ecology of Indigenous Education*. Durango, CO: Kivaki Press.

Cajete, G. (1999). *Reflections on Indigenous Ecology. A People's Ecology: Explorations in Sustainable Living*. Santa Fe, NM: Clear Light Publishers.

Cajete, G. (2000). *Native Science: Natural Laws of Interdependence*. Santa Fe, NM: Clear Light Publishers.

Cajete, G. (2015). *Indigenous Community: Rekindling the Teachings of the Seventh Fire.* St. Paul, MN: Living Justice Press.

Cameron, K., & Dutton, J. (eds) (2003). *Positive Organizational Scholarship: Foundations of a New Discipline.* New York: Berrett-Koehler Publishers.

Campbell, Donald T. (1996). Unresolved issues in measurement validity: An autobiographical overview. *Psychological Assessment*, 8(4), 363.

Castle, J., Clements, M., & Hendry, D. (2019). *Forecasting: An Essential Introduction.* Yale University Press.

Charmaz, K. (2006). *Constructing Grounded Theory: A Practical Guide through Qualitative Analysis.* London: Sage.

Chouinard, Ivron, (2005). *Let My People Go Surfing.* Penguin Putnam Inc.

Christensen, Peter, & Larsen, Jens (2014) *Helle Helle og Naja Marie Aidt.* Gyldendal Uddannelse.

Christensen, Peter, & Larsen, Jens (2016) *Kim Fupz Aakeson og Jesper Wung Sung.* Gyldendal Uddannelse.

Christensen, Peter, & Larsen, Jens (2020). *Caspar Eric og Theis Ørntoft – portrætsamtaler og lyrikanalyser.* Gyldendal Uddannelse.

Clark, J. (2005). Teaching and research: The Canterbury declaration and Popper's legacy for teacher educators. *New Zealand Annual Review of Education*, 14(2004), 111–130.

Compton, W. C., & Hoffman, E. (2019). *Positive psychology: The science of happiness and flourishing.* London: SAGE Publications.

Cooperrider, D. (2001, October). *Appreciative inquiry: The positive core of change.* Paper presented at the meeting of the Minnesota OD Network, University of St. Thomas, MN.

Cooperrider, David L., & Whitney, Diana (2019). A positive revolution in change: Appreciative inquiry. Draft accessed March 11, 2019 at www.academia.edu/38504721/A_Positive_Revolution_in_Change_Appreciative_Inqui?email_work_card=view-paper.

Corazon, S. S., Stigsdotter, U. K., Jensen, A. G. C., & Nilsson, K. (2010). Development of the nature-based therapy concept for patients with stress-related illness at the Danish, Healing Forest Garden Nacadia Projekt 2010. *Journal of Therapeutic Horticulture*, 20.

Corbin, J., & Strauss, A. (2007). *Basics of Developing Grounded Theory.* London: Sage.

Cottle, S. (2009). Global crises in the news: Staging new wars, disasters and climate change. *International Journal of Communication*, 3, 24.

Czarniawska, B. (ed.) (1997). *A Narrative Approach to Organization Studies.* London: Sage Publications.

Czarniawska, B. (2004). *Narratives in Social Science Research.* London: Sage Publications.

Deleuze. Gilles (1990). *Logic of Sense.* New York: Columbia University Press.

Deleuze, Gilles (1991). *Bergsonism*, Hugh Tomlinson and Barbara Habberjam (tr.). New York: Zone Books.

Deleuze, Gilles (1994). *Difference and Repetition*, Paul Patton (tr.), New York: Columbia University Press.

Deleuze, Gilles (1995). *Negotiations.* New York: Columbia Press.

Deleuze, Gilles (1997). *Essays Critical and Clinical*, D. W. Smith & M. A. Greco (tr.). Minneapolis: University of Minnesota Press.

Deleuze, Gilles, & Guattari, Felix (1987). *A Thousand Plateaus: Capitalism and Schizophrenia.* University of Minnesota Press.

Deleuze, Gilles, & Guattari, Felix. (1994). *What is Philosophy*, Hugh Tomlinson & Graham Burchell (tr.). New York: Columbia University Press.

Dennett, Daniel C. (1993). *Consciousness Explained*. London: Penguin.

de Solla Price, Derek J. (1963). *Little Science, Big Science ... and Beyond*. New York: Columbia University. Accessed March 24, 2019 at www.andreasaltelli.eu/file/repository/Little_science_big_science_and_beyond.pdf

Dewey, John (1929). *The Quest for Certainty*. Oxford: Minton, Balch.

Didion, Joan (1990). *Slouching Towards Bethlehem*. New York: Macmillan.

Didion, Joan (2003). *Where I Was From*. New York: A.A. Knopf.

Didion, Joan (2007). *The Year of Magical Thinking*. New York: Vintage.

Drass, Kriss A., & Ragin, Charles C. (1992). *Qualitative Comparative Analysis 3.0*. Evanston, IL: Institute for Policy Research, Northwestern University.

Dweck, Carol (2016). What having a "growth mindset" actually means. *Harvard Business Review*, 13, 213–226.

Dykeman, Wilmar (1955). *French Broad*. New York: Rinehart.

Eccles, John Carew (1945). Principles of scientific method: Notes on five lectures by Dr. K. R. Popper, given at the University of Otago from 22nd to 26th May, 1945. Accessed March 8, 2019 at http://popper-prior.nz/items/show/208.

Eccles, John Carew (1970/2013). *Facing Reality: Philosophical Adventures by a Brain Scientist*. Berlin/Heidelberg, Germany: Springer Science & Business Media.

Engberg-Pedersen, T. (1983). *Aristotle's Theory of Moral Insight*. Oxford: OUP.

Flora, K. (2019). Second wave of positive psychology: beyond the dichotomy of positive and negative and the consequences in the practice of psychotherapy. *Counselling Psychology Quarterly*, 32(3-4).

Flyvbjerg, Bent (2001). *Making Social Science Matter*. Cambridge University Press.

Franzosi, R. (ed.) (2010). *Quantitative Narrative Analysis*. London: Sage.

Freire, Paulo (1970/2000). *Pedagogy of the Oppressed*. New York: The Continuum International Publishing Group Inc.

Gabriel, Y. (2000). *Storytelling in Organisations*. Oxford: Oxford University Press.

Gabriel, Y. (2016). Narrative ecologies and the role of counter-narratives: The case of nostalgic stories and conspiracy theories. In Frandsen, S., Kuhn, T., & Lundholt, M. W. *Counter-Narrative and Organizations*. Routledge.

Garfinkel, Harold (1967). *Studies in Ethnomethodology*. Englewood Cliffs, NJ: Prentice-Hall, Inc.

Gee, James Paul (2004). *An Introduction to Discourse Analysis: Theory and Method*. Routledge.

Giddens, A. (1990). *The Consequences of Modernity*. Cambridge: Polity Press.

Giddens, A. (1991). *Modernity and Self-identity: Self and Society in the Late Modern Age*. Cambridge: Polity Press.

Gladstone, J. S. (2014). Native American transplanar wisdom. In C. Spiller & R. Wolfgramm (eds) *Indigenous Spiritualties at Work: Transforming the Spirit of Business Enterprise* (pp. 21–32). Charlotte, NC: Information Age Publishing.

Glaser, B. G. (1992). *Basics of Grounded Theory: Emergence vs. Forcing*. Mill Valley, CA: Sociology Press.

Glaser, B. G. (2001). *The Grounded Theory Perspective: Conceptualization Contrasted with Description*. Mill Valley, CA: Sociology Press

Glaser, B. G. (2002). Constructivist grounded theory? *Forum: Qualitative Sozialforschung/ Forum: Qualitative Social Research*, 3(3). www.qualitative-research.net/fqs-texte/3-02/3-02glaser-e.htm

Glaser, B. G. (2003). *The Grounded Theory Perspective II: Description's Remodeling of Grounded Theory Methodology*. Mill Valley, CA: Sociology Press.

Glaser, B. G. (2004). Naturalist inquiry and grounded theory. *Forum: Qualitative Sozialforschung/ Forum: Qualitative Social Research*, 5(1). www.qualitative-research.net/fqs-texte/1-04/1-04glaser-e.htm.

Glaser, B. G. (2005). *The Grounded Theory Perspective III: Theoretical Coding*. Mill Valley, CA: Sociology Press.

Glaser, B. G. (2007). Doing formal theory. In A. Bryant, & K. Charmaz (eds) *The Sage Handbook of Grounded Theory* (Part II, pp. 97–113). London: Sage Publications.

Glaser, B. G. (2008). *Doing Quantitative Grounded Theory*. Mill Valley, CA: Sociology Press.

Glaser, B. G., & Holton, J. (2004). Remodeling grounded theory. *Forum: Qualitative Sozialforschung/ Forum: Qualitative Social Research*, 5(2). www.qualitative-research.net/index.php/fqs/article/view/607/1315

Gössling, S., 2002. Global environmental consequences of tourism. *Global Environmental Change*, 12(4), 283–302.

Gössling, S., 2013. Advancing a clinical transport psychology. *Transportation Research Part F: Traffic Psychology and Behaviour*, 19, 11–21.

Gössling, S. (2017a). *The Psychology of the Car: Automobile Admiration, Attachment, and Addiction*. Cambridge, MA/Oxford: Elsevier.

Gössling, S. (2017b). ICT and transport behaviour: A conceptual review. Submitted.

Friedman, Michael (1991). The re-evaluation of logical positivism. *Journal of Philosophy*, 88 (10), 505–519.

Hacohen, Malachi Haim (2000). *Karl Popper – The Formative Years, 1902–1945*. Cambridge: Cambridge University Press.

Haraway, Donna (1991). *Cyborgs, Simians, and Women: The Reinvention of Nature*. New York: Routledge.

Haraway, Donna (2016). *Staying with the Trouble*. Duke University Press Books.

Hathorn, K., & Nanda, U. (2008). A guide to evidence-based art. Accessed September 16, 2019 at https://artshealthnetwork.ca/ahnc/guide_to_evidenced_based_art_.pdf

Hegel, Georg Wilhelm Friedrich (1807/1977). *Phenomenology of Spirit*. London/NY: Oxford University Press.

Heidegger, Martin (1923/1988/1999). *Ontology – The Hermeneutics of Facticity*. Bloomington/Indianapolis: Indiana University Press.

Heidegger, Martin (1927/1962). *Being and Time*, John Macquarrie and Edward Robinson (tr.). New York: Harper Row.

Heidegger, Martin (2003). *Four Seminars: Le Thor 1966, 1968, 1969, Zahringen 1973*, Andrew Mitchell and Francios Raffoul (tr.). Bloomington/Indianapolis: Indiana University Press.

Heidegger, Martin (1977). *The Question Concerning Technology*, William Lovitt (tr.). New York: Harper Row.

Hein, L., Larsen, Jens, Stadil, Christian, & Larsen, Jens (2012). *Kanten, karmaen og kunsten. En skitse til det forstandinge lederskab, in Forstandig Ledelse Frivillig ledelse*. Djøf Forlag.

Heisenberg, W. (1928). Zur theorie des ferromagnetismus. *Zeitschrift für Physik*, 49(9–10), 619–636.

Henderson, Tonya L., & Boje, David M. (2016). *Managing Fractal Organizing Processes*. NY/London: Routledge.

Hillon, Y. C., Kisiel, G., & Hillon, M. E. (2016). A discursive framework for research in management consulting. *Recherches en Sciences de Gestion*, 6, 109–124.

Hitchin, L. (2014). Method and story fragments. In Izak, M., Hitchin, L., & Anderson, D. (eds) *Untold Stories in Organizations* (pp. 213–238). London: Routledge.

Holton, Judith A. (2008). Grounded theory as a general research methodology. *The Grounded Theory Review*, 7(2), 67–89.

Hustvedt, S. (2012). *Living, Thinking, Looking*. Picador.

James, W. (1907). Pragmatism, a new name for some old ways of thinking, popular lectures. Accessed September 5, 2018 at www.gutenberg.org/files/5116/5116-h/5116-h.htm#link2H_4_0006

Jørgensen, K., & Boje, D. (2009). Genealogies of becoming: Antenarrative inquiry in organizations. *Tamara: Journal for Critical Organization Inquiry*, 8(1).

Jørgensen, K. M. (2011). Antenarrative writing: Tracing and representing living stories. In D. M. Boje (ed.) *Storytelling and the Future of Organizations: An Antenarrative Handbook* (pp. 284–297). Routledge.

Jørgensen, K. M., & Boje, D. M. (in press, 2019). Storytelling sustainability in problem-based learning. In R. V. Turcan, & J. P. Reilly (eds) *Populism in Higher Education Curriculum Development – Problem Based Learning as a Mitigating Response.*

Kahneman, Daniel (2011). *Thinking, Fast and Slow*. Farrar, Straus and Giroux.

Kallis, G., Kostakis, V., Lange, S., Muraca, B., Paulson, S., & Schmelzer, M. (2018). Research on degrowth. *Annual Review of Environment and Resources*, 43, 291–316.

Kant, Immanuel (1785/1993). *Grounding for the Metaphysics of Morals: ON a Supposed Right to Lie because of Philanthropic Concerns*, James W. Ellington (tr.). Indianapolis/Cambridge: Hackett Publishing Company, Inc.

Kant, Immanuel (1889). *Kant's Critique of Practical Reason and Other Works on the Theory of Ethics*. London: Longmans, Green and Co.

Kelbessa, Workineh (2011). *Indigenous and Modern Environmental Ethics: A Study of the Indigenous Oromo Environmental Ethic and Modern Issues of Environment and Development*. Ethiopian Philosophical Studies, I. Washington DC: The Council for Research in Values and Philosophy.

Kelle, U. (2007). "Emergence" vs. "forcing" of empirical data? A crucial problem of" grounded theory" reconsidered. *Historical Social Research, Supplement*, 19, 133–156.

Kierkegaard, Søren (1941). *Frygt og Bæven* [Fear and Trembling]. Princeton, NY: Walter Lowrie.

King, Stephen (2000). *On Writing*. Charles Scribner's Sons.

Kirkeby, O. F. (2000). *Management Philosophy: A Radical-Normative Perspective*. Springer Science & Business Media.

Kirkeby, O. F. (2008). *The Virtue of Leadership*. Copenhagen Business School Press DK.

Kirkeby, O. F. (2009). *The New Protreptic: The Concept and the Art*. Copenhagen Business School Press DK.

Kirkeby, O. F., Larsen, J., Dam Hede, T., & Mejlhede, M. (2008). *Protreptik - Filosofisk Coaching i Ledelse*. SL Forlag.

Kuhn, Thomas (1962). *The Structure of Scientific Revolutions*. Accessed March 13, 2019 at https://projektintegracija.pravo.hr/_download/repository/Kuhn_Structure_of_Scientific_Revolutions.pdf

Larsen, Jens (2001). *Sangskriver – Elleve Samtaler* [Songwriter – Eleven Conversations]. Lindhardt and Ringhof.

Larsen, Jens (2010). *Succes og Brændte Broer* [Success and Burned Bridges]. People's Press.

Larsen, J., Strand, A., & Aagaard, J. (2018). The break: Work–life balance and leadership anno 2016: Reconfiguring contemporary leadership through the 2,400-year-old coaching concept of protreptic, walking, and material storytelling. In *The Emerald Handbook of Quantum Storytelling Consulting*. Emerald Group Publishing.

Latour, Bruno (2018). *Down to Earth Politics in the New Climate Regime*. Polity.

Leopold, Aldo (1949). *A Sand Country Almanac*. Oxford University Press.

Lincoln, Yvonna S., & Guba, Egon G. (1985). Establishing trustworthiness. *Naturalistic Inquiry*, 289, 331.

Love, Tyron R. (2017a). *Māori values, care and compassion in organisations: a research strategy*. In the proceedings of the European Group for Organizational Studies Symposium. Copenhagen Business School, Copenhagen, Denmark.

Love, Tyron R. (2017b). *Mana, Māori (Indigenous New Zealand) and critical studies of management in Aotearoa New Zealand*. In the proceedings of the Critical Management Studies Conference. Britannia Adelphi Hotel, Liverpool, United Kingdom.

Love, Tyron R. (2018a). *Organizing Indigenous-Māori Identities at Work*. In the proceedings of the European Group for Organizational Studies Symposium. Tallinn, Estonia. July 5–7, 2018.

Love, Tyron R. (2018b). *Anteresearch in Indigenous Organization Studies*. In the proceedings of the Gender, Work and Organisation Conference. June 13–16, 2018.

Love, Tyron R. (2019). *Indigenous Organization Studies: Exploring Management, Business and Community*. Cham, Switzerland: Palgrave Macmillan.

Love, Tyron R. (Forthcoming a). Indigenous knowledges, priorities and processes: State of the field. *Qualitative Research in Organizations and Management*.

Love, Tyron R. (Forthcoming, b). Care and compassion at work: theorizing indigenous knowledges in colonial contexts. In M. Fotaki, G. Islam, & A. Antoni (eds) *Business Ethics and Care in Organizations*. New York: Routledge.

Love, Tyron R., Finsterwalder, J., & Tombs, A. (2017). Māori knowledge and consumer tribes. *MAI: A New Zealand Journal of Indigenous Research*, 7(1), 44–50.

Lowe, I. (2015). Causal layered analysis, climate change and limits to growth. *CLA*, 109–122.

Lyotard, Jean François (1979/1984). *The Postmodern Condition: A Report on Knowledge*. MN: University of Minnesota Press.

Macfarlane, Angus Hikairo (2012). "Other" education down-under: Indigenizing the discipline for psychologists and specialist educators. *Other Education: The Journal of Educational Alternatives*, 1(1), 205–225.

Mangaliso, Mzamo P. (2001). Building competitive advantage from Ubuntu: Management lessons from South Africa. *Academy of Management Perspectives*, 15(3), 23–33.

Marcuse, Herbert (1964). *One Dimensional Man: Studies in the Ideology of Advanced Industrial Society*. Boston, MA: Beacon Press.

Merleau-Ponty, M. (2003). *Nature: Course Notes from the Collège de France*. Northwestern University Press.

Metcalf, Henry C., & Urwick, L. (2004). *Dynamic Administration. The Collected Papers of Mary Parker Follett*. Routledge.

Milojević, I., & Inayatullah, S. (2015). Narrative foresight. *Futures*, 73, 151–162.

Morson, Gary Saul (2005). Sideshadows: The determination of free will. *The New Criterion*, 23, 17–25.

Mumby, D. K. (2011). What's cooking in organizational discourse studies? A response to Alvesson and Kärreman. *Human Relations*, 64(9), 1147–1161.

Nielsen, Stine Maria Louring, & Mullins, Michael Finbarr (2017). Beyond the dichotomy of figurative and abstract art in hospitals. The potential of visual art as a generator of well-being. *ARCH* 17.

Nietzsche, Friedrich (1910). *Human All too Human: A Book for All Spirits*. Edinburgh & London: T. N. Foulis.

Nietzsche, Friedrich (1968). *The Will to Power*. New York: Vintage Books.

Nussbaum, Barbara (2003). African culture and Ubuntu. *World Business Academy Perspectives*, 17(1), 1–12.

Nørtrander, Tor (2017). *Se Fremad*. Peoples Press.

Oppezzo, Marily, & Schwartz, Daniel L. (2014). Give your ideas some legs: The positive effect of walking on creative thinking. *Journal of Experimental Psychology: Learning, Memory, and Cognition*, 40(4).

Peirce, C. S. (1931–1935, 1958). *Collected Papers of Charles Sanders Peirce*. Cambridge, MA: Harvard University Press.

Penrose, R. (2011). Godel, the mind, and the laws of physics. In Matthias Baaz, Christos H. Papadimitriou, Hilary W. Putnam, Dana S. Scott, & Charles L. Harper Jr. (eds) *Kurt Gödel and the Foundations of Mathematics: Horizons of Truth* (pp. 339–360). Cambridge/NY/Melbourne…: Cambridge University Press.

Pihkala, S., & Karasti, H. (2018). Politics of mattering in the practices of participatory design. *August Proceedings of the 15th Participatory Design Conference: Short Papers, Situated Actions, Workshops and Tutorial*, 2, 13. ACM.

Plato (n.d.). *The Dialogues of Plato*, Benjamin Jowett (tr.). Accessed January 12, 2018 at http://webs.ucm.es/info/diciex/gente/agf/plato/The_Dialogues_of_Plato_v0.1.pdf

Popper, Karl R. (1935/1959/1992/2000). *The Logic of Scientific Discovery*. Routledge Classics. Accessed March 6, 2019 at http://strangebeautiful.com/other-texts/popper-logic-scientific-discovery.pdf and from www.math.chalmers.se/~ulfp/Review/logicscdis.pdf

Popper, Karl R. (1945/2008). *After the Open Society: Selected Social and Political Writings*. London/ New York: Routledge.

Popper, Karl R. (1945/2012). *The Open Society and its Enemies*. London/ New York: Routledge.

Popper, Karl R. (1956/1982). Quantum theory and the schism in physics. In W. W. Bartley, III (ed.) *Postscript to the Logic of Scientific Discovery*. London/Sydney/Auckland: Hutchinson & Co. (Publishers) Ltd.

Popper, Karl R. (1956/1983). *Realism and the Aim of Science*. In W. W. Bartley, III (ed.) *Postscript to the Logic of Scientific Discovery*. London/Sydney/Auckland: Hutchinson & Co. (Publishers) Ltd.

Popper, Karl R. (1963). *Conjectures and Refutations: The Growth of Scientific Knowledge*. London: Routledge and Kegan Paul.

Popper, Karl R. (1972). *Objective Knowledge*. Oxford: Oxford University Press. Accessed March 7, 2019 at https://pdfs.semanticscholar.org/845d/20c52e47cfb379ba1e384de92ed78eaac3ad.pdf

Popper, Karl R. (1978). The three worlds. Accessed March 10, 2019 at https://tannerlectures.utah.edu/_documents/a-to-z/p/popper80.pdf

Popper, Karl R. (1979/2014). *Die beiden Grundprobleme der Erkenntnistheorie, Hrsg* [The Two Fundamental Problems of the Theory of Knowledge], Andreas Pickel (tr.). London: Routledge. Accessed March 6, 2019 at https://content.taylorfrancis.com/books/download?dac=C2010-0-41626-X&isbn=9781135626761&format=googlePreviewPdf

Popper, Karl R. (1994). *The Myth of the Framework: In Defense of Science and Rationality*. London/New York: Routledge.

Popper, Karl R. (2008). *After the Open Society: Selected Social and Political Writings Karl Popper*. Abingdon, UK/New York: Routledge.

Pot, W. D., Dewulf, A., Biesbroek, G. R., & Verweij, S. (2019). What makes decisions about urban water infrastructure forward looking? A fuzzy-set qualitative comparative analysis of investment decisions in 40 Dutch municipalities. *Land Use Policy*, 82, 781–795.

Prádanos, L. I. (2015). The pedagogy of degrowth: Teaching Hispanic studies in the age of social inequality and ecological collapse. *Arizona Journal of Hispanic Cultural Studies*, 19(1),153–168.

Ragin, Charles C., Drass, Kriss A., & Davey, Sean (2006). *Fuzzy-Set/Qualitative Comparative Analysis 2.0.* Tucson, Arizona: Department of Sociology, University of Arizona.

Riach, K., Rumens, N., & Tyler, M. (2014). Un/doing chrononormativity: Negotiating ageing, gender and sexuality in organizational life. *Organization Studies*, 35(11), 1677–1698. Accessed March 29 2019 at https://journals.sagepub.com/doi/pdf/10.1177/0018726716632050

Riach, K., Rumens, N., & Tyler, M. (2016). Towards a Butlerian methodology: Undoing organizational performativity through anti-narrative research. *Human Relations*, 69 (11), 2069–2089. Accessed March 28, 2019 at https://journals.sagepub.com/doi/pdf/10.1177/0018726716632050

Ringgard, Dan (2014). *Litteratur* [Litterature]. Aarhus Universitets Forlag.

Ringgaard, Dan (2010). *Stedsans* [Sense of the Place]. Aarhus Universitets Forlag.

Ripple, W. J., Wolf, C., Newsome, T. M., Galetti, M., Alamgir, M., Crist, E., ... & 15,364 scientist signatories from 184 countries. (2017). World scientists' warning to humanity: A second notice. *BioScience*, 67(12), 1026–1028.

Riso, D. R., & Hudson, R. (1996). *Personality Types: Using the Enneagram for Self-Discovery.* The Enneagram Institute.

Roberts, P. (2013). Academic dystopia: Knowledge, performativity, and tertiary education. *Review of Education, Pedagogy, and Cultural Studies*, 35(1), 27–43.

Rockström, J., Steffen, W., Noone, K., Persson, Å., Chapin III, F. S., Lambin, E. F., ... & Nykvist, B. (2009). A safe operating space for humanity. *Nature*, 461: 472–475. Accessed March 9, 2019 at https://pdxscholar.library.pdx.edu/cgi/viewcontent.cgi?article=1063&context=iss_pub

Roffe, Jonathan (2010). Multiplicity. In Adrian Parr (ed.) *The Deleuze Dictionary Edition* (pp. 181–182). UK: Edinburgh University Press.

Rosile, G. A. (2016). *Tribal Wisdom for Business Ethics.* Bingley, UK: Emerald Group Publishing Limited.

Rosile, G. A., & Boje, David M. (2002). Restorying and postmodern organization theatre: Consultation in the storytelling organization. In Ronald R. Sims (ed.) *Changing the Way We Manage Change* (pp. 271–290). Westport, CN/London: Quorum Books.

Rosile, G. A., Boje, D. M., & Claw, C. M. (2018). Ensemble leadership theory: Collectivist, relational, and heterarchical roots from indigenous contexts. *Leadership*, 14 (3), 307–328.

Rosile, G. A., Boje, D. M., Carlon, D. M., Downs, A., & Saylors, R. (2013). Storytelling diamond: An antenarrative integration of the six facets of storytelling in organization research design. *Organizational Research Methods*, 16(4), 557–580.

Sartre, Jean Paul (1960/2004). *Critique of Dialectical Reason, Vol. 1: Theory of Practical Ensembles.* London/New York: Verso.

Savall, H. (1975/2010). *Work and People: An Economic Evaluation of Job-Enrichment.* Charlotte, NC: Information Age Press.

Savall, H. (2018). *Radical Origins to Economic Crises: German Bernacer, A Visionary Precursor.* Cham, Switzerland: Palgrave Macmillan.

Savall, H., & Zardet, V. (2008). *Mastering Hidden Costs and Socio-Economic Performance.* Charlotte, NC: Information Age Press.

Savall, H., & Zardet, V. (eds) (2011). *The Qualimetrics Approach: Observing the complex object.* Charlotte, NC: Information Age Press.

Savall, H., Peron, M., Zardet, V., & Bonnet, M. (2018). *Socially Responsible Capitalism*. London: Routledge.

Savall, H., Zardet, V., & Bonnet, M. (2008). *Releasing the Untapped Potential of Enterprises Through Socio-Economic Management*. London: International Labor Organization and Socio-Economic Institute of Firms and Organizations.

Schmelzer, M. (2015). The growth paradigm: History, hegemony, and the contested making of economic growthmanship. *Ecological Economics*, 118, 262–271.

Schoenmakers, B., Buntinx, F., & DeLepeleire, J. (2010). Supporting the dementia family caregiver: the effect of home care intervention on general well-being. *Aging and Mental Health*, 14(1), 44–56.

Scholes, R. (1980). Language, narrative, and anti-narrative. *Critical Inquiry*, 7(1), 204–212.

Schopenhauer, Arthur (1928). *The Philosophy of Schopenhauer*. New York: The Modern Library.

Schultz, M., & Hernes, T. (2019). Temporal interplay between strategy and identity: Punctuated, subsumed, and sustained modes. *Strategic Organization*, 18(1), 106–135. https://doi.org/10.1177/1476127019843834

Schumacher, E. F. (1973). *Small is Beautiful. A Study of Economics as if People Mattered*. New York: Vintage.

Seal, W., & Mattimoe, R. (2016). The role of narrative in developing management control knowledge from fieldwork: A pragmatic constructivist perspective. *Qualitative Research in Accounting & Management*, 13(3), 330–349.

Seidel, S., & Urquhart, C. (2013). On emergence and forcing in information systems grounded theory studies: The case of Strauss and Corbin. *Journal of Information Technology*, 28(3), 237–260.

Sele, Kathrin, & Grand, Simon (2016). Unpacking the dynamics of ecologies of routines: Mediators and their generative effects in routine interactions. *Organization Science*, 27 (3), 722–738.

Sharpe, B. (2013). *Three Horizons*. Devon, UK: Triarchy Press.

Shiva, Vandana (2008). From water crisis to water culture. *Cultural Studies*, 22(3–4), 498–509.

Skarmeas, D., Leonidou, C. N., & Saridakis, C. (2014). Examining the role of CSR skepticism using fuzzy-set qualitative comparative analysis. *Journal of Business Research*, 67(9), 1796–1805.

Spencer, Herbert (1851/1970/2014). *Social Statistics (or the Conditions Essential to Human Happiness)*. Robert Schalkenbach Foundation.

Stadil, Christian, & Larsen, Jens (2013). *Frivillig Ledelse*. Djøf Forlag.

Stein, Gertrude (1930). *Narration: Four Lectures by Gertrude Stein*. Introduction by Thornton Wilder. Chicago, IL: University of Chicago Press.

Sternfeld, Robert (1966). *Frege's Logical Theory*. With foreword by George Kimball Plochmann. Carbondale & Edwardsville, IL: Southern Illinois University Press.

Stoll-Kleemann, S., O'Riordan, T., & Jaeger, C. C. (2001). The psychology of denial concerning climate mitigation measures: evidence from Swiss focus groups. *Global Environmental Change*, 11(2), 107–117.

Strand, Anete Mikkala Camille (2012). *The Between: On Dis/continuous Intra-Active Becoming Of/Through an Apparatus of Material Storytelling*. Unpublished Doctoral Dissertation, Aalborg University, Denmark.

Strauss Anselm C., & Corbin Juliet (1990). *Basics of Qualitative Research: Grounded Theory Procedures and Techniques*. Newbury Park, CA: Sage Publications.

Strauss Anselm C., & Corbin Juliet (1994/1998). *Basics of Qualitative Research: Techniques and Procedures for Developing Grounded Theory*. Thousand Oaks, CA: Sage Publications.

Suddaby, Roy (2006). What grounded theory is not. *Academy of Management Journal*, 49(4), 633–642.

Svane, M. (2014). Quantum organizational world-making-through material embodied storytelling practices. Quantum Storytelling Conference, New Mexico University, December 17–19, 2014.

Svane, M., & Boje, D. (2014). *Merger strategy, cross-cultural involvement and polyphony. Between Cultures and Paradigms*. IACCM 2014, University of Warwick, UK.

Svane, M., & Boje, D. M. (2015). Tamara land fractal change management: In between managerialist narrative and polyphonic living stories. Online at http://vbn.aau.dk/files/225730097/Tamara_Land_Fractal_Change_Management_Las_Vegas_Paper.pdf

Svane, M., & Boje, D., & Gergerich, E. M. (2015). Counternarrative and antenarrative inquiry in two cross-cultural contexts. Accepted for publication in Special Issue on counternarrative, *European Journal of Cross-Cultural Competence*.

Svane, M., Gergerich, E., & Boje, David M. (2017). Fractal change management and counter-narrative in cross-cultural change. In Frandsen, Sanne, Kuhn, Timothy, & Wolff Lundholt, Marianne (eds) *Counter-Narratives and Organization* (pp. 129–154). New York: Routledge.

Talese, G. (2007). Telling true stories. In Mark Kramer, & Wendy Call (eds) *A Nonfiction Writers' Guide*. Nieman Foundation at Harvard University.

Taylor, Douglas F. (2014). Defining ubuntu for business ethics: A deontological approach. *South African Journal of Philosophy*, 33(3), 331–345.

Thaler, R. H., & Sunstein, C. R. (2009). *Nudge*. Penguin Books.

Toelken, K. (2012). Organizational discourses during planned change: A resiliency team case study. *American Communication Journal*, 14(2), 58–79.

Toulmin, S. (1972). Rationality and scientific discovery. *PSA: Proceedings of the Biennial Meeting of the Philosophy of Science Association*, 1972, 387–406.

Toulmin, S., Rieke, R., & Janik, A. (1980). Toulmins bold experiment. *Informal Logic*, 3(2).

Trafimow, D. (2003). Hypothesis testing and theory evaluation at the boundaries: Surprising insights from Bayes's theorem. *Psychological Review*, 110(3), 526.

Trafimow, D. (2012). The role of auxiliary assumptions for the validity of manipulations and measures. *Theory & Psychology*, 22, 486–498.

Trafimow, D. (2014). Considering quantitative and qualitative issues together. *Qualitative Research in Psychology*, 11(1), 15–24.

Trafimow, D. (2018). Confidence intervals, precision and confounding. *New Ideas in Psychology*, 50, 48–53.

Trafimow, D. (2019). Five nonobvious changes in editorial practice for editors and reviewers to consider when evaluating submissions in a post p< 0.05 universe. *The American Statistician*, 73(sup1), 340–345.

Trafimow, D., & Rice, S. (2009). A test of the null hypothesis significance testing procedure correlation argument. *The Journal of General Psychology*, 136(3), 261–270.

Trafimow, D., & Uhalt, J. (in press). The quality of auxiliary assumptions depends upon connections to nonobservational terms in theories and observational terms in empirical hypotheses. *Theory & Psychology*.

Turunen, Marja (2015). *Toward a Consciousness-Based View of Organizing*. Doctoral Dissertation, Aalto University, Finland.

Tutu, Desmond (2012). *No Future without Forgiveness*. New York: Random House.

TwoTrees, Kaylynn Sullivan (1997). *Presentation at the Organizational Behavior Teaching Conference*. Case Western Reserve, Ohio.

TwoTrees, Kaylynn Sullivan (2000). Seven directions practice: A practice for the crossroads. *The Fourth R*, 92(August, Sept, October).

TwoTrees, Kaylynn Sullivan, & Kolan, Matthew (2016). The trees are breathing us: An indigenous view of relationship in nature and business. In Grace Ann Rosile (ed.) *Tribal Wisdom for Business Ethics* (pp. 211–222). Bingley, UK: Emerald Group Publishing Limited.

Valaei, N., Rezaei, S., Ho, R. C., & Okumus, F. (2019). Beyond structural equation modelling in tourism research: Fuzzy set/qualitative comparative analysis (fs/QCA) and data envelopment analysis (DEA). In *Quantitative Tourism Research in Asia. Perspectives on Asian Tourism* (pp. 297–309). Singapore: Springer.

van Hulst, Merlijn, & Yberma, Sierk (2020). From what to where: A setting-sensitive approach to organizational storytelling. *Organization Studies*, 41(3), 365–391.

van Maanen, John (1988). *Tales of the Field: On Writing Ethnography*. Chicago, IL: University of Chicago Press.

van Maanen, John (1991). *The Smile Factory: Work at Disneyland*. Beverly Hills, CA: Sage.

von Wright, Georg Henrik (1941/1965). *The Logical Problem of Induction*. Oxford: Basil Blackwell.

Wardekker, A., & Lorenz, S. (2019). The visual framing of climate change impacts and adaptation in the IPCC assessment reports. *Climatic Change*, 1–20.

Waring, M., & Steinem, G. (1988). *If Women Counted: A New Feminist Economics*. San Francisco: Harper & Row.

Weick, Karl E. (1995). *Sensemaking*. Thousand Oaks, CA: Sage.

Weick, Karl E. (2012). Organized sensemaking: A commentary on processes of interpretive work. *Human Relations*, 65(1), 141–153.

Wolfe, F. A. (1988). *Taking the Quantum Leap: The New Physics for Nonscientists*. Harper Perennial.

Worley, C. G., Zardet, V., Bonnet, M., & Savall, A. (2015). *Becoming Agile: How the SEAM Approach to Management Builds Adaptability*. John Wiley & Sons.

Yin, R. K. (2014). *Case Study Research: Design and Methods*. Thousand Oaks, CA: Sage.

Yin, R. K. (2015/2017). *Qualitative Research from Start to Finish*. Guilford Publications.

Yolle, Maurice (2019, in review). The socio-cultural dynamics of development: Part 2 cultural political evolution.

Index

Page numbers in italics refer to figures.